SRA Reading Mastery® Transformations

Reading

Textbook A

Siegfried Engelmann

Steve Osborn

Jean Osborn

Leslie Zoref

McGraw Hill

Acknowledgments

Many thanks to Lynda Gansel, Marjorie Mayo, and
Crystal Weber for their help in preparing
the manuscript.

CREDITS

Thank You M'am
"Thank You M'am" from SHORT STORIES by Langston Hughes. Copyright © 1996 by Ramona Bass and
Arnold Rampersad. Reprinted by permission of Hill and Wang, a division of Farrar, Straus and Giroux.
Reprinted by permission of Farrar, Straus, and Giroux.

Additional rights by permission of Harold Ober Associates Incorporated.

Open Range/In Time of Silver Rain
"Open Range" from TENGGREN'S COWBOYS AND INDIANS by Kathryn and Byron Jackson, copyright ©
1948 and renewed 1976 by Penguin Random House LLC. Used by permission of Golden Books, an imprint
of Random House Children's Books, a division of Penguin Random House LLC. All rights reserved. "Any
third party use of this material, outside of this publication, is prohibited. Interested parties must apply
directly to Penguin Random House LLC for permission."

"In Time of Silver Rain" from THE COLLECTED POEMS OF LANGSTON HUGHES by Langston Hughes, edited
by Arnold Rampersad with David Roessel, Associate Editor, copyright 1994 by the Estate of Langston
Hughes. Used by permission of Alfred A. Knopf, an imprint of the Knopf Doubleday Publishing Group, a
division of Penguin Random House LLC. All rights reserved. "Any third party use of this material, outside
of this publication, is prohibited. Interested parties must apply directly to Penguin Random House LLC for
permission." "In Time of Silver Rain" from THE COLLECTED POEMS OF LANGSTON HUGHES. Copyright 1994
by the Estate of Langston Hughes.

Additional rights by permission of Harold Ober Associates Incorporated.

PHOTO CREDITS
171 (t)Library of Congress Prints and Photographs Division [LC-USZ62-50927]; **174** (t)Library of Congress
Prints and Photographs Division [LC-USZ62-50927], (tr)Ingram Publishing; **176** (t)Library of Congress
Prints and Photographs Division [LC-USZ62-98684]; **219** (tr)Photos.com/Getty Images; **221** (tr)Library of
Congress Prints and Photographs Division [LC-USZ62-87246].

mheducation.com/prek-12

Copyright © 2021 McGraw-Hill Education

Send all inquiries to:
McGraw-Hill Education
8787 Orion Place
Columbus, OH 43240

ISBN: 978-0-07-905423-4
MHID: 0-07-905423-4

Printed in the United States of America.

2 3 4 5 6 7 8 9 10 LWI 26 25 24 23 22 21

Table of Contents

A WORD LISTS

1 State Names

1. Colorado
2. Florida
3. Indiana
4. Maine

2 Compound Words

1. backyard
2. homework
3. sketchbook
4. weekend

3 Vocabulary Words

1. assignment
2. instead
3. kayak
4. kayaking
5. poster
6. sketchbook
7. vacation

B READING LITERATURE: Short Story

Ron's Summer Vacation
Ozzie Reid
Chapter 1

Summer vacation was over, and the first day of school was almost over. Ron sat at his new desk in Ms. Brown's fourth-grade classroom, waiting for the school bell to ring. He had already finished reading a story on his tablet, and he didn't have any homework yet, so he just looked around the room.

Ms. Brown had hung several travel posters on the wall behind her desk. One poster showed kids playing on a big, sandy beach next to the ocean. "Visit Florida," the poster said.

Another poster showed a boy and a girl standing on top of a mountain, looking all around. "Colorado has GREAT views," it said. A third showed a boy paddling a kayak down a swiftly moving river, under the words, "For a real vacation, paddle up to Maine."

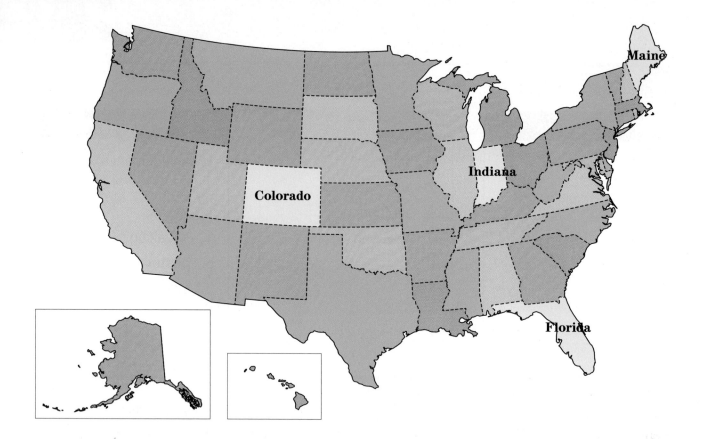

Vacation! The word made Ron's eyes light up. It sounded so great, so full of promise. Then Ron remembered. Ever since his father died in a car wreck six years ago, his family hadn't taken a single summer vacation. They had spent every one of those summers at home in Flatville, Indiana, not doing much of anything.

Oh sure, on some weekends Ron's mother would drive him and his sister Debby to Flatville State Park, where they'd hike around in the woods for a few hours. But Ron didn't think those weekend trips counted as real vacations. For him, vacations were when you spent two weeks climbing mountains in Colorado or a month relaxing on a beach in Florida or the whole summer kayaking down a wild river in Maine. Now those were vacations. They were fun. They were exciting. They cost a lot of money.

Money! The word made Ron frown. He didn't know much about money, but he did know that his mom never seemed to have any. At the beginning of every year, his mom said, "Maybe we'll have enough money to take a real vacation this summer." But by the time summer rolled around, she wasn't talking about vacations anymore. Instead, she said, "Sorry, Ron, we'll have to stay in Flatville this summer. Maybe next year."

Every summer she said that. She said it in the summer after Ron finished kindergarten and when he finished first, second, and third grades. He'd spent every one of those summers hanging around Flatville. Now here he was at the beginning of fourth grade, looking at the posters on his classroom wall and dreaming of a real vacation. ♦

The posters made Ron think about his sister Debby, who was three years older than he was. Sometimes Ron wished he had a brother instead—a brother he could play sports with, a brother who liked to fool around and have fun. But he didn't have a brother. All he had was Debby, and Debby was no fun at all.

Ever since their father died, Debby's idea of fun was to draw pictures. Every day, she sat by her bedroom window with a sketchbook and drew whatever she saw. Some days she drew the trees in the backyard. Some days she drew clouds. Some days she drew robins hunting in the grass for worms.

Ron had to admit that Debby was a pretty good artist. She was only in seventh grade, but she could already draw pictures that looked just like the real thing. Her trees looked like real trees, with branches, leaves, blossoms, and fruit. Her clouds looked fluffy or full of rain, with different areas of light and dark. Even her robins seemed ready to fly off the page.

Compared with other kids her age, Debby was miles ahead in art. Of course, she did spend more time drawing than other kids–a lot more time. In fact, Debby spent almost every spare hour of the day drawing in her room. She had started a few years ago by drawing simple pictures of objects in the house, such as cups, chairs, and books. But she got tired of drawing those objects, so she started looking out her window.

Ron wondered how much longer Debby would be happy with her window. Although she could see a lot from there, it wasn't like being out in the country. If she were out in the country, she could be drawing pictures of forests or mountains or swiftly moving rivers. But the only way

she could draw those pictures was to look at the real thing. And the only way to see the real thing was to take a vacation.

Vacation! There was that awful word again! Ron tried to put it out of his mind. Suddenly, he noticed Ms. Brown talking to the class.

"Because this is the first day of school," she said, "I'm going to give you a really easy homework assignment. I'd like you to write a paragraph or two about your summer vacation. Describe the places you visited. Tell about all the wonderful times you had. I'm sure it will be very easy since it's so fresh in your mind."

Then Ms. Brown called on several students to describe their summer vacations. A lot of the students hadn't done much, but Natalie Smith had played on a beach in Michigan. Kiko Meyer had climbed Pike's Peak in Colorado. Fred Arnsworth had gone kayaking in Alaska.

Ron sank lower in his chair. He hoped Ms. Brown wouldn't call on him. What would he say if she did? That he'd spent the whole summer in Flatville? That he hadn't had a vacation in six years? That his sister drew pictures of their backyard? He didn't want to tell her any of those things. The other students would only laugh.

Just then, the bell rang.

"Oh, dear, we're out of time," said Ms. Brown. "Remember to bring me your vacation stories by tomorrow morning. Now close your desks and line up by the door. The sooner you're ready, the sooner we can leave."

C COMPREHENSION

Write the answers.

1. How do you know that Ron is the main character in the story?

2. Why do you think the word **money** made Ron frown?

3. How do you think Ron felt when other kids talked about their vacations? Why did he feel that way?

4. Why did Ron think that Debby was a good artist?

5. Why was Ron worried about his homework assignment?

D WRITING

Write a paragraph that answers this main question:

- If you could take a vacation anywhere in the world, where would you go?

Your paragraph should also answer these questions:

1. What do you like about your vacation spot?

2. What does your vacation spot look like?

3. What kinds of things can you do in your vacation spot?

Write at least four sentences.

END OF LESSON 1

A | WORD LISTS

1 | Word Practice

1. cell phone
2. computer
3. e-mail
4. Internet

2 | Compound Words

1. backpack
2. classroom
3. downtown
4. driveway
5. hallway
6. notebook

3 | Word Endings

1. really
2. slowly
3. swiftly
4. usually

4 | Vocabulary Words

1. cashier
2. expecting
3. rapids
4. startled
5. usual
6. vanish

5 | Vocabulary Review

1. instead
2. kayaking

B | READING LITERATURE: Short Story

Ron's Summer Vacation
Chapter 2

Ron threw his notebook into his backpack and stood in line, waiting to leave the classroom. He didn't say anything to anybody, because he was worried about his homework assignment. When Ms. Brown finally opened the classroom door, Ron walked through with his eyes to the ground.

Out in the hallway, students were laughing and shoving each other and making noise. But Ron just kept on walking, right down the hallway and out the front door.

Outside, he could see parents waiting for their children. Some were standing near the front door, but others just stayed in their cars in the parking lot, listening to their radios or talking on their cell phones.

One woman in an expensive car was talking on a cell phone and looking at her gold watch. Ron figured her car had air conditioning, because all her windows were closed. He wondered what it would be like to drive home in an expensive, air-conditioned car while talking on the phone. His mom's car was a rusty older model that only got air-conditioned in the winter, when the heater didn't work.

Right now, his mom's car was parked at her job. She worked as a cashier in a grocery store several miles from their house. She worked from nine o'clock in the morning to six o'clock in the evening, so she never picked up Ron from school. Instead, he usually went home in a school bus. If he didn't take the bus, he had to walk.

Ron looked over at the school buses lined up in the driveway. Students were standing next to the doors, waiting to get on. Somehow, Ron didn't feel like riding the bus today. He didn't want to talk to anybody, and he wasn't in a hurry to get home. So he decided to walk.

Ron's house was about a mile from school. Usually he could walk home in a half hour or less. He would go east on Center Street for three blocks, then south on Oak Street for five blocks, then east again for a half block on Shady Lane. His address was 367 Shady Lane.

Today, Ron set off on Center Street as usual. But when he got to Oak Street, he decided to head north instead of south. He hadn't walked on this part of Oak Street much before, but he knew that it went downtown. He thought that he might look at some of the store windows in the downtown mall or the posters outside the movie theater. ♦

As Ron walked, he kept thinking about his homework assignment. What was he going to write? He couldn't think of anything to say except that he'd spent the whole summer in Flatville, going to the state park, watching TV, and hanging out with his friends.

Just then, Ron looked up and saw that he was passing the library. He remembered that the library had several computers in a special room. People used the computers to surf the Internet, write e-mail, and work on projects.

Ron stopped walking and thought about going into the library. Why not? He could write his homework assignment on one of the computers. His story might be boring to read, but at least he'd be done with it. If he finished the story this afternoon, he'd have the evening free to watch TV, play outside, or read a book.

When Ron entered the library, he looked around for the computer room. He couldn't find it right away, but he did see a clock. It was just a few minutes after four. Suddenly, Ron remembered that Debby was expecting him to be home by four. His mom usually called around four-thirty to make sure that Ron and Debby were safe.

Ron didn't have a cell phone, so he thought about running home as fast as he could, but then he saw a pay phone on the wall. He had some change in his pocket, so he called Debby and told her that he'd be home by six, after he'd finished working in the library. That was fine with Debby. She said she was already sitting in her room, drawing a picture of the neighbors' swing set.

Ron hung up and found the computer room in a corner of the library. When he walked into the room, a woman at the desk showed him how to use the writing program on the computer. Ron had already

used the same program at school, so it didn't take him long to get ready.

Except for the woman at the desk, Ron was the only person in the room. He stared at the computer screen, wondering how to begin. "I spent my summer vacation in one of the hottest vacation spots in America" was his first sentence. Then he wrote another sentence: "It's called Flatville, Indiana."

Ron laughed at what he had written. What a joke. Flatville was hot all right, but Ron didn't think that anyone had ever taken a vacation there. What would a person do? Flatville didn't have any mountains or beaches, and the only river was the Little Muddy, a small creek that flowed slowly through the middle of town.

It was called the Little Muddy because the water was almost always brown with mud.

The first two sentences of Ron's story weren't really true, but at least they were a good beginning. He decided to write some more sentences that weren't really true. Why not? The real story was so boring that he got tired just thinking about it.

Ron stared at the screen for a minute and then started writing again. "I did something new and exciting every day," he wrote. "But the most exciting event was when I paddled my kayak down the swiftly moving rapids of the Little Muddy."

Ron laughed again. He could almost see himself floating down the Little Muddy in a kayak. The water flowed so slowly that he would have to paddle like crazy just to move a few feet. He might even get stuck in the mud.

If only the Little Muddy was a wild river, with dangerous rapids and huge rocks–just like the river in the poster of Maine. Ron closed his eyes and imagined what it would be like to paddle down a wild river in Maine. He would have to grip the paddle as hard as he could and keep switching it from side to side to guide the kayak. If he made one slip, he might crash into the rocks and flip over.

Ron closed his eyes tighter and made a picture of the river in his mind. He could almost hear the roar of the rapids and feel the cold, clear water spraying in his face.

His arms were moving as fast as they could, and the wind was whistling by his ears.

That was a great picture. Ron thought he'd describe it for his story, so he opened his eyes and looked at the computer screen. But instead of words, the screen showed a picture of a wild river in Maine.

Ron couldn't believe what he saw. He reached out to touch the screen, but it vanished in front of his hand. Instead of hitting the screen, his hand just waved in the air. And then it got wet.

Startled, Ron looked around. He wasn't in the computer room anymore. He was sitting in a kayak, paddling down a wild river in Maine.

C COMPREHENSION

Write the answers.

1. Why did Ron decide to walk instead of taking the bus?

2. How do you think Ron felt about the woman in the air-conditioned car?

3. Why did Ron write sentences that weren't true?

4. Why wouldn't people want to kayak in the Little Muddy?

5. Name at least two ways that the Little Muddy was different from the wild river.

D WRITING

At the end of today's story, Ron was paddling a kayak down a wild river in Maine.

- Pretend you are Ron paddling your kayak down that river, which is called the Big Rock River. A river guide is next to you in her kayak. The river is wild. It has big rocks and fast-moving water. You are good at paddling your kayak, but you suddenly have a problem.

Write a story that tells what kind of problem you have and how you solve the problem.

Write at least five sentences.

A WORD LISTS

1 Word Practice	2 Word Endings	3 Vocabulary Words	4 Vocabulary Words
1. blue jay	1. closely	1. boulder	1. bounding
2. bobcat	2. completely	2. lack	2. budge
3. cardinal	3. hardly	3. notice	3. celebration
4. robin	4. instantly	4. shrug	4. cupboard
5. wildflower	5. quickly	5. supplies	5. sober
	6. suddenly		
	7. swiftly		

B VOCABULARY FROM CONTEXT

1. The animals were **bounding** swiftly down the tunnel.
   - sitting   • running   • walking

2. He tried to pull the post out of the ground, but the post would not **budge.**
   - glisten   • disappear   • move

3. They had a great **celebration** after winning the game.
   - school   • party   • sleep

4. The room contained a rusty stove and a **cupboard** for the dishes.
   - cup   • ceiling   • cabinet

5. The sun and wind had taken the sparkle from her eyes and left them a **sober** gray.
   - serious   • happy   • red

C WORD ENDINGS

1. The picture was **perfect,** so it was painted ▢ .

2. When he was hungry, he would get **anxious,** so he waited for dinner ▢ .

3. The young man was **polite,** so he acted ▢ .

4. She had a **loud** voice, so she talked ▢ .

5. The noise was **sudden,** so we heard it ▢ .

6. The car was very **slow,** so it went very ▢ .

Ron's Summer Vacation
Chapter 3

Ron still couldn't believe that he was really paddling a kayak down a wild river in Maine. He looked around again. He was surrounded by a forest of pine trees that stretched as far as he could see. Many different kinds of birds flew from tree to tree or sat in the branches, whistling and chirping. Some were red, some were blue, and others were black, brown, or gray. Ron thought that some of the birds were cardinals, blue jays, and robins, but he wasn't sure about the others.

The forest floor was covered with pinecones, pine needles, bushes, and wildflowers.

Far away, Ron saw a group of deer grazing. He wondered if there were other animals in the woods, like bears or bobcats or snakes. Thinking about those animals made Ron afraid for a second, but he soon forgot his fear and looked at the river around his kayak.

The water was as clear as glass. It seemed to be several feet deep, and Ron could see rocks of many shapes and sizes at the bottom of the river. Swimming above the rocks were dozens of fish. They looked so close that Ron thought he might be able to reach out and grab one. He put his hand in the water and instantly took it out. Boy, was that water cold!

Ron noticed that he was wearing just a life jacket, a T-shirt, a swimming suit, and a pair of sneakers without socks. He also noticed that the water was moving quickly, even though the river was fairly calm.

There weren't any rapids or boulders in the water, and Ron's kayak just kept moving forward in a straight line.

Ron looked down the river to see where he was going. He couldn't see very far ahead, because a bend in the river blocked his view. But Ron could hear the sound of roaring rapids. He guessed that the rapids started soon after the bend in the river.

The sound of the rapids made Ron's heart beat faster, and it also made him a little afraid. He wondered how well he could paddle through the rapids, so he examined his kayak closely. It was a small plastic kayak, with just one seat in the middle, where Ron was sitting. The inside of the kayak was completely empty: no food, no maps, no supplies of any kind. For a moment, the lack of supplies made Ron glad because nothing would get wet or lost if the kayak tipped over.

The next moment, however, Ron started to worry about his lack of supplies. What if he got hungry? What if he got lost? What if night fell and he didn't have any light or anywhere to sleep? What if there were bears? ♦

Those questions bothered Ron, but he didn't want to think about them. Instead, he tried to find out how well he could guide the kayak. He looked at his paddle, which had a wide blade at each end. The two blades were connected by a long handle that Ron held in the middle. When Ron stroked the paddle through the water on the right side of the kayak, the kayak

turned a little bit left. When he stroked the paddle on the left side, the kayak turned a little bit right.

When Ron wanted to go straight, he made a right stroke, then a left stroke, then another right stroke, then another left stroke, and so on. As long as he made equal numbers of left and right strokes, the kayak went straight.

To turn the kayak, Ron had to make strokes on just one side of the kayak. First he practiced turning right by making several strokes on the left side. Then he practiced turning left by making strokes on the right side.

Ron crossed from one side of the river to the other, and then back again. After a while, he decided to go straight as fast as he could. Left, right, left, right went his

paddle as Ron put his head down and picked up speed. He was having so much fun that he didn't notice that the kayak had gone around the bend in the river. He also didn't notice that someone was yelling his name.

"Ron!" the person yelled.

Ron kept paddling.

"Ron! Ron! Over here!" the person yelled even louder.

Ron looked around. Who was calling his name?

"RON!" the person yelled at the top of her lungs.

Ron followed the sound of the voice and saw a girl standing on the left bank of the river, waving her arms up and down and yelling his name. He looked more closely, and he couldn't believe what he saw. It was his sister Debby. What was she doing here? And what did she want?

"Ron!" she yelled again. "You have to come out! We have to go home!"

Home? What was she talking about? Ron was just starting to have fun. He didn't want to go home. He'd only been on vacation in Maine for a few minutes, and he didn't want it to end so soon.

Ron pretended he couldn't hear Debby. He laid the paddle on his lap and cupped his hands behind his ears. Then he shrugged his shoulders as if to say, "I can't hear you."

Debby started yelling again. Ron saw that she was standing next to a kayak just like his own. Behind her was a little shed filled with kayaks. A man was in the shed, working on one of the kayaks. Ron wondered who the man was and what he was doing with all those kayaks.

"Ron!" Debby yelled again. "Get out right now! You can't go any farther! You have to stop here!"

Ron thought fast. He knew that Debby wanted him to get out, but she was only his sister. If his mother had been there, he would have stopped. But Debby was just,

well, Debby. Why should he listen to her? Besides, he was having too much fun.

While Ron was turning these ideas over in his mind, he suddenly noticed that the water was moving much faster. Debby kept yelling at him, but he was moving farther and farther away from her, at a faster and faster rate.

Ron looked back over his shoulder and could hardly see Debby anymore. Then he looked forward. There, just a few hundred feet in front of him, the river narrowed into swiftly moving rapids between huge boulders. Ron could hear the roar and see the water pounding against the rocks again and again, spraying into the air.

Ron began to feel afraid. The roar got louder and louder. The kayak moved faster and faster. He had to decide what to do. He wanted to try the rapids, but he didn't know if he was good enough.

At the last second, he made up his mind to head for the left bank of the river. But it was too late. The kayak was moving too quickly, and he couldn't turn it or make it stop. He was headed into the rapids. He couldn't go anywhere else.

E COMPREHENSION

Write the answers.

1. Why was Ron afraid when he thought about the animals that lived in the woods?

2. Why did Ron worry about his lack of supplies?

3. How did Ron feel about the rapids when he first heard them? Why did he feel that way?

4. Why didn't Ron want to come out of the river?

5. Why didn't Ron obey Debby?

F WRITING

Use details from the story to explain how Ron guided his kayak.

Your explanation should answer these questions:

1. What tool did Ron use to guide his kayak?

2. What did that tool look like?

3. How did Ron make the kayak go straight?

4. How did Ron make the kayak turn right?

5. How did Ron make the kayak turn left?

Write at least five sentences.

END OF LESSON 3

4

A | WORD LISTS

1 | Compound Words

1. playground
2. slingshot
3. waterfall

2 | Word Endings

1. barely
2. furiously
3. loudly
4. probably
5. quickly
6. tightly

3 | Vocabulary Words

1. approach
2. current
3. dangerous
4. disappeared
5. ignored
6. manager

B | VOCABULARY FROM CONTEXT

1. It's **dangerous** to ride your bike on a street with lots of traffic.
   - easy
   - safe
   - not safe

2. Near the rapids, the **current** got faster.
   - flow of water
   - raisin
   - riverbank

3. We thought the book had **disappeared,** but then we found it under the couch.
   - vanished
   - dismissed
   - reappeared

4. They couldn't **approach** the fire because it was too hot.
   - put out
   - see
   - come close to

5. The man **ignored** his ringing telephone.
   - paid no attention to
   - copied
   - obeyed

6. At the store, the **manager** told the other workers what to do.
   - customer
   - boss
   - cashier

Ron's Summer Vacation
Chapter 4

Ron knew he had made some mistakes. He should have listened to Debby. He should have stopped when she called to him. He should have known that the river was too dangerous. But he didn't have time to worry about all that right now, because he was headed straight into the rapids. He had to use every muscle in his body to guide the kayak, and he had to think fast.

The water was moving so quickly that Ron could hardly steer. He could only go with the current and hope that he didn't crash into any boulders. He held his paddle tightly with both hands.

The first few feet of the rapids weren't that bad. Ron's kayak stayed in the middle, far from the rocks along the edge. But then the rapids narrowed and the water moved even faster. Ron looked ahead and saw a huge boulder sticking out of the middle of the river. Half the river flowed around the right side of the boulder, and the other half flowed around the left.

Both sides looked dangerous, with the water spraying high into the air and roaring loudly. Ron decided to try for the right side of the boulder. Using all his strength, he made several quick strokes on the left side of the kayak. Nothing happened. He was still going in a straight line, and he was headed directly toward the boulder!

Ron quickly moved his paddle over to the right. He was only a few feet from the boulder, and he had to turn fast. He grabbed the handle as hard as he could, and he paddled furiously. At the last second, the kayak turned left and swept around the left side of the boulder, with only inches to spare.

Now Ron was really frightened. He was going many times faster than when he had started, back in the calm part of the river. His kayak was filling with cold water, and he was soaking wet from all the spray. He could just barely see the boulder as he swept around it, carried along by the current.

Ron felt as if he were zooming down a huge, curving playground slide. But the slide didn't seem to have any end, and Ron had no idea where he was headed.

Suddenly, Ron could no longer see the boulder, so he figured that he must have passed it safely. But he didn't dare to look back, because he was too afraid of what might be coming next. ♦

Ron stared down the river as far as he could. He didn't see any more boulders, just fast-moving rapids with rocks on both sides. If he stayed in the middle of the river, he should be all right.

But just when Ron thought he might be safe for a little while, he noticed that the river seemed to disappear a few hundred yards away. He could hear a really loud roar coming from that spot, and he could see spray shooting into the air.

Ron wondered why the river disappeared so suddenly. Could it be going into a big hole? Or did it just stop all of a sudden? Then the answer struck Ron like a bolt of lightning. That must be a waterfall! The river must come to a certain point and then drop down, down to the rocks below!

Time was running out. Ron knew that he couldn't kayak over the waterfall, no matter how high or low it was. He had to get out of the river. But how? The current was moving faster and faster, and try as he might, Ron couldn't make the kayak turn. He paddled backwards and forwards, then forwards and backwards. He tried turning right. Then he tried turning left. Nothing worked.

Ron thought about jumping out of the kayak, but that would be even worse. He wouldn't be able to swim against the current, and the water would smash him against the rocks. At least the kayak protected him a little.

Meanwhile, the edge of the waterfall came closer and closer. As Ron approached, he saw a boulder sticking just a few feet out of the water right at the edge of the

waterfall. His only chance was to smash the kayak against the boulder and hope that it would stop him from going over. Besides, the current was taking him straight toward the boulder, so he had no other choice.

This time, Ron didn't try to turn the kayak. He just kept his eyes on the boulder and waited to see what would happen. He was only ten feet away, five, four, three, two, one.

The kayak hit the boulder straight on. Then the kayak flipped into the air. Ron shot out of the kayak like a rock from a slingshot. The world was spinning so fast that Ron couldn't even see where he was going. All of a sudden, he hit water–deep, cold water. Thanks to the life jacket, he floated back up to the surface of the water.

Ron saw that he had flown over the waterfall, which was only about twenty feet high, and landed in a large, round pool. He could see the kayak lying upside

down at the edge of the pool. The front part was smashed, and the sides didn't look too good either. The paddle was nowhere in sight. At the far end of the pool, the river kept flowing, but Ron couldn't even bear to look at it.

Ron swam to the edge of the pool and pulled himself out onto a rocky beach. He was shivering from the cold water, but he didn't seem to have any broken bones. He just sat on the ground for a while and caught his breath. Then he took off his wet life jacket, shirt, and shoes. He figured the warm sun would quickly dry both him and his clothes.

Ron poured the water out of his shoes. Then he wrung out his life jacket and shirt and laid them on top of some rocks to dry. After that, he found a smooth spot on top of a small boulder and sat down to think.

Ron figured that Debby and the man from the kayak shed would soon come looking for him. Debby had probably run over to the man and told him that Ron had paddled into the rapids. Now the two of them were probably running along the riverbank, looking for Ron.

He felt like such a fool. What was he going to say to Debby when she found him at the bottom of the waterfall, with the kayak smashed and his clothes soaking wet? How was he going to explain why he had just ignored her as he paddled by?

As Ron thought about these questions, he noticed that he was getting very sleepy. Kayaking was hard work. His arms were tired, and his legs were sore. He stood up and walked to a sandy spot where he could lie down. The life jacket was already pretty dry, so he used it as a pillow.

Ten seconds later, Ron was fast asleep.

D COMPREHENSION

Write the answers.

1. Why was Ron worried about Debby at the end of the chapter?

2. Why did the river seem to disappear at the waterfall?

3. When Ron was approaching the waterfall, why didn't he jump out of the kayak?

4. What did Ron hope would happen when the kayak smashed into the boulder at the edge of the waterfall?

5. The story says that Ron couldn't bear to look at the river anymore. Why do you think he felt that way?

E WRITING

• At the end of today's story, Debby was looking for Ron.

Write what you think Debby will say to Ron if she finds him.

Debby's comments to Ron should answer these questions:

1. How does Debby feel about Ron passing the kayak shed?

2. How does Debby feel about Ron entering the rapids?

3. What does Debby think could have happened to Ron?

4. How does Debby feel about finding Ron?

Write at least five sentences.

END OF LESSON 4

A WORD LISTS

1	Hard Words
1.	challenge
2.	conflict
3.	establish
4.	intently
5.	rough
6.	situation

2	Word Endings
1.	cackle
2.	candle
3.	incredible
4.	sparkle
5.	startle
6.	tunnel
7.	twinkle

3	Vocabulary Words
1.	accept
2.	dominant
3.	inherit
4.	respect
5.	sibling

B READING LITERATURE: Short Story

Ron's Summer Vacation
Chapter 5

"Ron!" said the voice. "Ron!"

Ron was dreaming about Flatville. Strangely, the dream was so pleasant that he didn't want to wake up.

"Ron!" said the voice again. "Are you okay?"

He knew that voice. It was Debby's. Ron thought it was the sweetest voice he'd ever heard. He woke up.

"I'm fine," Ron said as he opened his eyes.

Debby and the man from the kayak shed were standing over him. They both looked out of breath and worried.

Ron stood up slowly and kept his eyes on the ground. He didn't know what Debby would say, but he figured she would be plenty mad at him.

Much to Ron's surprise, Debby reached out and gave him a big hug that seemed to last forever. Then she pulled back and asked again, "Are you sure you're okay?"

Ron nodded his head yes, even though he felt really ashamed. He couldn't believe how stupid he'd been.

"We've been looking for you for a long time," Debby said. "We didn't know if you were dead or alive. It's a good thing that Mr. Mason was able to help me."

Ron turned to look at Mr. Mason. He had gray hair and glasses, and he didn't look too happy. "You're a very lucky boy," he said. "You could easily have been killed. Only the best kayakers can go down these rapids. It's no place for a beginner."

"I know," Ron said, and the three of them looked over at the damaged kayak on the rocks.

Debby said, "Didn't you hear me back at Mr. Mason's kayak rental shed? I kept calling your name, but you didn't answer. Don't you remember that Mom told us to get out of the river at the shed? That's where we were supposed to return the kayaks to Mr. Mason."

Ron hung his head. He didn't know what to say. Of course he had heard Debby. Of course he should have left the river while it was safe. But he didn't do any of those things. Instead, he had just kept on going, right into the rapids.

Then Ron remembered something strange. Only a few hours ago, he was sitting in the library, writing about his summer vacation. After that, he was suddenly here in Maine, paddling a kayak. Should he tell Debby and Mr. Mason about the library? Or should he just keep it to himself? ♦

Ron decided not to mention the library, at least for now. After a moment, he lifted up his head and said, "I'm sorry, Debby, I don't know what came over me. I just wanted to stay in the kayak and make the vacation last a little longer." Debby looked at Ron strangely. "Longer?" she laughed. "Ron, we've already been in Maine for three weeks. Mom's waiting for us back at the cabin. We're driving home first thing tomorrow morning."

Ron hung his head again. Now he was really confused. How could they have been here for three weeks? All he could remember was the last few hours.

"Well, at least your body is okay," Debby said, "even if your mind is on vacation."

"Let's go back to the shed," said Mr. Mason. "I'll come back and get the kayak tomorrow."

Debby, Ron, and Mr. Mason began walking back up the riverbank toward the shed. As they walked, Ron told them his story. He didn't want to tell them about the library, so he started with the part about paddling past the shed. He told them about the first boulder in the middle of the rapids and how he had gone to the left. Then he told them about the second boulder at the edge of the waterfall. Finally, he described how he had flown through the air and landed in the pool.

"You're a lucky boy," Mr. Mason kept saying. Ron could tell that Mr. Mason wasn't happy, and then he figured out why. Mr. Mason's kayak was badly damaged, and it was Ron's fault.

When the three of them got back to the shed, Ron asked Mr. Mason, "What about the kayak? Do we have to pay you for that?"

"Well," Mr. Mason began, "let me talk to your mother. I think we can work something out."

"I have an idea!" Debby said suddenly. "Just wait here!"

Ron and Mr. Mason watched as Debby ran over to one of the kayaks. She reached in, pulled out her sketchbook, and came back.

Debby opened the sketchbook to the first page and showed a drawing to Mr. Mason. "How do you like this picture?" she asked. "Do you think it's worth one kayak?"

Mr. Mason looked at the drawing. "Why, that's beautiful!" he said. "It looks just like the river!"

Ron peeked over Mr. Mason's shoulder to look at the picture. Debby had drawn the river and the forest near the shed, just the way they were. The picture showed the sunlight sparkling on the water and the birds flying through the trees. Coming down the river was a boy paddling a kayak.

"That's just beautiful!" Mr. Mason said again. "I'll take it!"

Debby blushed and said, "I've been working on it all vacation. It's so great to be outdoors, instead of just looking at the world through my window."

Ron smiled at Debby. He was really proud of her. Then he looked at the picture again. He thought he'd seen the picture somewhere before, but he didn't know where. Then he remembered. It was the same picture that he'd seen on the computer screen when he was in the library.

He looked at the picture harder and harder and then reached out to touch it. But instead of touching paper, his fingers touched glass. He looked again and saw that the picture was on the computer screen. He was back in the library, back where he had begun his vacation.

Ron let out a startled cry. The woman at the desk smiled at him and said, "You've been sleeping at the computer. Did you finish your story?"

"I...I don't know," Ron answered. He looked at the screen again. Instead of the picture of the river, the screen showed the first few sentences of Ron's story. He read the first sentence, the one that said, "I spent my summer vacation in one of the hottest vacation spots in America."

Ron thought about that first sentence. Then he wrote a new second sentence. It said, "That spot is called the library."

After he'd written that sentence, the rest was easy. He explained how he'd gone to the library and dreamed that he was paddling a kayak in Maine. Then he told everything that had happened in his dream. It wasn't a real vacation, but it was almost as good as the real thing.

When he finished his story, Ron raced home just in time to meet his mother coming home from work.

"Ron! Debby!" she said, as she walked through the front door. "I have wonderful news! They've made me a manager at the store, and I'm going to make a lot more money! I think I can finally take us on a real vacation! How would you like to go to Maine next summer?"

"I'd love to," said Ron. "I hear it's a beautiful place."

C COMPREHENSION

Write the answers.

1. Why could Debby have been mad at Ron?

2. Why do you think Debby wasn't mad at Ron when she found him?

3. Why do you think Ron didn't mention the library to Debby and Mr. Mason?

4. How was Debby's picture of the river different from the pictures she drew in her room?

5. Why did Ron think the library was one of the hottest vacation spots in America?

D WRITING

- Ron explained how he got from the kayak shed to the pool, but the story doesn't show exactly what he said.

Pretend you are Ron. Explain how you got from the kayak shed to the pool.

Your explanation should answer these questions:

1. Why did you paddle past the shed?

2. Why couldn't you get out of the river before you entered the rapids?

3. How did you get by the first big boulder?

4. What happened when you got to the second boulder?

Write at least five sentences.

A | WORD LISTS

1	Hard Words
1.	acceptable
2.	depend
3.	explore
4.	frequent
5.	natural
6.	reminder

2	Vocabulary Words
1.	acknowledge
2.	aggressive
3.	ancestor
4.	behavior
5.	express
6.	intention

3	Vocabulary Words
1.	affection
2.	dominance
3.	interaction
4.	social

B | VOCABULARY FROM CONTEXT

1. To be sure, dogs do show **affection** to humans. But some of their behaviors have more to do with power than love.

2. One way a dog shows **dominance** is by making itself look bigger.

3. Puppies learn about **social interaction** through play. They explore how to get along in their pack. They learn which behaviors are acceptable and which are not.

C | READING INFORMATIONAL TEXT: Science

Dogspeak

Suppose you have a dog that jumps up on you when you come home. It leans heavily against you as you stand or sit. If you are in a chair or on the floor, the dog puts its paw on your leg or shoulder.

Why does your dog do these things? Is it expressing deep and faithful love for its master? Think again. Your dog wants to be the boss of you.

To be sure, dogs do show affection to humans. But some of their behaviors have more to do with power than love. Dogs constantly try to establish their rank within a group.

Establishing rank is part of a dog's natural makeup that has been passed down for centuries. Dogs inherit it from their wild ancestor, the wolf.

Within every wolf pack are two leaders and a group of followers. The leaders, called the alpha pair, are one male and one female.

The alpha wolves give frequent and clear reminders that they have the highest rank in the pack. They do this through their body language. Wolves and other animals use body language to show how they feel and what they may do.

One way a dog shows dominance is by making itself look bigger. It lifts its head high and thrusts out its chest.

When a dog meets a stranger, the hair on its back and shoulders might stand up. This change also makes the dog appear larger. The message is clear: "I'm bigger than you, and I'm in charge."

Small dogs do not always accept a lower rank. Often they jump on people or on other dogs to show that they are powerful. Another reason dogs jump is to try to make eye contact. A dog of high rank will look another dog in the eye. A dog that looks away accepts the idea that the dominant dog is in charge.

Keeping the Peace

Sometimes a dog does not want to give in, but it also does not want to fight. In this case, the dog might start to blink. By blinking, the dog can avoid a challenge without losing much respect. ♦

Dogs have other ways of showing they want to keep the peace. A dog of lower rank will turn its side toward a higher-ranking dog. This signals that the lower-ranking dog is not backing down, but acknowledges that the other dog has a higher rank.

At other times, a lower-ranking dog will pretend it does not notice a higher-ranking dog as it comes near. The lower-ranking dog may sniff the ground intently or stare into the distance. The lower-ranking dog's attention is focused away from the higher-ranking dog. This shows that the lower-ranking dog is not prepared to fight.

One of the most direct ways a dog avoids conflict is by scratching itself. An older dominant dog often does this to

avoid conflict with a younger dog. When a young dog starts to act aggressively, the older dog may simply sit and scratch itself, which shows that it is bored by the whole situation. As a rule, this behavior stops the young dog in its tracks. The older dog shows that it has no fear and no intention of fighting. It proves it is dominant by taking control. There will be no fight—end of the situation.

Learning Through Play

Puppies learn about social interaction through play. They explore how to get along in their pack. They learn which behaviors are acceptable and which are not. If a puppy bites one of its brothers or sisters too hard, the injured pup will yelp and run away. That is punishment because puppies love to play. They learn that they must play nicely to keep the game going.

While play with siblings can get rough, puppies learn early not to treat Mom or Dad that way. Young puppies know they depend on adult dogs. They use body language to persuade older dogs to take care of them. One such action is asking for food by licking or nudging an adult dog's face. By asking the dominant dog for food, the puppy admits its lower rank.

An outranked dog may make a nudging motion in the direction of a leader. Real contact may not even take place. But by using this "puppy behavior," a dog sends the message that it trusts the leader to take care of it.

Claiming the Alpha Role

All pups become bolder as they grow. Some young dogs will try to claim the alpha role. Yet it is a job they may not really want. Indeed, an alpha dog can become stressed when it feels responsible for a pack of humans.

Some experts believe this stress is the cause of some problem behaviors in pet dogs. A dog that tears up the house when its owners leave might not be upset that its "parents" left it. Rather, it might be worried because it cannot take care of some members of its pack.

Humans who learn that dogs treat them like members of a pack will be rewarded with a close and loyal friend. But remember to stand tall and claim your place as leader. After that, you and your pal can sniff noses and have fun.

D | COMPREHENSION

Write the answers.

1. How do alpha dogs show their rank? Give at least two examples.

2. How do lower-ranking dogs show they want to keep the peace? Give at least two examples.

3. What important rule about play do puppies learn through social interaction?

4. What group do dogs think humans belong to?

5. Why might a dog be worried when its human "parents" leave the house?

E | WRITING

Write a passage that answers this main question:

- How is a human family like a pack of dogs?

Your passage should also answer these questions:

1. Who are the alpha people in the family?

2. How do the alpha people show their rank?

3. How does the family keep the peace?

Write at least five sentences.

END OF LESSON 6

A WORD LISTS

1 Hard Words	**2** Word Practice	**3** Word Endings	**4** Vocabulary Words
1. Calducci	1. awesome	1. allowance	1. arouse
2. enthusiasm	2. cafeteria	2. appearance	2. bewildered
3. leather	3. ease	3. confidence	3. customary
4. thoroughly	4. fringe		4. flustered
	5. secret		5. fret
			6. sneer

B VOCABULARY FROM CONTEXT

1. Tora was **bewildered** by all the new features on her cell phone.

2. It is **customary** for the teacher to have a desk.

3. Mr. Soto began to **fret** when his children didn't come home from school on time. He was worried about them.

C STORY BACKGROUND

Fables

"The Jacket" is a modern **fable**—a story that teaches us a lesson. That lesson is called the **moral**. The moral of "The Jacket" tells about the self-confidence and power we each have inside of us.

Walter is a timid student until he gets a magic jacket. The story tells what Walter learns about himself by wearing the jacket.

The Jacket

Steven Otfinoski

Part 1

My name is Walter. I'm in the sixth grade, and until a few weeks ago, I was the number-one nerd at school. Then I put on the jacket and everything changed. But I think I'd better start at the beginning. Otherwise, I'm sure you won't believe what happened to me. I can hardly believe it myself.

It all started one Friday during lunch period. I was standing in line in the school cafeteria when "Gorilla" Gordon walked up to me. His real name is Gus, but everyone calls him Gorilla because he looks and acts like one. Of course, most kids only call him that behind his back. You live longer that way.

"Hi, punk," Gorilla said. "How about moving aside and letting me ahead of you? I'm really hungry today."

"Sure, Gus," I smiled. "Go right ahead."

To add insult to injury, Gorilla stomped on my foot as he walked past. It hurt, but I didn't say a word. Besides being a nerd, I was a coward, too.

After getting my lunch, I sat down at a table next to the new kid in school. His name is Bob, and he's a pretty nice guy. At least he didn't get up and leave when I sat down next to him like the other kids do.

"Why do you take that stuff from that big ape?" Bob asked me. He had seen what happened in line.

"Simple," I replied. "If I didn't, he'd cream me."

"He's not so tough," said Bob. "If you only stood up to him, I bet he'd crumble in a minute."

I wasn't enjoying this conversation at all and wished I'd taken my customary seat at an empty table. "That's easy for you say," I told Bob. "You're bigger. Guys like Gorilla don't pick on you."

"Size doesn't have anything to do with it," replied Bob. "It's all in how you

see yourself. I think I know someone who can help you."

Bob reached into his pocket, pulled out a small white business card, and handed it to me. I read the fine black print.

CALDUCCI'S CLOTHING SHOP
19 River Road
"Clothes that give confidence"

I looked up at Bob, bewildered. "I don't need any new clothes," I told him.

Bob just grinned. "Yes, you do," he said. "Mr. Calducci helped me, and he can help you too."

It sounded crazy, but I had to admit that Bob had aroused my curiosity. So Saturday morning I hopped on my bike and pedaled down to River Road. ♦

Calducci's Clothing Shop certainly wasn't much to look at. The shop window was dirty, and the sign above it looked as if it would fall apart if you breathed on it. But then I saw it in the window—the most awesome jacket I had ever laid eyes on. It was made of black leather with fringe the colors of the rainbow and beaded cuffs. **KING of the Mountain** was written across the back in glowing letters.

"Like to try it on?" someone spoke quietly. I looked up and saw a balding, middle-aged man with a black mustache. He was standing in the doorway.

"Are you Mr. Calducci?" I asked.

"That's me," he said, smiling. "Come on inside and I'll show you the jacket."

I hesitated. "I'm sure it's too expensive for me," I mumbled.

"Let's not talk about money," said the man, ushering me into the store. "One thing at a time."

So I tried on the jacket. It was a perfect fit. This was strange, because in the window it looked several sizes bigger. My skin tingled when I put it on. It felt like

there was a current of electricity running through me. It was exciting and a little scary at the same time.

"This jacket was made for you, young man," said Mr. Calducci.

"Maybe," I said, "but it wasn't made for my allowance. I'm sure I can't afford it."

"So, don't buy it," replied the store owner. "I'll tell you what. You can take it on loan."

I had never heard of a store that loans clothes, but I wasn't going to argue with him.

"You mean like a rental?" I asked.

"Yes, something like that," said Mr. Calducci. "See how you like it, and we'll talk later."

I thanked him and left wearing the jacket.

That night, I joked and talked at dinner more than I can ever remember. I actually felt completely at ease with my parents, and we didn't have *one* argument. My parents even believed my story about the jacket! It was truly amazing. I couldn't explain it, but the new jacket gave me a confidence that I'd never felt before.

The next day I woke up feeling full of enthusiasm. I actually looked forward to going to school. That was a switch! I put on my jacket over my school clothes and looked in the mirror. I wondered what the other kids would think of it.

You might say my taste in clothes before this was definitely on the nerdish side. What I wore pretty much reflected my personality. No one seemed to notice me much, which is just the way I liked it.

But did they ever notice me now! I was the center of attention the moment I strolled into class. And the amazing part was I thoroughly enjoyed it!

Our teacher, Ms. Bateman, gave us a surprise quiz that morning. I normally get so flustered during quizzes that I automatically get half the answers wrong. Or else I fret so long over one question that I never finish in time. But not now. I felt cool as a cucumber in my new jacket and answered every question with ease. When Ms. Bateman returned the corrected quizzes just before lunchtime, I had a perfect 100.

"Good work, Walter," said Ms. Bateman. "I'm pleased to see your study habits are improving."

How could I tell her my study habits had nothing to do with it—that it was all the jacket's doing?

In the lunch line, everyone wanted to get a closer look at my jacket. Kids who never noticed I was alive before were suddenly treating me like their best friend. That's when Gorilla Gordon made his appearance.

"Where'd you get the cool threads, punk?" Gorilla sneered. "The used clothing store?"

I looked at Gorilla and then at the other kids. No one said a word. I suddenly realized I wasn't scared of this bully one bit.

"Look, Gorilla," I said, looking him right in the eye, "why don't you find a nice tall tree to climb up into, and leave the jungle floor to us intelligent humans?"

You should have seen the expression on Gorilla's face! Once he got over the shock of having Walter the Nerd talk back to him, however, he got good and angry.

He reached out and grabbed me by the front of my jacket.

Before I knew what I was doing, I pulled his hands away and flipped him over my shoulder. He let out a groan as he hit the floor and just lay there stunned for a moment.

The circle of students cheered. "Guess that'll teach you to mess with the king!" yelled one boy.

Gorilla got up to the sound of jeering laughter, gave me a nasty look, and stalked away. That day I didn't have any problem finding company for lunch. Nearly everyone wanted to sit at my table and talk with me. In one day, I had gone from being Mr. Nobody to the Personality Kid.

At one point, I glanced up and saw Bob sitting across at another table. I smiled at him and he winked back at me. We were the only two people in school who knew the secret of my success.

E COMPREHENSION

Write the answers.

1. How is Gus like a gorilla?

2. What did Bob think would happen to Gorilla if Walter stood up to him?

Many things changed for Walter after he started wearing the jacket.

3. How did Walter change when he ate dinner with his parents?

4. How did Walter change during the surprise quiz?

5. How did Walter change when Gorilla tried to bully him?

F WRITING

Write a passage that answers this question:

• Do you think Walter's jacket is magic?

Use details from the story to answer these questions in your passage:

1. What was strange about the size of the jacket?

2. How did Walter's body feel when he put on the jacket?

3. How did Walter's attitude toward school change when he wore the jacket?

4. What was Walter able to do to Gorilla while wearing the jacket?

Write at least four sentences.

A WORD LISTS

1 Hard Words	**2** Vocabulary Words
1. assembly	1. candidate
2. athlete	2. expectant
3. auditorium	3. improvise
4. brilliant	4. ovation
5. election	5. philosophical
6. revenge	6. podium
	7. potential

B READING LITERATURE: Fable

The Jacket

Part 2

After I stood up to Gorilla, I wore my jacket everywhere. At school, at home. I even slept in it. I quickly became the best student in my class and the top athlete on the playing field during recess. Everyone was my friend—everybody but Gorilla Gordon—and when the time came to elect a class president for all the sixth grades, I was the leading candidate.

The day before the election was to be held, each candidate was supposed to give a short speech in a special assembly. I wrote my speech the night before. (It was brilliant, of course!) When I finished, I folded the speech and put it in my jacket pocket.

The next morning at school, all my friends were congratulating me as if I had already won the election. Before the assembly, I took my place backstage with the other three candidates.

Ms. Bateman asked me if I'd carry the wooden speaker's podium from backstage to center stage. It must have weighed fifty tons, and it was tough trying to lift it with my jacket on. So I took off the jacket and carefully folded it over a chair backstage. Then I lugged the podium out to the middle of the stage as the students took their seats in the auditorium.

Imagine my surprise when I came backstage and found my jacket was gone! Who could have taken it? I immediately thought of Gorilla Gordon. This was his revenge for showing him up in the cafeteria that day! I had to find him and get it back.

But just then Ms. Bateman appeared. "We're ready to begin, Walter," she said. "You'll speak second, all right?"

"But I can't," I stammered.

"What do you mean?" asked the teacher.

"My jacket's gone!" I told her.

"It is?" she said. "Maybe you just misplaced it. I'm sure it's around here someplace."

"You don't understand," I said. "My speech was in the pocket of my jacket."

"Oh," said Ms. Bateman. "Well, I'm sure you can improvise. You're such an excellent public speaker."

Now, the King of the Mountain was an excellent public speaker. But without that jacket, I wasn't king of anything. The moment of truth had come.

"Well," I said to myself, trying to be philosophical, "it was fun while it lasted." ♦

The first candidate finished her speech. Ms. Bateman gave me the signal to come out on stage. That twenty-foot walk to the podium was the longest walk of my life.

I gazed out over the expectant faces of my classmates. They looked eager, anxious to hear what I was going to say. Just realizing they already liked me, even before I opened my mouth, was comforting. Maybe all wasn't lost yet, I thought to myself.

"Fellow students," I began at last. "You've all noticed a big change in me over these past few weeks. Well, it wasn't really me that changed, but the way I felt about myself. My jacket says 'King of the Mountain.'

I think we're all kings of the mountain in our own ways. Maybe all anyone needs is a little confidence to scale the mountain. If you elect me your class president, I'll make it my goal to help you reach the top. If we work together, I think we can make our school number one. Thank you."

That was it. Short and sweet. There was a long moment of silence. I really blew it, I thought to myself. Then suddenly the applause started. Everybody in the auditorium was clapping and shouting. Some kids were even giving me a standing ovation. It was incredible!

As I made way for the next speaker, I noticed Gorilla Gordon down in front, clapping right along with everyone else. He didn't look like someone who had just stolen my jacket, but then maybe he was a better actor than I thought.

That afternoon, I looked all over school for the jacket. But it was nowhere to be found. I went home a worried wreck. The next day at school I had even more reason to worry. The votes were counted and I won the election by a landslide. Now I really felt like a fake. How was I ever going to make good as class president without my jacket to give me confidence?

After class, I rushed down River Road to Calducci's Clothing Shop. I figured whatever kind of wizard Mr. Calducci was, he could make me another jacket like the first one. But to my amazement, there was my jacket in the window where I had first seen it!

"Hello, young man," said Mr. Calducci when I entered the shop. "I'm surprised to see you back here."

"Not as surprised as I am," I told him. "How on earth did my jacket get back here?"

"That's simple," he explained. "I picked it up backstage before your speech. I told you it was only a loan."

I was stunned. "But why did you take it at the very moment I needed it most?"

Mr. Calducci smiled and shook his head. "You had no more use for it—as your speech proved. Frankly, I think your speech was a big improvement over the one you wrote. You made a discovery about yourself in that speech. The jacket was just a way to show you what you had inside all along."

It was beginning to sink in. Mr. Calducci was right. The jacket helped me to realize my potential. Now that I had confidence in myself, I didn't need it anymore.

"So the jacket always comes back to you?" I asked.

"Of course," he said. "All my clothes are strictly on short-term loan."

"I don't know how to thank you," I told him.

"The best way you can thank me is to tell someone else about my shop— someone else who needs a shot of self-confidence," said Mr. Calducci.

I said I would do that. Before I left, I took one last look at the jacket in the window. It didn't look so special anymore. It looked just like any other jacket.

That was a week ago. I haven't found anyone yet who needs Mr. Calducci's help. Maybe you know someone who could use a little self-confidence? Say, you look a little down in the dumps yourself. Why don't you take this card I have here? I know you won't be sorry ...

C COMPREHENSION

Write the answers.

1. "The Jacket" is a fable. What is a fable?

2. How does Walter feel about himself at the beginning of the story?

3. How does Walter's feeling about himself change when he wears the jacket?

4. Why didn't Walter need the jacket by the end of the story?

5. What is the moral of "The Jacket"?

D WRITING

Write a passage that answers this question:

- Why do you think Walter changed after he started wearing the jacket?

Use details from the story to answer these questions in your passage:

1. Was the jacket magic?

2. What did Walter believe about the jacket?

3. How did Walter's belief about the jacket change the way he felt about himself?

4. What happened when Walter stopped wearing the jacket?

Write at least four sentences.

END OF LESSON 8

A WORD LISTS

1	Hard Words
1.	aunt
2.	Dorothy
3.	Kansas
4.	surroundings
5.	Toto
6.	whirlwind

2	Word Endings
1.	people
2.	sprinkle
3.	terrible
4.	tinkle

3	Word Endings
1.	happy
2.	happi • ly
3.	angry
4.	merry

4	Vocabulary Words
1.	arise
2.	attic
3.	cyclone
4.	horizon
5.	in spite of
6.	mass

B STORY BACKGROUND

From Kansas to Oz

Today you will start reading a famous novel called *The Wonderful Wizard of Oz*. The version you will read is shorter than the original book, but the story remains the same.

The Wonderful Wizard of Oz begins in the state of Kansas more than a hundred years ago. At that time, people had almost none of the machines that we use today. They didn't have cars or televisions. They didn't have radios, cell phones, or computers. They used candles to light their houses, and they kept warm in the winter by building fires in their fireplaces.

The map shows where Kansas is located. Kansas is a prairie, which is a mostly flat grassland with almost no trees.

More than a hundred years ago, many people moved to Kansas to become farmers. But life was hard for the early farmers in Kansas because the winters were cold and the summers were hot and dry. During the late summer, the hot sun would turn the green grass gray, and the land would dry up and crack. The streams and ponds would also dry up, and the wind would blow great clouds of dust.

The Wonderful Wizard of Oz

L. Frank Baum

Adapted for young readers

Chapter 1

Kansas

Dorothy lived in the middle of the great Kansas prairies with Uncle Henry, who was a farmer, and Aunt Em, who was Uncle Henry's wife. Their house was small, for the lumber to build it had to be carried many miles by wagon. There were four walls, a floor, and a roof, which made one room. This room contained a rusty cooking stove, a cupboard for the dishes, a table, four chairs, and the beds. Uncle Henry and Aunt Em had a big bed in one corner, and Dorothy had a little bed in another corner.

There was no attic at all and no cellar—except a small hole, dug in the ground, called a cyclone cellar. The family could go into the cellar in case one of those great whirlwinds arose, mighty enough to crush any building in its path. The cellar was reached by a trapdoor in the middle of the floor. A ladder inside led down into a small, dark hole.

When Dorothy stood in the doorway and looked outside, she could see nothing but the great, gray prairie on every side. No trees or houses could be seen on the flat country that reached the edge of the sky in all directions.

The sun had baked the plowed land into a gray mass with little cracks running through it. Not even the grass was green, for the sun had burned the tops of the grass blades until they were the same gray color as the land. Once, the house had been painted white, but the sun blistered the paint and the rains washed it away, and now the house was as dull and gray as everything else.

When Aunt Em came here to live, she was young and pretty. The sun and wind had changed her, too. They had taken the sparkle from her eyes and left them a sober gray. They had taken the red from her cheeks and lips, and they were gray also. She was thin and she never smiled, now. ♦

Dorothy was an orphan, which was why she had come to live with her aunt and uncle. At first, Aunt Em had been so startled by Dorothy's laughter that she would scream and press her hand upon her heart whenever Dorothy laughed. Aunt Em was still amazed that Dorothy could find anything to laugh about.

Uncle Henry never laughed. He worked hard from morning till night and did not know what joy was. He was gray also, from his long beard to his rough boots. He looked stern, and he rarely spoke.

It was Toto who made Dorothy laugh and kept her from growing as gray as her surroundings. Toto was not gray. He was a little black dog, with long, silky hair and small black eyes that twinkled merrily on either side of his funny, small nose. Toto played all day long, and Dorothy played with him and loved him dearly.

Today, however, Dorothy and Toto were not playing. Uncle Henry sat on the doorstep and looked anxiously at the sky, which was even grayer than usual. Dorothy stood in the door with Toto in her arms and looked at the sky, too. Aunt Em was washing the dishes.

E COMPREHENSION

Write the answers.

1. Why was Dorothy's house small?

2. Why was the land around Dorothy's house gray?

3. Why had Dorothy's house turned from white to gray?

4. How had the sun and wind changed Aunt Em?

5. Why was Uncle Henry looking anxiously at the sky?

F WRITING

Write a passage that describes Dorothy's house.

Use details from the novel to answer these questions in your passage:

1. Where is the house located?

2. What is the house made of?

3. What color is the house?

4. How many rooms does the house have?

5. What furniture does the house have?

Write at least five sentences.

END OF LESSON 9

A WORD LISTS

1 Hard Words

1. danger
2. gorgeous
3. magician
4. pressure
5. sorceress

2 Words with Same Spelling

1. bowed/bowed
2. close/close
3. dove/dove

3 Vocabulary Words

1. bondage
2. cradle
3. for

4 Vocabulary Words

1. brilliant
2. deaf
3. dismally
4. ripple

B VOCABULARY FROM CONTEXT

1. The **brilliant** feathers of the birds were every color you could imagine.
   - gray
   - bright
   - unhappy

2. The wind shrieked so loudly that the girl nearly became **deaf.**
   - unable to see
   - unable to hear
   - unable to smell

3. The lonely dog put his head in the air and whined **dismally.**
   - eagerly
   - rapidly
   - sadly

4. The wind made **ripples** in the grass that rose and fell.
   - small waves
   - bricks
   - dandelions

Cyclones

Chapter 2 of *The Wonderful Wizard of Oz* tells about a cyclone. Here are some facts about cyclones.

A cyclone is a strong wind that spins around and around. One kind of cyclone looks like a giant funnel. This kind of cyclone is also called a tornado or a twister.

A cyclone moves forward quickly and destroys almost everything in its path. The wind that forms a cyclone may spin as fast as 300 miles an hour.

The middle of the cyclone is called the eye of the cyclone. Most eyes are narrow, but some are wider than a house. The air in the eye is still, but it is surrounded by the spinning wind.

The picture shows the parts of a cyclone.

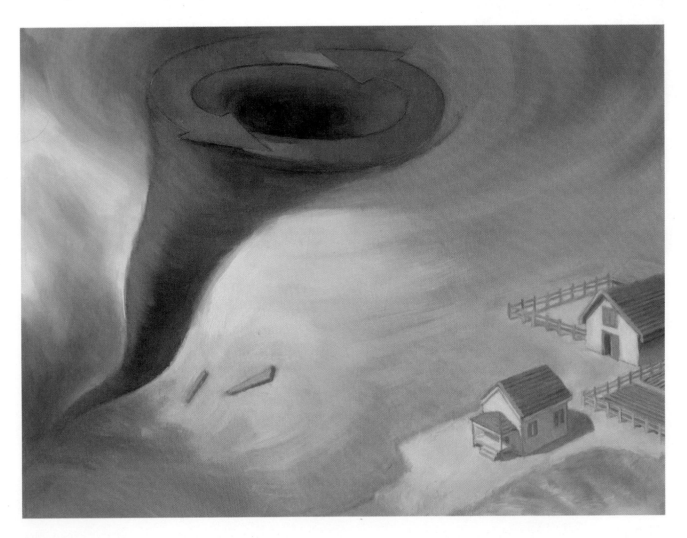

Chapter 2

The Cyclone

Uncle Henry and Dorothy kept looking at the sky. After a while, they heard a low wailing wind from the north. They could see where the long grass bent in waves before the coming storm.

There now came a sharp whistling from the south. As Uncle Henry and Dorothy turned their eyes that way, they saw ripples in the grass coming from that direction also.

Suddenly Uncle Henry stood up.

"There's a cyclone coming, Em," he called to his wife. "I'll go look after the animals." Then he ran toward the sheds where the cows and horses were kept.

Aunt Em dropped her work and came to the door. One glance told her of the danger close at hand.

"Quick, Dorothy!" she screamed. "Run for the cellar!"

Toto jumped out of Dorothy's arms and hid under the bed inside the house, and the girl went after him. Aunt Em was badly frightened. She threw open the trapdoor in the floor and climbed down the ladder into the small, dark hole.

Dorothy caught Toto at last and started to follow her aunt. When she was halfway across the room, there came a great shriek from the wind, and the house shook so hard that Dorothy lost her footing and sat down suddenly on the floor.

Then a strange thing happened.

The house whirled around two or three times and rose slowly through the air. Dorothy felt as if she were going up in a balloon.

The north and south winds met where the house stood and made it the exact center of the cyclone. In the middle of a cyclone the air is generally still, but the great pressure of the wind on every side of the house raised it higher and higher until the house was at the very top of the cyclone. The house stayed at the top, and then it was carried miles and miles away as easily as you could carry a feather.

It became very dark, and the wind howled horribly, but Dorothy found she was riding quite easily. After the first few whirls and one other time when the house tipped badly, she felt as if she were being rocked gently, like a baby in a cradle.

Toto did not like it. He ran about the room, here and there, barking loudly. But Dorothy sat quite still on the floor and waited to see what would happen.

Once Toto got too near the open trapdoor and fell in. At first, Dorothy thought she had lost him, but soon she saw one of his ears sticking up through the hole. The strong pressure of the air was keeping him from falling. ♦

Dorothy crept to the hole, caught Toto, and dragged him into the room again. Then she closed the trapdoor so that no more accidents could happen.

Hour after hour passed away, and slowly Dorothy got over her fright. She still felt quite lonely, and the wind shrieked so loudly that she nearly became deaf. At first she wondered if she would be smashed to pieces when the house fell again. But as the hours passed and

nothing terrible happened, she stopped worrying and decided to wait calmly and see what would happen. At last she crawled over the swaying floor to her bed and lay down on it. Toto followed and lay down beside her.

In spite of the swaying of the house and the wailing of the wind, Dorothy soon closed her eyes and fell fast asleep.

E INFERENCES

Work the items.

The smoke was getting into Ben's eyes and making him cough. He felt the wall. It was hot. He followed the wall slowly toward the door. He bumped into the car. It was hot. At last he opened the door and fell on the ground outside. He could hear sirens down the street and people hollering.

1. What was getting in Ben's eyes and making him cough?

2. What did you use to answer question 1: explicit statement or inference?

3. Why was Ben trying to get out of the garage?

4. What did you use to answer question 3: explicit statement or inference?

5. What object did Ben bump into?

6. What did you use to answer question 5: explicit statement or inference?

7. Who was coming to help Ben?

8. What did you use to answer question 7: explicit statement or inference?

9. What did Ben hear when he was outside?

10. What did you use to answer question 9: explicit statement or inference?

F COMPREHENSION

Write the answers.

1. Why did Uncle Henry run toward the animals before the cyclone hit?

2. Why didn't Dorothy go into the cellar right away?

3. Why did Dorothy decide to wait calmly while the cyclone carried the house?

4. How did Toto behave differently from Dorothy when the cyclone lifted the house?

5. What kept Toto from falling through the trapdoor?

G WRITING

Write a passage about the brave things Dorothy did in this chapter.

Use evidence from this chapter to answer these questions in your passage:

1. What did Dorothy do when Toto ran away?

2. How did Dorothy act while the house was spinning around?

3. What did Dorothy do when Toto fell through the hole?

Write at least four sentences.

END OF LESSON 10

11

A WORD LISTS

1	Hard Words
1.	calmly
2.	gracious
3.	marvelous
4.	wizard

2	Word Practice
1.	bowed/bowed
2.	grown-up
3.	jolt
4.	Munchkins
5.	paused
6.	polished

3	Related Words
1.	magic
2.	magical
3.	magician

4	Precious Stones
1.	diamonds
2.	emeralds
3.	rubies

5	Vocabulary Review
1.	bondage
2.	brilliant
3.	deaf
4.	dismally
5.	ripples

6	Vocabulary Words
1.	cheering
2.	civilized
3.	inquire

7	Vocabulary Words
1.	brook
2.	gorgeous
3.	messenger
4.	sorceress
5.	sprinkled

B VOCABULARY FROM CONTEXT

1. The **brook** was filled with bubbling, sparkling water that rushed along.
   - small croak
   - small stream
   - small puddle

2. Everything was beautiful, especially the **gorgeous** flowers.
   - very pretty
   - very loud
   - very ugly

3. A **messenger** came and brought me the news.
   - person who is messy
   - person who can't move
   - person who delivers messages

4. She was such a powerful witch that people said she was the greatest **sorceress** in the land.
   - tree
   - magician
   - man

5. Her white dress was **sprinkled** with bright little stars.
   - dotted
   - blackened
   - rough

Chapter 3

The Munchkins

A sudden jolt awakened Dorothy. It was so sudden that it might have hurt her if she had not been lying on the soft bed. The jolt made her catch her breath and wonder what had happened. Toto put his cold little nose into her face and whined dismally.

Dorothy sat up and noticed that the house was not moving; nor was it dark, for bright sunshine came in the window, filling the little room. She sprang from her bed, and with Toto following at her heels, she ran across the room and opened the door.

Then Dorothy looked around and gave a cry of amazement. Her eyes grew bigger and bigger at the wonderful sights she saw. The cyclone had set the house down in a country of marvelous beauty. There were lovely patches of green grass all around, with large trees bearing rich fruits. Gorgeous flowers were everywhere, and birds with brilliant feathers sang and fluttered in the trees and bushes. A small brook was close by, rushing and sparkling along between green banks. The sound of the brook was very cheering to the girl who had lived so long on the dry, gray prairies.

While Dorothy stood looking eagerly at the beautiful sights, she noticed a group of strange people coming toward her. They were not as big as the grown-ups Dorothy was used to, but neither were they very small. In fact, they seemed about as tall as Dorothy, who was tall for her age, although they looked many years older.

The group consisted of three men and one woman, and all were oddly dressed.

They wore round hats that rose to a small point a foot above their heads. Little bells around the hat brims tinkled sweetly when the people moved. The hats of the men were blue. The woman's hat was white, and she wore a white gown that was sprinkled with little stars that glistened in the sun like diamonds.

The men were dressed in blue, of the same shade as their hats, and they wore well-polished boots with blue bands at the tops. The men, Dorothy thought, were about as old as Uncle Henry, for two of them had beards. But the woman looked much older: her face was covered with wrinkles, her hair was nearly white, and she walked rather stiffly.

When the men came near where Dorothy was standing, they paused and whispered among themselves. They acted as if they were afraid to come closer. But the old woman walked up to Dorothy, made a low bow, and said in a sweet voice, "You are welcome, most noble sorceress, to the Land of the Munchkins. We are grateful to you for having killed the Wicked Witch of the East and for setting our people free from bondage."

Dorothy listened to this speech with wonder. What could the woman possibly mean by calling her a sorceress and saying that she had killed the Wicked Witch of the East? She was just a harmless little girl who had been carried by a cyclone many miles from home, and she had never killed anything in her life.

But the old woman seemed to expect an answer, so Dorothy said, "You are very kind, but there must be some mistake. I have not killed anyone."

"Your house did, anyway," replied the old woman with a laugh. "Look!" she continued, pointing to the corner of the house. "There are her two feet, still sticking out from under your house."

Dorothy looked and gave a little cry of fright. There, indeed, under the corner of the house, two feet were sticking out, wearing silver shoes with pointed toes.

"Oh, dear! Oh, dear!" cried Dorothy, clasping her hands together. "The house must have fallen on her. What shall we do?"

"There is nothing to be done," said the woman calmly.

"But who was she?" asked Dorothy.

"She was the Wicked Witch of the East, as I said," answered the woman. "She has held all the Munchkins in bondage for many years, making them slave for her night and day. Now they are all set free, and we are grateful to you."

"Who are the Munchkins?" inquired Dorothy.

"They are the people who live in this Land of the East, where the Wicked Witch ruled."

"Are you a Munchkin?" asked Dorothy.

"No, but I am their friend, although I live in the Land of the North. When the Munchkins saw that the Witch of the East was dead, they sent a swift messenger to me, and I came at once. I am the Witch of the North." ♦

"Oh, gracious!" cried Dorothy. "Are you a real witch?"

"Yes, indeed," answered the woman. "But I am a good witch, and the people love me. I am not as powerful as the Wicked Witch was; if I had been, I would have set the Munchkins free myself."

"But I thought all witches were wicked," said the girl, who was half-frightened at facing a real witch.

"Oh, no, that is not true. There are only four witches in all the Land of Oz, and two of them, those who live in the Land of the North and the Land of the South, are good witches. I know this is true, for I am one of them myself and cannot be mistaken. The witches who live in the Land of the East and the Land of the West are wicked witches. But now that you have killed one of them, there is only one wicked witch in all the Land of Oz—the one who lives in the Land of the West."

"But," said Dorothy, after a moment's thought, "Aunt Em told me that the witches all died years and years ago."

"Who is Aunt Em?" inquired the old woman.

"She is my aunt who lives in Kansas, where I came from," said Dorothy.

The Witch of the North seemed to think for a time, with her head bowed and her eyes upon the ground. Then she looked up and said, "I do not know where Kansas is, for I have never heard of that country. But tell me, is it a civilized country?"

"Oh, yes," replied Dorothy.

"Then that explains it. In the civilized countries, I believe there are no witches left—nor wizards nor sorceresses nor magicians. But, you see, the Land of Oz has never been civilized, for we are cut off from all the rest of the world. Therefore, we still have witches and wizards."

"Who are the wizards?" asked Dorothy.

"Oz himself is the Great Wizard," answered the Witch, sinking her voice to a whisper. "He is more powerful than all the rest of us together. He lives in the Emerald City."

D COMPREHENSION

Write the answers.

1. Describe how the Land of Oz looked different from Kansas.

2. Why did the Witch of the North think Dorothy was a sorceress?

3. Why were the Munchkins grateful to Dorothy?

4. How are civilized countries different from the Land of Oz?

5. What kind of powers do you think the Witch of the North has?

E WRITING

Write a passage that compares Kansas with the Land of Oz.

Use details from the novel to answer these questions in your passage:

1. What does Kansas look like?

2. What does the Land of Oz look like?

3. What kind of people live in Kansas?

4. What kind of people live in Oz?

Write at least five sentences.

END OF LESSON 11

12

A   WORD LISTS

1 | Hard Words

1. delicious
2. desert
3. handkerchief

2 | Word Practice

1. exact
2. gracious
3. magical
4. sunbonnet

3 | People in Oz

1. Gillikins
2. Munchkins
3. Quadlings
4. Winkies

4 | Vocabulary Review

1. brook
2. civilized
3. gorgeous
4. messenger
5. sprinkled

5 | Vocabulary Words

1. gingham
2. leather
3. silk
4. velvet

6 | Vocabulary Words

1. balanced
2. pave
3. slate

7 | Vocabulary Words

1. brisk
2. charm
3. journey
4. sob
5. solemn
6. trot

B   VOCABULARY FROM CONTEXT

1. She walked at such a **brisk** pace that she arrived at the city an hour before the others.
   - slow
   - happy
   - fast

2. Her shoes had a secret **charm** that kept her out of danger.
   - shoelace
   - magic power
   - heel

3. They took a long **journey** through the forest and past the fields.
   - ribbon
   - moment
   - trip

4. Dorothy began to **sob,** and large tears fell from her eyes.
   - cry
   - smile
   - listen

5. She looked grim as she counted in a **solemn** voice.
   - clear
   - serious
   - happy

6. The dog's legs were so short that he had to **trot** to keep up with his master.
   - sleep
   - run slowly
   - eat

C READING LITERATURE: Novel

Chapter 4

The Yellow Brick Road

Dorothy was going to ask another question, but just then the Munchkins, who had been standing silently by, gave a loud shout and pointed to the corner of the house where the Wicked Witch had been lying.

"What is it?" asked the good witch. She looked and began to laugh. The feet of the dead witch had disappeared entirely and nothing was left but the silver shoes.

"She was so old," explained the Witch of the North, "that she dried up quickly in the sun. That is the end of her. But the silver shoes are yours, and you shall have them to wear."

The Witch of the North reached down and picked up the shoes. After shaking out the dust, she handed them to Dorothy. "The Witch of the East was proud of these silver shoes," said the old woman. "They have some kind of magical charm, but I do not know what it is."

Dorothy carried the shoes into the house and placed them on the table. Then she came out again to the Munchkins and said, "I am anxious to get back to my aunt and uncle, for I am sure they will worry about me. Can you help me find my way?"

The Munchkins and the witch first looked at one another, and then at Dorothy, and then they shook their heads.

"I am afraid," said the witch, "that a great desert surrounds the whole Land of Oz, and no one can live to cross it."

The witch reached behind her back and pulled out a slate. A map of the Land of Oz suddenly appeared on it.

One Munchkin pointed to the Land of the East on the map and said, "This is where we are now. You can see that the desert is not far from here."

The second Munchkin pointed to the Land of the South. "The South is where the Quadlings live," he said. "They have the same desert, for I have been there and seen it."

"I am told," said the third Munchkin, "that the West also has the same desert. And that country, where the Winkies live, is ruled by the Wicked Witch of the West. She would make you her slave if you passed her way."

"The North is my home, and the Gillikins live there," said the witch. "This same great desert is also at its edge. The only part of the Land of Oz that doesn't touch the desert is the Emerald City, which is in the middle of Oz. I am sorry, my dear, but it appears that you will have to live with us, because you cannot cross the desert."

Dorothy began to sob at this, for she felt lonely among all these strange people.

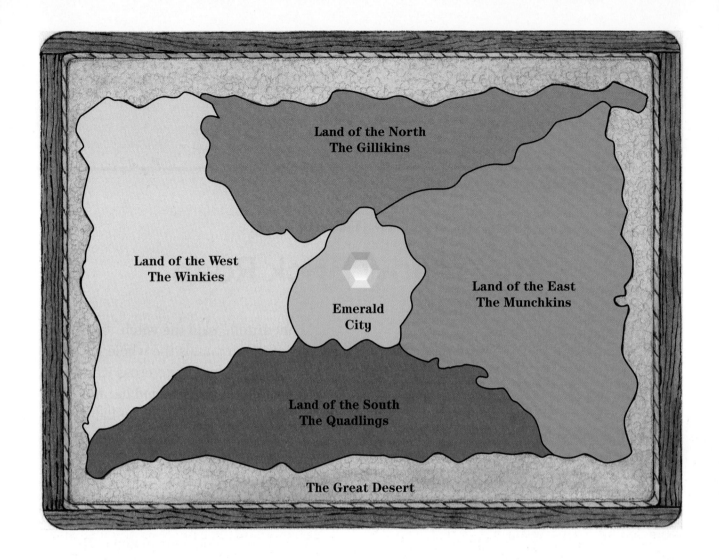

Land of the North
The Gillikins

Land of the West
The Winkies

Land of the East
The Munchkins

Emerald
City

Land of the South
The Quadlings

The Great Desert

Her tears seemed to make the kindhearted Munchkins sad, for they immediately took out their handkerchiefs and also began to weep.

As for the witch, she put the slate on the ground, took off her round hat, turned it upside down, and balanced the point on the end of her nose. Then she counted "One, two, three" in a solemn voice.

All at once, the map on the slate faded away, and big white letters appeared in its place. The letters said: LET DOROTHY GO TO THE EMERALD CITY.

The old woman read the words on the slate and asked, "Is your name Dorothy, my dear?"

"Yes," answered the child, looking up and drying her tears.

"Then you must go to the Emerald City. Perhaps Oz will help you."

"Where is this city?" asked Dorothy.

"It is in the exact center of the country, and it is ruled by Oz, the Great Wizard I told you about."

"Is Oz a good man?" inquired Dorothy, anxiously.

"He is a good wizard. Whether he is a man or not I cannot tell, for I have never seen him."

"How can I get there?" asked Dorothy.

"You must walk. It is a long journey, through a country that is sometimes pleasant and sometimes dark and terrible. However, I will use all the magic arts I know to keep you from harm."

"Won't you go with me?" pleaded the girl, who had begun to think that the old woman was her only friend.

"No, I cannot do that," she replied. "But I will give you my kiss, and no one will dare injure a person who has been kissed by the Witch of the North."

She came close to Dorothy and kissed her gently on the forehead. Her lips left a round, shining mark on Dorothy's skin.

"The road to the Emerald City is paved with yellow brick," said the witch, "so you cannot miss it. When you get to see the Great Oz, do not be afraid. Just tell your story and ask him to help you. Goodbye, my dear."

The three Munchkins bowed low to Dorothy and wished her a pleasant journey, after which they walked away through the trees. The witch gave Dorothy a friendly little nod, whirled around on her left heel three times, and disappeared, much to the surprise of little Toto. But Dorothy, who knew that the woman was a witch, had expected her to disappear in just that way and was not surprised in the least. ♦

When Dorothy was left alone, she began to feel hungry. So she went into the house and cut herself some bread, which she spread with butter. She gave some of the bread to Toto. Then she took a pail from the shelf and carried it down to the little brook, where she filled it with clear, sparkling water.

Toto ran over to the trees and began to bark at the birds sitting there. Dorothy went to get him and saw such delicious fruit hanging from the branches that she gathered some of it. It was just what she wanted to complete her breakfast.

Then Dorothy went back to the house. She helped herself and Toto to a good drink of the cool, clear water, and she started to prepare for the journey to the Emerald City.

Dorothy had only one other dress, but that happened to be clean and was hanging on a peg beside her bed. It was gingham, with checks of white and blue; and although the blue was somewhat faded, it was still a pretty dress. The girl washed herself carefully, dressed herself in the clean gingham, and put her pink sunbonnet on her head. She took a little basket and filled it with bread from the cupboard and laid a white cloth over the top. Then she looked down at her feet and noticed how old her shoes were.

"They surely will never do for a long journey, Toto," she said. And Toto looked up into her face with his little black eyes and wagged his tail to show that he knew what she meant.

At that moment, Dorothy saw the Wicked Witch's silver shoes lying on the table.

"I wonder if they will fit me," she said to Toto. "They would be just the thing to take a long walk in."

She took off her old leather shoes and tried on the silver ones. They fit her just as well as if they had been made for her.

Finally, she picked up her basket.

"Come along, Toto," she said. "We will go to the Emerald City and ask the Great Oz how to get back to Kansas."

She closed the door, locked it, and put the key carefully in the pocket of her dress. And so, with Toto trotting along behind her, she started on her journey.

There were several roads nearby, but it did not take her long to find the one paved with yellow brick. Within a short time, she was walking briskly toward the Emerald City, her silver shoes tinkling merrily on the hard yellow roadbed. The sun shone brightly and the birds sang sweetly. Dorothy did not feel at all sad, even though she had been taken from her home and set down in a strange land.

D INFERENCES

Work the items.

Maria gripped the bat a little bit harder and looked at the pitcher. She watched as the pitcher went into his windup and threw very hard. The ball was moving fast, but she kept her eye on it as she swung the bat. Smack! The ball soared high in the air and went over the fence behind the outfielders. Maria ran around the bases and touched home plate. Her team was now ahead, one to nothing.

1. What did Maria grip a little bit harder?

2. What did you use to answer item 1: explicit statement or inference?

3. What game was Maria playing?

4. What did you use to answer item 3: explicit statement or inference?

5. What kind of hit did Maria get?

6. What did you use to answer item 5: explicit statement or inference?

7. What did Maria touch after she ran around the bases?

8. What did you use to answer item 7: explicit statement or inference?

9. Why was Maria's team now ahead?

10. What did you use to answer item 9: explicit statement or inference?

E COMPREHENSION

Write the answers.

1. Why did the feet of the dead witch disappear?

2. Why can't Dorothy leave the Land of Oz?

3. Give at least two examples of the good witch's magical powers.

4. Why wasn't Dorothy surprised when the witch suddenly disappeared?

5. Why was Dorothy happy at the end of the chapter?

F WRITING

Write a passage that answers this question:

- Where do you think Dorothy should live, in Kansas or the Land of Oz?

Use details from the novel to answer these other questions in your passage:

1. What is good about Kansas for Dorothy?

2. What is bad about Kansas for Dorothy?

3. What is good about the Land of Oz for Dorothy?

4. What is bad about the Land of Oz for Dorothy?

Write at least five sentences.

END OF LESSON 12

13

A WORD LISTS

1 | Hard Words
1. Boq
2. clumsiness
3. curiosity
4. ordinary
5. scarecrow
6. uncomfortable

2 | Word Endings
1. apparently
2. earnestly
3. gratefully
4. politely

3 | Vocabulary Review
1. brisk
2. journey
3. solemn
4. trot

4 | Vocabulary Review
1. gingham
2. leather
3. silk
4. velvet

5 | Vocabulary Words
1. apparent
2. crops
3. dome
4. fiddler
5. field of grain
6. injured

6 | Vocabulary Words
1. amused
2. earnestly
3. hearty
4. husky
5. represent
6. resolved
7. suspected

B VOCABULARY FROM CONTEXT

1. The dog looked so funny that she **amused** all of us.
   - saddened
   - bit
   - entertained

2. She wanted them to understand, so she told about her problem very **earnestly.**
   - sincerely
   - happily
   - timidly

3. Dorothy was so hungry that she ate a **hearty** supper.
   - tiny
   - late
   - large

4. He was a big man and he spoke in a **husky** voice.
   - small
   - high
   - deep or thick

5. The mask that she wore **represented** the face of a gorilla.
   - looked like
   - sounded like
   - smelled like

6. Although he felt like crying, he **resolved** to keep the tears back.
   - made his bed
   - made up his mind
   - made a joke

7. He wasn't sure, but he **suspected** that she was a witch.
   - thought
   - doubted
   - knew

C READING LITERATURE: Novel

Chapter 5

The Scarecrow

Dorothy was surprised, as she walked along, to see how pretty the country was. There were neat fences, painted a blue color, at the sides of the road, and beyond them were fields of grain and vegetables. Apparently, the Munchkins were good farmers and knew how to raise large crops.

Once in a while, Dorothy would pass a house, and the people would come out to look at her. They would bow low as she went by, for everyone knew she had destroyed the Wicked Witch and set them free from bondage.

The houses of the Munchkins were odd looking. Each was round, with a big dome for a roof. All were painted blue, for in this country of the East, blue was the favorite color.

Toward evening, when Dorothy was tired from her long walk and was beginning to wonder where she should pass the night, she came to a house that was larger than the rest. Many men and women were dancing on the green lawn in front of the house. Five little fiddlers played as loudly as possible, and the people were laughing and singing. A big table nearby was loaded with delicious fruits, nuts, cakes, and many other good things to eat.

The people greeted Dorothy kindly and invited her to dinner. Then they asked her to spend the night with them. The home belonged to one of the richest Munchkins in the land, and his friends were gathered with him to celebrate their freedom from the bondage of the Wicked Witch.

Dorothy ate a hearty supper and was waited on by the rich Munchkin himself, whose name was Boq. Then she sat down on a bench and watched the people dance.

When Boq saw her silver shoes, he said, "You must be a great sorceress."

"Why?" asked the girl.

"Because you wear silver shoes and have killed the Wicked Witch of the East. Besides, you have white in your dress, and only witches and sorceresses wear white."

"My dress is blue and white checked," said Dorothy, smoothing out the wrinkles in it.

"It is kind of you to wear that," said Boq. "Blue is the color of the Munchkins, and white is the witch color, so we know you are a friendly witch."

Dorothy did not know what to say to this, for all the people seemed to think that she was a witch. But she knew very well that she was only an ordinary little girl.

When Dorothy grew tired of watching the dancing, Boq led her into the house,

where he gave her a room with a pretty bed in it. The sheets were made of blue cloth, and Dorothy slept soundly on them till morning, with Toto curled up on the blue rug beside her.

She ate a hearty breakfast and watched a small Munchkin baby, who played with Toto and pulled his tail and laughed in a way that greatly amused Dorothy. Toto was a curiosity to all the people, for they had never seen a dog before.

"How far is it to the Emerald City?" the girl asked.

"I do not know," answered Boq solemnly. "I have never been there. It is better for people to keep away from Oz unless they have business with him. But it is a long way to the Emerald City, and the journey will take many days. The country here is rich and pleasant, but you must pass through rough and dangerous places before you reach the end of your journey."

Boq's statement worried Dorothy a little, but she knew that only the Great Oz could help her get to Kansas again, so she bravely resolved not to turn back.

She said goodbye to her friends and again started along the Yellow Brick Road. When she had gone several miles, she wanted to rest, so she climbed to the top of the fence beside the road and sat down. There was a large cornfield beyond the fence, and not far away she saw a Scarecrow, placed high on a pole to keep the birds away from the ripe corn.

Dorothy leaned her chin upon her hand and gazed thoughtfully at the Scarecrow, whose head was a small sack stuffed with straw. Eyes, nose, and mouth were painted on it to represent a face.

The Scarecrow had an old blue pointed Munchkin hat on his head, and he wore a faded blue suit of clothes, which was also stuffed with straw. On his feet were some old boots with blue tops, just like those that Munchkin men wore. The Scarecrow was raised above the stalks of corn by a pole stuck up his back.

While Dorothy was looking earnestly into the strange painted face of the Scarecrow, she was surprised to see one of the eyes slowly wink at her. She thought she was seeing things at first, for none of the scarecrows in Kansas ever winked at her. Then the Scarecrow nodded his head to her in a friendly way. She climbed down from the fence and walked up to him while Toto ran around the pole and barked.

"Good day," said the Scarecrow in a rather husky voice.

"Did you speak?" asked the girl in wonder.

"Certainly," answered the Scarecrow. "How do you do?"

"I'm pretty well, thank you," replied Dorothy politely. "How do you do?"

"I'm not feeling well," said the Scarecrow, with a smile, "for it is very boring to be stuck up here night and day to scare away crows."

"Can't you get down?" asked Dorothy.

"No, for this pole is stuck up my back. If you will please take away the pole, I will be very grateful to you."

Dorothy stretched her arms and easily lifted the Scarecrow off the pole. Because he was stuffed with straw, the Scarecrow was quite light. "Thank you very much," said the Scarecrow when he had been set down on the ground. "I feel like a new man."

Dorothy thought it was odd to hear a stuffed man speak and to see him bow and walk along beside her. ♦

"Who are you?" asked the Scarecrow when he had stretched himself and yawned. "And where are you going?"

"My name is Dorothy," said the girl, "and I am going to the Emerald City to ask the Great Oz to send me back to Kansas."

"Where is the Emerald City?" he inquired. "And who is Oz?"

"Why, don't you know?" she answered in surprise.

"No, indeed. I don't know anything. You see, I am stuffed with straw, so I have no brains at all," he said sadly.

"Oh," said Dorothy, "I'm awfully sorry for you."

The Scarecrow asked, "Do you think that if I go to the Emerald City with you, Oz would give me some brains?"

"I do not know," she answered, "but you may come with me if you like. If Oz will not give you any brains, you will be no worse off than you are now."

"That is true," said the Scarecrow. "You see," he continued, "I don't mind my legs and arms and body being stuffed, because I cannot get hurt. If anyone steps on my toes or sticks a pin into me, it doesn't matter, for I can't feel it. But I do not want people to call me a fool, and if my head stays stuffed with straw instead of with brains, how am I ever to know anything?"

"I understand how you feel," said the girl, who was truly sorry for him. "If you will come with me, I'll ask Oz to do all he can for you."

"Thank you," he answered gratefully.

They walked back to the road. Dorothy helped him over the fence, and they started along the Yellow Brick Road for the Emerald City.

Toto did not like the Scarecrow at first. He sniffed around the stuffed man as if he suspected there might be a nest of rats in the Scarecrow's straw, and he often growled at the Scarecrow in an unfriendly way.

"Don't mind Toto," said Dorothy to her new friend. "He never bites."

"Oh, I'm not afraid," replied the Scarecrow. "He can't hurt the straw. Do let me carry that basket for you. I won't mind it, for I can't get tired. I'll tell you a secret," he continued as he walked along. "There is only one thing in the world that I am afraid of."

"What is that?" asked Dorothy. "The Munchkin farmer who made you?"

"No," answered the Scarecrow. "The only thing I fear is a lighted match."

D COMPREHENSION

Write the answers.

1. Why did Boq think that Dorothy was a sorceress?

2. What would make you think that someone was a sorceress?

3. What is the purpose of a scarecrow?

4. Does the Scarecrow act like somebody who doesn't have any brains? Explain your answer.

5. Why do you think the Scarecrow was afraid of a lighted match?

E WRITING

Write a passage that explains how the Scarecrow could help Dorothy on her journey.

Use details from the novel to answer these questions in your passage:

1. How could the Scarecrow entertain Dorothy?

2. What could the Scarecrow do if Dorothy were in danger?

3. How else could the Scarecrow help Dorothy?

Write at least four sentences.

END OF LESSON 13

A WORD LISTS

1 Hard Words	2 Word Endings	3 Vocabulary Review	4 Vocabulary Words
1. fortunate	1. curiosity	1. earnestly	1. clumsiness
2. inconvenient	2. dreary	2. hearty	2. dreary
3. one-legged	3. hearty	3. husky	3. fortunate
4. shoulder	4. husky	4. represent	4. people of flesh and blood
	5. ordinary	5. resolved	5. spoil
		6. suspected	

B VOCABULARY FROM CONTEXT

1. Because of his **clumsiness,** he kept falling down.
   - gracefulness
   - awkwardness
   - skill

2. Our homes were gray and very **dreary** looking.
   - dull
   - happy
   - beautiful

3. After they were saved from the witch, they all felt **fortunate** to be alive.
   - lucky
   - surprised
   - disappointed

4. Cartoon characters are not **people of flesh and blood.**
   - drawings of people
   - make-believe people
   - real people

5. Milk will **spoil** if it gets too warm.
   - be ruined
   - freeze
   - spill

Chapter 6

The Road Gets Rough

After a few hours, the road began to get rough, and the walking became so difficult that the Scarecrow often stumbled over the yellow bricks, which were now very uneven. Sometimes, indeed, the bricks were broken or missing altogether, leaving holes that Toto jumped across and Dorothy walked around. But the Scarecrow, who had no brains, walked straight ahead and stepped into the holes and fell down on the yellow bricks. These falls never hurt him, however, and

Dorothy would pick him up and set him on his feet again, while he joined her in laughing merrily at his own clumsiness.

The farms were not nearly so well cared for here as they had been farther back. There were fewer houses and fewer fruit trees, and the farther the travelers went, the more dismal and lonesome the country became.

At noon, Dorothy and the Scarecrow sat down by the roadside, near a little brook, and Dorothy opened her basket and took out some bread. She offered a piece to the Scarecrow, but he refused.

"I am never hungry," he said, "and it is a lucky thing that I am not. For my mouth is only painted, and if I were to cut a hole in it so I could eat, the straw I am stuffed with would come out, and that would spoil the shape of my head."

Dorothy saw at once that this was true, so she only nodded and went on eating her bread.

When Dorothy had finished her dinner, the Scarecrow said, "Tell me something about yourself and the country you came from."

So she told him all about Kansas and how gray everything was there and how the cyclone had carried her to this strange Land of Oz. The Scarecrow listened carefully and said, "I cannot understand why you want to leave this beautiful country and go back to the dry, gray place you call Kansas."

"That is because you have no brains," answered the girl. "No matter how dreary and gray our homes are, we people of flesh and blood would rather live there than in any other country, no matter how beautiful it is. There is no place like home."

The Scarecrow sighed.

"Of course I cannot understand it," he said. "If your heads were stuffed with straw, like mine, you would probably all live in the beautiful places, and then Kansas would have no people at all. It is fortunate for Kansas that you have brains." ♦

D INFERENCES

Work the items.

Angela was pedaling as hard as she could up the steep road. She was wearing a helmet. Her backpack was heavy because it was filled with books and other items. Suddenly, her front tire hit a sharp rock. She could hear air rushing out of the tire. Angela pulled over to the side of the road and took a toolkit out of her backpack.

1. How hard was Angela pedaling up the road?

2. What did you use to answer item 1: explicit statement or inference?

3. What kind of vehicle was Angela riding?

4. What did you use to answer item 3: explicit statement or inference?

5. What was Angela's backpack filled with?

6. What did you use to answer item 5: explicit statement or inference?

7. What came rushing out of the tire?

8. What did you use to answer item 7: explicit statement or inference?

9. Why did Angela pull over to the side of the road?

10. What did you use to answer item 9: explicit statement or inference?

E COMPREHENSION

Write the answers.

1. Why did the Scarecrow walk straight into the holes in the road?

2. Why wasn't the Scarecrow hurt when he fell down?

3. Name at least three ways the country changed as Dorothy went farther down the road.

4. Why did the Scarecrow think that Dorothy might want to stay in Oz?

5. Why did Dorothy want to go back to Kansas?

F WRITING

Write a passage that answers this main question:

• Do you think the Scarecrow is smart?

Use details from the novel to answer these other questions in your passage:

1. Why does the Scarecrow think he's not smart?

2. In what ways is the Scarecrow not smart?

3. In what ways is the Scarecrow smart?

Write at least five sentences.

END OF LESSON 14

A WORD LISTS

1 | Hard Words

1. astonish
2. comrade
3. coward
4. passage

2 | Word Practice

1. embarrass
2. embarrassed
3. fastened
4. lifted
5. luckily
6. uplifted

3 | Related Words

1. comfort
2. comforted
3. uncomfortable

4 | Vocabulary Review

1. clumsiness
2. dreary
3. fortunate

5 | Vocabulary Words

1. companion
2. desert
3. inconvenient
4. maiden
5. mystery
6. ray of sunshine
7. satisfaction

6 | Vocabulary Words

1. comforted
2. declared
3. motionless

B VOCABULARY FROM CONTEXT

1. When she rocked the baby and sang to it, the baby stopped crying and felt **comforted.**
   - calm
   - irritated
   - worse

2. The Scarecrow **declared,** "I can see quite well."
   - asked
   - said
   - wondered

3. She stood so still that she seemed to be **motionless.**
   - without movement
   - without arms
   - without a voice

Chapter 7

The Forest

Dorothy and the Scarecrow were still sitting by the roadside. Dorothy said, "Won't you tell me a story while we are resting?"

The Scarecrow seemed a little embarrassed at first, but then he told her the story of his life. Here is what he said:

My life has been so short that I really don't know anything. I was only made the day before yesterday. What happened in the world before that time is all unknown to me. Luckily, when the farmer made my head, one of the first things he did was to paint my ears, so I heard what was going on.

There was another Munchkin with the farmer, and the first thing I heard was the farmer saying, "How do you like those ears?"

"They aren't straight," answered the other Munchkin.

"Never mind," said the farmer. "They are ears just the same," which was true.

"Now I'll make the eyes," said the farmer. So he painted my right eye, and as soon as it was finished, I found myself looking at him and at everything around me with a great deal of curiosity, for this was my first glimpse of the world.

"That's a rather pretty eye," remarked the other Munchkin. "Blue paint is just the color for eyes."

"I think I'll make the other eye a little bigger," said the farmer. When the second eye was done, I could see much better than before. Then the farmer made my nose and my mouth, but I did not speak.

I had fun watching them make my body and my arms and legs. And when they fastened on my head, at last, I felt very proud, for I thought I was just as good a man as anyone.

"This fellow will scare the crows," said the farmer. "He looks just like a man."

"Why, he is a man," said the other.

The farmer carried me under his arm to the cornfield and set me up on a tall stick. Then he and his friend walked away and left me alone.

I did not like to be deserted in this way, so I tried to walk after them. But my feet would not touch the ground, and I was forced to stay on that pole. It was a lonely life, and I had nothing to think of, since I had just been made a little while before. Many crows and other birds flew into the cornfield, but as soon as they saw me, they flew away again, thinking I was a Munchkin. This pleased me and made me feel that I was quite an important person.

After a while, an old crow flew near me. He looked at me carefully, landed on my shoulder, and said, "I wonder if that farmer thought he could fool me by putting you here. Any smart crow can see that you are only stuffed with straw." Then he hopped down at my feet and ate all the corn he wanted.

When the other birds saw that I had not harmed the old crow, they also came to eat the corn; and in a short time, there was a great flock of them around me.

I felt sad because it seemed that I was not such a good Scarecrow after all. But the old crow comforted me, saying, "If you only had brains in your head, you would be as good a man as any of them and a better man than some of them. Brains are the only things worth having in this world, whether you are a crow or a man."

After the crows had gone, I thought about what the old crow had said. I decided I would try hard to get some brains. Then you came along and pulled me off the stake, and from what you said, I am sure the great Oz will give me brains as soon as I get to the Emerald City.

"I hope the Wizard will help you," said Dorothy earnestly, after the Scarecrow had finished his story. "You seem very anxious to have brains."

"Oh, yes, I am anxious," returned the Scarecrow. "It is such an uncomfortable feeling to know that I am a fool."

"Well," said the girl, "let's go." And she handed the basket to the Scarecrow.

There were no fences at all by the roadside now, and there were no farms. Toward evening, Dorothy and the Scarecrow came to a great forest, where the trees grew so big and close together that their branches met over the road. It was almost dark under the trees, for the branches shut out the daylight.

"If this road goes in, it must come out," said the Scarecrow. "And since the Emerald City is at the other end of the road, we must go wherever it leads us."

"Anyone would know that about the road," said Dorothy.

"Certainly. That is why I know it," answered the Scarecrow. "If I had needed brains to figure it out, I never could have said it." ♦

After an hour or so, the light faded away, and the travelers found themselves stumbling along in the darkness. Dorothy could not see at all, but Toto could, for some dogs see very well in the dark. The Scarecrow declared that he could also see well, so Dorothy took hold of his arm and managed to get along.

She said, "If you see any house or any place where we can pass the night, you must tell me. It is very uncomfortable to walk in the dark."

Soon the Scarecrow stopped.

"I see a little cottage to the right of us," he said. "It is built of logs and branches. Shall we go there?"

"Yes, indeed," answered the girl. "I am all tired out."

So the Scarecrow led her through the trees until they reached the cottage, and Dorothy entered and found a bed of dried leaves in one corner. She lay down at once with Toto beside her and soon fell into a sound sleep. The Scarecrow, who was never tired, stood up in another corner and waited until morning came.

When Dorothy awoke, the sun was shining through the trees, and Toto was outside chasing birds. The Scarecrow was still standing in his corner, waiting for her.

"We must go and search for water," she said to him.

"Why do you want water?" he asked.

"To wash the road dust off my face, and to drink, so the dry bread will not stick in my throat."

"It must be inconvenient to be made of flesh," said the Scarecrow thoughtfully. "You must sleep and eat and drink. However, you have brains, and it is worth a lot of trouble to be able to think properly."

They left the cottage and walked through the trees until they found a little spring of clear water, where Dorothy drank and bathed and ate her breakfast. The girl saw that there was not much bread left in the basket, and she was thankful that the Scarecrow did not have to eat anything, for there was barely enough for herself and Toto for the day.

When Dorothy had finished her meal, she was startled to hear a deep groan nearby.

"What was that?" she asked.

"I don't know," replied the Scarecrow, "but we can go and see."

Just then another groan reached their ears. The sound seemed to come from behind them. They turned and walked through the forest a few steps, and Dorothy saw something shining in a ray of sunshine. She ran to the place and then stopped short with a cry of surprise.

One of the big trees had been partly chopped through, and standing beside it, with an uplifted axe in his hands, was a man made entirely of tin. He stood perfectly motionless, as if he could not move at all.

Dorothy looked at him in amazement, and so did the Scarecrow, while Toto barked sharply and made a snap at the tin legs, which hurt his teeth.

"Did you groan?" asked Dorothy.

"Yes," answered the Tin Woodman, "I did. I've been groaning for more than a year, and no one has ever heard me before or come to help me."

D COMPREHENSION

Write the answers.

1. Why did the Scarecrow feel proud when the farmer first made him?

2. Why wasn't the old crow scared of the Scarecrow?

3. The old crow said, "Brains are the only things worth having in this world." Do you agree with the old crow? Explain your answer.

4. What did the Scarecrow mean when he said, "It must be inconvenient to be made of flesh"?

5. Why do you think the Tin Woodman could not move?

E WRITING

Write the story of the Scarecrow's life.

Use details from the novel to answer these questions in your story:

1. Who made the Scarecrow and why?

2. When did the Scarecrow begin to see and hear the world?

3. What did the old crow tell the Scarecrow?

4. What did the Scarecrow decide to do?

Write at least five sentences.

END OF LESSON 15

16

A | WORD LISTS

1 | Hard Words
1. approve
2. guide
3. shiver
4. sorrow

2 | Word Practice
1. alas
2. cruel
3. halves
4. marriage

3 | Vocabulary Review
1. comforted
2. declared
3. deserted
4. inconvenient
5. maiden
6. motionless
7. satisfaction

4 | Vocabulary Words
1. awkward
2. courage
3. jagged
4. moved

5 | Vocabulary Words
1. comrade
2. misfortune
3. passage
4. shouldered his axe

B | VOCABULARY FROM CONTEXT

1. They met a **comrade,** who joined them on their journey.
   * foe
   * tree
   * friend

2. The woodman had the **misfortune** of getting his axe stuck in a tree.
   * good luck
   * bad luck
   * big fortune

3. The woodman cleared a **passage** through the thick shrubs and bushes.
   * passenger
   * idea
   * path

4. The woodman **shouldered his axe** and marched through the forest.
   * brought his axe to his shoulder
   * thought his axe was his shoulder
   * made his axe look like a shoulder

Chapter 8

The Tin Woodman

Dorothy was startled to hear the Tin Woodman speak, and she was moved by his sad voice.

"What can I do for you?" she inquired softly.

"Get an oilcan and oil my joints," he answered. "They are rusted so badly that I cannot move them at all. But if I am well oiled, I will soon be all right again. You will find an oilcan on a shelf in my cottage."

Dorothy at once ran back to the cottage and found the oilcan. Then she returned and asked anxiously, "Where should I begin?"

"Oil my neck joint first," replied the Tin Woodman.

So Dorothy oiled his neck. Because the neck was quite badly rusted, the Scarecrow took hold of the Tin Woodman's head and moved it gently from side to side until it turned freely.

"Now oil the joints in my arms," said the Tin Woodman. So Dorothy oiled them, and the Scarecrow bent them carefully until they were quite free from rust and as good as new. Then the woodman gave a sigh of satisfaction and lowered his axe, which he leaned against the tree.

"This is a great comfort," he said. "I have been holding that axe in the air ever since I rusted, and I'm glad to be able to put it down at last. Now, if you will oil the joints of my legs, I shall be all right."

So they oiled his legs until he could move them freely. The Tin Woodman thanked the travelers again and again for saving him, for he seemed a very polite man and very grateful.

"I might have stood there always if you had not come along," he said. "You have certainly saved my life. But how did you happen to be here?"

"We are on our way to the Emerald City to see the great Oz," Dorothy answered. "We stopped at your cottage to pass the night."

"Why do you wish to see Oz?" the Tin Woodman asked.

"I want him to send me back to Kansas, and the Scarecrow wants him to put a few brains into his head," she replied.

The Tin Woodman appeared to think deeply for a moment. Then he said, "Do you suppose Oz could give me a heart?"

"Why, I guess so," Dorothy answered. "It would be as easy as giving the Scarecrow brains."

"True," the Tin Woodman replied. "If you will allow me to join your party, I will also go to the Emerald City and ask Oz to help me."

"Come along," said the Scarecrow, and Dorothy said that she would be pleased to have him join them.

So the Tin Woodman shouldered his axe and asked Dorothy to put the oilcan in her basket. "For," he said, "if I should get caught in the rain and rust again, I would need the oilcan badly." Then they all walked through the forest until they came to the Yellow Brick Road.

It was a bit of good luck to have the Tin Woodman, for soon after the comrades had begun their journey, they came to a place where the trees and branches grew so thickly over the road that they could not pass.

But the Tin Woodman set to work with his axe and chopped so well that he soon cleared a passage.

Dorothy was thinking so earnestly as they walked along that she did not notice when the Scarecrow stumbled into a hole and rolled over to the side of the road. Indeed, he had to call to her to help him up again.

"Why didn't you walk around the hole?" asked the Tin Woodman.

"I don't know enough," replied the Scarecrow cheerfully. "My head is stuffed with straw, you know, and that is why I am going to Oz to ask him for some brains."

"Oh, I see," said the Tin Woodman. "But, after all, brains are not the best things in the world."

"Do you have any?" inquired the Scarecrow.

"No, my head is quite empty," answered the Tin Woodman. "But I once had brains, and also a heart. Having tried them both, I would much rather have a heart."

"And why would you rather have a heart?" asked the Scarecrow.

"I will tell you my story, and then you will know."

So while they were walking through the forest, the Tin Woodman told the following story:

• • •

I was born the son of a woodman who chopped down trees in the forest and sold the wood for a living. When I grew up, I too became a woodchopper, and after my father died, I took care of my old mother as long as she lived. Then I made up my mind that instead of living alone I would marry, so that I would not become lonely.

There was a Munchkin girl who was so beautiful that I soon grew to love her with all my heart. She promised to marry me as soon as I could earn enough money to build a better house for her; so I set to work harder than ever. But the girl lived with an old woman who did not want her to marry anyone, for the woman was so lazy that she wanted the girl to remain with her and do the cooking and the housework.

So the old woman went to the Wicked Witch of the East and promised the witch two sheep and a cow if she would prevent the marriage. The Wicked Witch agreed to help, and she put a spell on my axe. One day, when I was chopping away, the axe slipped and cut off my left leg.

At first, this seemed a great misfortune, for I knew a one-legged man could not do very well as a woodchopper. So I went to a tinsmith and had him make me a new leg out of tin. The leg worked very well, once I was used to it; but my action angered the Wicked Witch because I could still marry the pretty Munchkin girl. ◆

When I began chopping again, my axe slipped and cut off my right leg. Again I went to the tinsmith, and again he made me a leg out of tin. After this, the axe cut off my arms, one after the other, but I had them replaced with tin arms. The Wicked Witch then made the axe slip and cut off my head, and at first I thought that was the end of me. But the tinsmith happened to come along, and he made me a new head out of tin.

I thought I had tricked the Wicked Witch then, and I worked harder than ever. But I did not know how cruel my enemy could be. She thought of a new way to kill my love for the beautiful Munchkin maiden and made

my axe slip again so that it cut right through my body, splitting me into halves.

Once more the tinsmith came to my aid and made me a body of tin. He fastened my tin arms and legs and head to my tin body, by means of joints, so that I could move around as well as ever. But, alas! Now I had no heart, so I lost all my love for the Munchkin girl and did not care whether I married her or not. I suppose she is still living with the old woman, waiting for me to come after her.

My body shone so brightly in the sun that I felt very proud of it; and it did not matter now if my axe slipped, for it could not cut me. There was only one danger— my joints could rust. But I kept an oilcan in my cottage and took care to oil myself whenever I needed it. However, one day I forgot to oil myself. I got caught in a rainstorm, and before I knew it, my joints had rusted, so I was forced to stand in the woods until you came to help me. Standing there for a year was terribly hard, but while I stood there, I had time to think that the greatest loss I had known was the loss of my heart.

When I was in love, I was the happiest man on Earth. But you cannot love if you do not have a heart, and so I am resolved to ask the Wizard of Oz to give me one. If the Wizard gives me a heart, I will go back to the Munchkin maiden and marry her.

• • •

Both Dorothy and the Scarecrow were greatly interested in the story of the Tin Woodman, and now they knew why he was so anxious to get a new heart.

"All the same," said the Scarecrow, "I will ask for brains instead of a heart, for a fool would not know what to do with a heart if he had one."

"I shall take the heart," answered the Tin Woodman. "Brains do not make you happy, and happiness is the best thing in the world."

Dorothy did not say anything, for she did not know which of her two friends was right, and she wondered if she would ever get back to Kansas and Aunt Em.

What worried her most was that the bread was nearly gone, and another meal for herself and Toto would empty the basket. To be sure, neither the Tin Woodman nor the Scarecrow ever ate anything, but she was not made of tin or straw, and she could not live unless she was fed.

D GLOSSARY WORDS

Find the following words in your glossary. Then write the definitions.

1. gloomy   2. snug   3. cluster

E INFERENCES

Work the items.

Carlos walked down an aisle, looking at the cans of soup and boxes of rice. Then he walked down several more aisles with food on both sides. Finally he found what he was looking for. He couldn't wait to pour some over his cereal. He bought a quart and took it home. He watched the sunrise as he ate a bowl of cereal.

1. What did Carlos look at in the first aisle?

2. What did you use to answer item 1: explicit statement or inference?

3. What kind of store was Carlos visiting?

4. What did you use to answer item 3: explicit statement or inference?

5. What kind of liquid did Carlos buy?

6. What did you use to answer item 5: explicit statement or inference?

7. How much liquid did Carlos buy?

8. What did you use to answer item 7: explicit statement or inference?

9. What time of day was it when Carlos ate?

10. What did you use to answer item 9: explicit statement or inference?

F COMPREHENSION

Write the answers.

1. What kind of weather would make the Tin Woodman stop working? Why?

2. How did the Tin Woodman help the travelers as they walked through the forest?

3. Why did the Tin Woodman think that a heart was more important than brains?

4. Why did the Scarecrow think that brains were more important than a heart?

5. Which do you think is more important: brains or a heart? Explain your answer.

G WRITING

Write a passage that explains how the Woodman became the Tin Woodman.

Use details from the novel to answer the following questions in your passage:

1. Who did the Woodman want to marry?

2. Who put a spell on the Woodman's axe and why?

3. What did the axe do to the Woodman?

4. Who repaired the Woodman?

Write at least five sentences.

A WORD LISTS

1 | Word Practice

1. adventure
2. ashamed
3. disease
4. fierce
5. guide

2 | Word Practice

1. Kalidahs
2. peculiar
3. relief
4. welcome

3 | Word Endings

1. cottages
2. fences
3. hinges
4. manages
5. places

4 | Vocabulary Review

1. comrade
2. misfortune
3. passage

5 | Vocabulary Words

1. approve of
2. astonished
3. coward
4. remarkable

6 | Vocabulary Words

1. shiver
2. sorrow
3. strides
4. unbearable

B VOCABULARY FROM CONTEXT

1. Toto did not **approve of** the new comrade and tried to bite him.
   - smell
   - look at
   - like

2. When Dorothy saw the Scarecrow wink at her, she was **astonished.**
   - not interested
   - surprised
   - hopeful

3. The Lion was such a **coward** that he was afraid of everybody.
   - brave person
   - fearful person
   - nice person

4. The dog was **remarkable** because it had a coat of seven different colors.
   - ordinary
   - boring
   - amazing

5. When Abby went outside without a coat on, she began to **shiver** from the cold.
   - tremble
   - run
   - sweat

6. When Hector's friends left, he felt great **sorrow** and started to cry.
   - happiness
   - anger
   - sadness

7. The Lion's **strides** were so long that he took one step each time Dorothy took three steps.
   - steps
   - breaths
   - hooves

8. When Aunt Em couldn't stand being alone anymore, she cried, "This is **unbearable**."
   - something I don't mind
   - something I can't stand
   - something I like

C READING LITERATURE: Novel

Chapter 9

The Cowardly Lion

All this time, Dorothy and her companions had been walking through the thick woods. The road was still paved with yellow brick, but the bricks were covered by dried branches and dead leaves from the trees, and it was difficult to walk.

There were very few birds in this part of the forest, for the birds of Oz love the open country, where there is plenty of sunshine. Now and then the travelers would hear a deep growl from some wild animal hidden among the trees. These sounds made Dorothy's heart beat fast, for she did not know what made the sounds. But Toto knew, and he walked close to Dorothy's side and did not even bark.

"How long will it be," Dorothy asked the Tin Woodman, "before we are out of the forest?"

"I cannot tell," he answered, "for I have never been to the Emerald City. My father went there once when I was a boy, and he said it was a long journey through a dangerous country. But I am not afraid so long as I have my oilcan, and nothing can hurt the Scarecrow. As for you, you have the mark of the good witch's kiss on your forehead, and that will protect you from harm."

"But Toto!" said Dorothy anxiously. "What will protect him?"

"We must protect him ourselves if he is in danger," replied the Tin Woodman.

Just as he spoke, a terrible roar came from the forest, and the next moment, a great Lion bounded into the road. With one blow of his paw, he sent the Scarecrow spinning over and over to the edge of the road, and then he struck at the Tin Woodman with his sharp claws. But, to the Lion's surprise, he could make no dent in the tin, although the Tin Woodman fell over in the road and lay still.

Little Toto, now that he had an enemy to face, ran barking toward the Lion, and the great beast opened his mouth to bite the dog. But Dorothy, fearing Toto would be killed, rushed forward and slapped the Lion on his nose as hard as she could while she cried out, "Don't you dare bite Toto! You ought to be ashamed of yourself, a big beast like you, to bite a poor little dog!"

"I didn't bite him," said the Lion as he rubbed his nose with his paw where Dorothy had hit it.

Dorothy said, "No, but you tried to. You are nothing but a big coward."

"I know that I am a coward," said the Lion, hanging his head in shame. "I've always known it. But how can I help it?"

"I don't know, I'm sure. To think of your striking a stuffed man, like the poor Scarecrow!"

"Is he stuffed?" asked the Lion in surprise, as he watched her pick up the Scarecrow, set him on his feet, and pat him into shape again.

"Of course he's stuffed," replied Dorothy, who was still angry.

"So that's why he went over so easily," remarked the Lion. "It astonished me to see him whirl around like that. Is the other one stuffed, too?"

"No," said Dorothy. "He is made of tin." And she helped the Tin Woodman up.

"That's why he nearly ruined my claws," said the Lion. "When they scratched against the tin, it made a cold shiver run down my back. What is that little animal you are so fond of?"

"He is my dog," answered Dorothy.

"Is he made of tin, or stuffed?" asked the Lion.

"Neither. He's just a dog," said the girl.

"Oh! He's a curious animal and seems remarkably small, now that I look at him. No one would think of biting such a little thing except a coward like me," continued the Lion sadly.

"What makes you a coward?" asked Dorothy, looking at the great beast in wonder, for he was as big as a small horse.

"It's a mystery," replied the Lion. "I suppose I was born that way. All the other animals in the forest naturally expect me to be brave, for the Lion is supposed to be the King of Beasts. I soon learned that if I roared very loudly every living thing was frightened and got out of my way."

The Lion continued, "Whenever I meet people, I'm awfully scared. But I just roar at them, and they always run away as fast as they can go. If the elephants and the tigers and the bears had ever tried to fight me, I would have run myself—I'm such a coward. But just as soon as they hear me roar, they all try to get away from me, and of course I let them go."

The Scarecrow said, "But that isn't right. The King of Beasts shouldn't be a coward."

"I know it," answered the Cowardly Lion, wiping a tear from his eye with the tip of his tail. "It is my great sorrow and makes my life very unhappy. But whenever there is danger, my heart begins to beat fast."

"Perhaps you have heart disease," said the Tin Woodman.

"It may be," said the Lion.

"If you have," continued the Tin Woodman, "you ought to be glad, for it proves you have a heart. As for me, I have no heart, so I cannot have heart disease." ♦

Thoughtfully, the Lion said, "Perhaps if I had no heart I would not be a coward."

"Do you have brains?" asked the Scarecrow.

"I suppose so. I've never looked to see," replied the Lion.

"I am going to the great Oz to ask him to give me some brains," remarked the Scarecrow, "for my head is stuffed with straw."

"And I am going to ask him to give me a heart," said the Tin Woodman.

"And I am going to ask him to send me back to Kansas," added Dorothy.

"Do you think Oz could give me courage?" asked the Cowardly Lion.

"Just as easily as he could give me brains," said the Scarecrow.

"Or give me a heart," said the Tin Woodman.

"Or send me back to Kansas," said Dorothy.

"Then, if you don't mind, I'll go with you," said the Lion, "for my life is simply unbearable without a bit of courage."

"You will be very welcome," answered Dorothy, "for you will help to keep away the other wild beasts. It seems to me they must be more cowardly than you are if they let you scare them so easily."

"They really are," said the Lion. "But that doesn't make me any braver, and as long as I know that I am a coward, I will be unhappy."

So once more the little party set off on their journey, the Cowardly Lion walking with proud strides at Dorothy's side. Toto did not approve of this new comrade at first. He could not forget how he had almost been crushed between the Lion's great jaws, but after a time, he became more relaxed. Soon, Toto and the Cowardly Lion became good friends.

The group traveled peacefully for the rest of that day. Once, the Tin Woodman stepped on a beetle that was crawling along the road and killed the poor little thing. This made him very unhappy, for he was always careful not to hurt any living creature; and as he walked along, he wept several tears of sorrow. These tears ran slowly down his face and over the hinges of his jaw, and they rusted the hinges.

When Dorothy asked him a question, the Tin Woodman could not open his mouth, for his jaws were tightly rusted together. He became greatly frightened at this and made many motions to Dorothy to help him, but she could not understand, nor could the Lion. But the Scarecrow took the oilcan from Dorothy's basket and oiled the Tin Woodman's jaws, so after a few moments, he could talk as well as before.

"This will teach me a lesson," he said, "to look where I step. For if I should kill another bug or beetle, I would surely cry again, and crying rusts my jaws so that I cannot speak."

After that, the Tin Woodman walked very carefully, with his eyes on the road, and when he saw a tiny ant going by, he would step over it, so as not to harm it. He knew very well that he had no heart, and therefore, he took great care never to be cruel or unkind to anything.

"You people with hearts," he said, "have something to guide you and need never do wrong. But I have no heart, and so I must be very careful. When Oz gives me a heart, of course, I won't have to be so careful."

D GLOSSARY WORDS

Find the following words in your glossary. Then write the definitions.

1. cluster   2. meadow   3. scarlet

E COMPREHENSION

Write the answers.

1. Why did Dorothy slap the Lion on the nose and yell at him?

2. Why do you think the Lion is called the King of Beasts?

3. Why was the Tin Woodman never cruel or unkind?

4. Do you think the Tin Woodman needs a heart? Why or why not?

5. Do you think the Scarecrow needs brains? Why or why not?

F WRITING

Write a passage that describes the Lion.

Use details from the novel to answer the following questions in your passage:

1. Is the Lion brave or cowardly?

2. How does the Lion scare other animals?

3. What would happen if the other animals tried to fight the Lion?

4. What does the Lion want and why?

Write at least five sentences.

END OF LESSON 17

A WORD LISTS

1 | Word Practice

1. adventure
2. attempt
3. fierce
4. Kalidahs

2 | Word Practice

1. prefer
2. relief
3. shaggy
4. snarl

3 | Related Words

1. delight / delightful
2. despair / despairingly
3. faint / faintest
4. monster / monstrous

4 | Word Endings

1. cottages
2. distances
3. edges
4. fences
5. places

5 | Vocabulary Review

1. approve of
2. astonished
3. remarkable
4. sorrow
5. strides
6. unbearable

6 | Vocabulary Words

1. crouch
2. gloomy
3. snug

7 | Vocabulary Words

1. dreadful
2. peculiar
3. splendid

B VOCABULARY FROM CONTEXT

1. When Stella saw the awful things the tigers did, she said, "Those beasts do some **dreadful** things."
   - horrible
   - great
   - silly

2. They saw **peculiar** looking beings who had three eyes and four arms.
   - ordinary
   - regular
   - strange

3. Dorothy built a **splendid** fire that made large flames and gave off a lot of heat.
   - ugly
   - marvelous
   - small

Chapter 10

The Kalidahs

The travelers had to camp out that night under a large tree in the forest, for there were no houses near. The tree made a good shelter, and the Tin Woodman chopped a great pile of wood with his axe. Dorothy built a splendid fire that warmed her and made her feel less lonely. She and Toto ate the last of their bread, and now she did not know what they would do for breakfast.

"If you wish," said the Lion, "I will go into the forest and kill a deer for you. You can roast it by the fire, since your tastes are so peculiar that you prefer cooked food, and then you will have a very good breakfast."

"Don't, please don't," begged the Tin Woodman. "I would certainly weep if you killed a poor deer, and then my jaws would rust again."

But the Lion went away into the forest and found his own supper, and no one ever knew what it was, for he didn't mention it.

The Scarecrow found a tree full of nuts and filled Dorothy's basket with them so that she would not be hungry for a long time. She thought this was very kind and thoughtful of the Scarecrow, but she laughed heartily at the awkward way in which the poor creature picked up the nuts. His padded hands were so clumsy and the nuts were so small that he dropped almost as many as he put into the basket.

But the Scarecrow did not mind how long it took him to fill the basket. The nut tree was far away from the fire, and he feared a spark from the fire might get into his straw and burn him up. He only came near the fire to cover Dorothy with dry leaves when she lay down to sleep. These kept her very snug and warm, and she slept soundly until morning.

When it was daylight, the girl bathed her face in a little rippling brook, and soon after, they all started toward the Emerald City.

This was to be an important day for the travelers. They had hardly been walking an hour when they saw a great ditch in front of them that crossed the road and divided the forest as far as they could see on either side. It was a very wide ditch, and when they crept up to the edge and looked into it, they could see it was also very deep, with many big, jagged rocks at the bottom.

The sides were so steep that nobody could climb down, and for a moment, it seemed that their journey must end.

"What shall we do?" asked Dorothy despairingly.

"I haven't the faintest idea," said the Tin Woodman. And the Lion shook his shaggy mane and looked thoughtful.

The Scarecrow said, "We cannot fly, that is certain. Neither can we climb down into this great ditch. Therefore, if we cannot jump over it, we must stop where we are."

"I think I could jump over it," said the Cowardly Lion, after measuring the distance carefully in his mind.

"Then we are all right," answered the Scarecrow, "for you can carry us all over on your back, one at a time."

"Well, I'll try it," said the Lion. "Who will go first?"

"I will," declared the Scarecrow. "For if you found that you could not jump over the ditch, Dorothy would be killed, or the Tin Woodman badly dented on the rocks below. But if I am on your back, it will not matter so much, for the fall would not hurt me at all."

"I am terribly afraid of falling myself," said the Cowardly Lion, "but I suppose there is nothing to do but try it. So get on my back and we will make the attempt."

The Scarecrow sat on the Lion's back, and the big beast walked to the edge of the ditch and crouched down.

"Why don't you run and jump?" asked the Scarecrow.

"Because that isn't the way we lions do these things," he replied. Then he sprang forward through the air and landed safely on the other side. They were all greatly pleased to see how easily the Lion had jumped, and after the Scarecrow got down from his back, the Lion sprang across the ditch again.

Dorothy thought she should go next, so she took Toto in one arm and climbed on the Lion's back, holding tightly to his mane with her free hand. The next moment she was flying through the air. And then, before she had time to think about it, she was safe on the other side. The Lion went back a third time and got the Tin Woodman. Then they all sat down for a few moments to give the beast a chance to rest. The Lion's great leaps had made his breath short, and he panted like a big dog that has been running too long.

The forest was very thick on this side, and it looked dark and gloomy. After the Lion had rested, they started along the

Yellow Brick Road, silently wondering if they would ever come to the end of the woods and reach the bright sunshine again. To add to their discomfort, they soon heard strange noises coming from the forest, and the Lion whispered to them that the Kalidahs lived in this part of the country. ♦

"What are the Kalidahs?" asked Dorothy.

"They are monstrous beasts with bodies like bears and heads like tigers," replied the Lion. "Their claws are so long and sharp that they could tear me in two as easily as I could kill Toto. I'm terribly afraid of the Kalidahs."

"I'm not surprised that you are," replied Dorothy.

The Lion was about to reply when suddenly they came to another ditch across the road. This ditch was so broad and deep that the Lion knew at once that he could not leap across it.

So they sat down to consider what they should do. After serious thought, the Scarecrow said, "Here is a large tree, standing close to the ditch. If the Tin Woodman can chop it down so that the top falls on the other side of the ditch, we can walk across it easily."

"That is a first-rate idea," said the Lion. "One would almost think you had brains in your head, instead of straw."

The Tin Woodman set to work at once, and his axe was so sharp that he soon chopped most of the way through the tree. Then the Lion put his strong front legs against the tree and pushed with all his might. The big tree tipped and fell with a crash across the ditch, with its top branches on the other side.

They had just started to cross this tree bridge when a sharp growl made them all look up. To their horror, they saw two great beasts running toward them. These beasts had bodies like bears and heads like tigers.

"Those are the Kalidahs!" said the Cowardly Lion, beginning to tremble.

"Quick!" cried the Scarecrow, "Let's cross over."

So Dorothy went first, holding Toto in her arms. The Tin Woodman followed, and the Scarecrow came next. The Lion, although he was certainly afraid, turned to face the Kalidahs, and then he gave a roar that was so loud and terrible that Dorothy screamed and the Scarecrow fell over backward. Even the Kalidahs stopped short and looked at him in surprise.

But seeing they were bigger than the Lion and remembering that there were two of them and only one of him, the Kalidahs again rushed forward. The Lion crossed over the tree and turned to see what they would do next. Without stopping an instant, the fierce beasts also began to cross the tree, and the Lion said to Dorothy, "We will lose, for they will surely tear us to pieces with their sharp claws. But stand close behind me, and I will fight them as long as I am alive."

"Wait a minute!" called the Scarecrow. He had been thinking what to do, and now he asked the Woodman to chop away the end of the tree that rested on their side of the ditch. The Tin Woodman began to use his axe at once, and just as the two Kalidahs were nearly across, the tree fell with a crash into the ditch, carrying the ugly, snarling beasts with it. Both fell onto the sharp rocks at the bottom.

"Well," said the Cowardly Lion, heaving a sigh of relief, "I see we are going to live a little while longer, and I am glad, for it must be a very uncomfortable thing not to be alive. Those creatures frightened me so badly that my heart is pounding."

"Ah," said the Tin Woodman, sadly. "If I only had a heart."

D GLOSSARY WORDS

Find the following words in your glossary. Then write the definitions.

1. timid

2. lining

3. advance

E COMPREHENSION

Write the answers.

1. Explain how the Lion helped the travelers cross the first ditch.

2. Explain how the Lion, the Tin Woodman, and the Scarecrow worked together as a team to cross the second ditch.

3. Give at least two examples of brave things the Lion did in this chapter.

4. Do you think the Lion really needs courage? Why or why not?

5. Why did the Kalidahs fall into the second ditch?

F WRITING

Write a passage that answers this main question:

- Do you think the Tin Woodman really needs a heart?

Use details from the novel to answer these other questions in your passage:

1. Why doesn't the Tin Woodman have a heart now?

2. Does the Tin Woodman act like someone without a heart? Why or why not?

3. What does the Tin Woodman think will happen when he gets a heart?

Write at least five sentences.

A WORD LISTS

1 Word Practice
1. beckon
2. curtsy
3. fortunately
4. hurriedly
5. scent

2 Compound Words
1. cornfield
2. downstream
3. hereafter
4. indeed
5. wildcat

3 Vocabulary Words
1. cluster
2. cozy
3. dazzle
4. meadow
5. raft
6. scarcely
7. scarlet

4 Vocabulary Words
1. delightful
2. glare
3. refreshed

B VOCABULARY FROM CONTEXT

1. They were pleased to see this **delightful** meadow before them.
   - ugly
   - wonderful
   - sad

2. The **glare** of the lights almost blinded her.
   - sound
   - feeling
   - brightness

3. The next morning, Dorothy said, "I feel great. The long sleep made me feel **refreshed.**"
   - tired
   - lonesome
   - full of energy

C READING LITERATURE: Novel

Chapter 11

The River

The adventure with the Kalidahs made the travelers more anxious than ever to get out of the forest. They walked so fast that Dorothy became tired and had to ride on the Lion's back. To their great joy, the trees became thinner the farther they went, and in the afternoon, they suddenly came upon a broad river, flowing swiftly just before them.

On the other side of the water, they could see the Yellow Brick Road running through a beautiful country with green meadows dotted with bright red flowers and trees full of delicious fruits. They were greatly pleased to see this delightful land before them.

"How shall we cross the river?" asked Dorothy.

"That is easily done," replied the Scarecrow. "The Tin Woodman must build us a raft so we can float to the other side."

So the Woodman took his axe and began to chop down small trees to make a raft. While he was busy at this, the Scarecrow found a tree full of fine fruit on the riverbank. This pleased Dorothy, who had eaten nothing but nuts all day, and she made a hearty meal of the ripe fruit.

It takes time to make a raft, even when one is as hard-working as the Woodman, and when night came, the work was not done. So they found a cozy place under the tree, where Dorothy, Toto, and the Lion slept well until morning. Dorothy dreamed of the Emerald City and the Wizard of Oz, who would soon send her back to her own home.

Dorothy, Toto, and the Lion awakened the next morning, refreshed and full of hope, and Dorothy had a breakfast of peaches and plums from the trees beside the river. Behind them was the dark forest they had passed safely through, but in front of them was a lovely, sunny country that seemed to beckon them on to the Emerald City.

To be sure, the broad river now cut them off from this beautiful land. But the raft was nearly done, and after the Tin Woodman had cut a few more logs and fastened them together with wooden pins, they were ready to start. Dorothy sat down in the middle of the raft and held Toto in her arms. When the Lion stepped upon the raft it tipped badly, for he was big and heavy; but the Scarecrow and the Tin Woodman stood upon the other end to balance it.

The Scarecrow and the Tin Woodman had long poles in their hands to push the raft through the water. They got along quite well at first, but when they reached the middle of the river, the swift current swept the raft downstream, farther and farther away from the Yellow Brick Road. The water soon grew so deep that the long poles could barely touch the bottom.

"This is bad," said the Tin Woodman, "for we are getting farther from the road to the Emerald City. If we lose our way, I couldn't get a heart."

"And I would get no brains," said the Scarecrow.

"And I would get no courage," said the Cowardly Lion.

"And I would never get back to Kansas," said Dorothy.

"We must certainly get to the Emerald City if we can," the Scarecrow said. And he pushed his pole in so deeply that it stuck fast in the mud at the bottom of the river. Before he could pull it out again or let go, the raft was swept away, and the poor Scarecrow was left clinging to the pole in the middle of the river.

"Goodbye!" the Scarecrow called after them, and they were very sorry to leave him. Indeed, the Tin Woodman began to cry, but fortunately, he remembered that he might rust, and so he dried his tears.

Meanwhile, the Scarecrow started to think. "I am now worse off than when I first met Dorothy," he thought. "Then, I was stuck on a pole in a cornfield, where I could try to scare the crows. But surely there is no use for a Scarecrow stuck on a pole in the middle of a river. I am afraid I will never have any brains, after all!" ♦

D GLOSSARY WORDS

Find the following words in your glossary, then write the definitions.

1. countless

2. tint

3. untilled

E VOCABULARY SENTENCES

For each word, write a sentence that uses the word.

1. suspected

2. clumsiness

3. fortunate

4. dull

5. inconvenient

6. declared

7. comforted

8. deserted

F COMPREHENSION

Write the answers.

1. How did the Scarecrow and the Tin Woodman work together to help the travelers cross the river?

2. Why do you think Dorothy dreamed about the Emerald City and the Wizard of Oz when she was sleeping by the river?

3. What do you think happened in Dorothy's dream?

4. What was the same about when the Scarecrow was in the cornfield and when he was in the middle of the river?

5. Explain why the Scarecrow thought he was worse off now than when he first met Dorothy.

G WRITING

Write a story that tells what you think will happen to the travelers in the next chapter.

Be sure your story answers the following questions:

1. What will happen to the Scarecrow?

2. What will happen to the other travelers?

3. Will the travelers get back together?

4. Why or why won't they get back together?

Write at least five sentences.

END OF LESSON 19

A WORD LISTS

1 | Word Practice

1. blossoms
2. carpet
3. poison
4. poisonous
5. shallow

2 | Vocabulary Review

1. beckon
2. cluster
3. dazzle
4. delightful
5. dreadful

3 | Vocabulary Review

1. glare
2. refreshed
3. scarcely
4. scarlet

4 | Vocabulary Words

1. curtsy
2. fond of
3. mistress
4. odor
5. scent

5 | Vocabulary Words

1. permit
2. shrill
3. spicy
4. therefore
5. timid

B READING LITERATURE: Novel

Chapter 12

The Field of Flowers

The raft floated downstream, and the poor Scarecrow was left far behind. Then the Lion said, "Something must be done to save us. I think I can swim to the shore and pull the raft after me if you will only hold on to the tip of my tail."

So the Lion sprang into the water, and the Tin Woodman caught hold of his tail. Then the Lion began to swim with all his might toward the shore. It was hard work, even though he was so big, but after a while, he pulled them out of the current. ✿

When they reached the shallow water, Dorothy took the Tin Woodman's long pole and helped push the raft to the land.

They were all tired when they finally reached the shore and stepped onto the pretty green grass. But their troubles were not over. The current had carried them a long way past the Yellow Brick Road that led to the Emerald City.

"What shall we do now?" asked the Tin Woodman as the Lion lay down on the grass to let the sun dry him.

"We must get back to the road," said Dorothy.

"The best plan would be to walk along the riverbank until we come to the road again," remarked the Lion.

So when they were rested, Dorothy picked up her basket, and they started along the grassy bank, back to the road from which the river had carried them. It was a lovely country, with plenty of flowers and fruit trees and sunshine to cheer them, and if they had not felt so sorry for the poor Scarecrow, they would have been very happy.

They walked along as fast as they could. Dorothy only stopped once to pick a beautiful flower. After a time, the Tin Woodman cried out, "Look!"

Then they all looked at the river and saw the Scarecrow hanging onto his pole in the middle of the water, looking very lonely and sad.

"What can we do to save him?" asked Dorothy.

The Lion and the Woodman both shook their heads, for they did not know. So they sat down on the bank and gazed at the Scarecrow until a Stork flew by.

When the Stork saw them, it stopped to rest at the water's edge.

"Who are you and where are you going?" asked the Stork.

"I am Dorothy," answered the girl. "These are my friends, the Tin Woodman and the Cowardly Lion. We are going to the Emerald City."

"This isn't the road," said the Stork as she twisted her long neck and looked sharply at the strange party.

"I know it," answered Dorothy. "But we have lost the Scarecrow and are wondering how we will get him again."

"Where is he?" asked the Stork.

"Over there in the river," answered Dorothy.

"If he wasn't so big and heavy, I would get him for you," remarked the Stork.

"He isn't a bit heavy," said Dorothy eagerly. "He is stuffed with straw, and if you will bring him back to us, we will thank you ever and ever so much."

"Well, I'll try," said the Stork. "But if I find he is too heavy to carry, I shall have to drop him into the river again."

So the big bird flew into the air and over the water until she came to where the Scarecrow was hanging onto his pole. Then the Stork grabbed the Scarecrow with her great claws and carried him up into the air and back to the bank, where Dorothy and the Lion and the Tin Woodman and Toto were sitting.

When the Scarecrow found himself among his friends again, he was so happy that he hugged them all, even the Lion and Toto. And as they walked along, he sang.

"I was afraid I would have to stay in the river forever," he said, "but the kind Stork saved me, and if I ever get any brains, I shall find the Stork again and return the favor."

"That's all right," said the Stork, who was flying along beside them. "I always like to help anyone in trouble. But I must go now because my babies are waiting for me. I hope you will find the Emerald City and that Oz will help you."

"Thank you," replied Dorothy, and then the kind Stork flew into the air and was soon out of sight.

They walked along listening to the singing of the bright-colored birds and looking at the lovely flowers, which now became so thick that the ground was covered with them. There were big yellow and white and blue and purple blossoms and also great clusters of scarlet flowers, which were so brilliant in color they almost dazzled Dorothy's eyes. ◆

"Aren't they beautiful?" the girl asked as she breathed in the spicy scent of the flowers.

"I suppose so," answered the Scarecrow. "When I have brains, I will probably like them better."

"If I only had a heart, I would love them," added the Tin Woodman.

"I always did like flowers," said the Lion. "They seem so helpless. But there are none in the forest as bright as these."

They now came upon more and more of the big scarlet flowers and fewer and fewer of the other flowers. Soon they found themselves in the middle of a great meadow of scarlet flowers.

Now, when there are many of these flowers together, their odor is so powerful that anyone who breathes them falls asleep; and if the sleeper is not carried away from the flowers, he sleeps on and on forever. But Dorothy did not know this, nor could she get away from the flowers.

Her eyes soon grew heavy, and she felt she must sit down to rest and sleep.

But the Tin Woodman would not let her do this.

"We must hurry and get back to the Yellow Brick Road before dark," he said, and the Scarecrow agreed with him. So they kept walking until Dorothy could stand no longer. Her eyes closed, and she forgot where she was, and she fell among the flowers, fast asleep.

"What shall we do?" asked the Tin Woodman.

"If we leave her here, she will die," said the Lion. "The smell of the flowers is killing us all. I can scarcely keep my eyes open, and the dog is asleep already."

It was true—Toto had fallen down beside his mistress. But the Scarecrow and the Tin Woodman, since they weren't made of flesh, were not troubled by the odor of the flowers.

"Run fast," said the Scarecrow to the Lion, "and get out of this deadly flower bed as soon as you can. We will bring Dorothy with us, but if you should fall asleep, you are too big to be carried."

So the Lion bounded forward as fast as he could go. In a moment, he was out of sight.

"Let us make a chair with our hands and carry her," said the Scarecrow. So they picked up Toto and put him in Dorothy's lap. Then they made a chair with their hands for the seat and their arms for the chair's arms, and they carried the sleeping girl between them through the flowers.

On and on they walked, and it seemed that the great carpet of deadly flowers that surrounded them would never end. They followed the bend of the river, and at last came upon their friend the Lion, lying fast asleep among the flowers. The odor of the flowers had been too strong for the huge beast, and he had given up at last. He had fallen only a short distance from the end of the field, where the sweet grass spread in beautiful green fields before them.

"We can do nothing for him," said the Tin Woodman, sadly. "He is much too heavy to lift. We must leave him here to sleep on forever, and perhaps he will dream that he has found courage at last."

"I'm sorry," said the Scarecrow. "The Lion was a very good comrade for one so cowardly. But let us go on."

They carried the sleeping girl to a pretty spot beside the river, far enough from the field so that she could not breathe any more of the deadly flowers, and here they laid her gently on the soft grass and waited for the fresh breeze to wake her up.

C GLOSSARY

Find the following words in your glossary. Then write the definitions.

1. advance   2. shears

D COMPREHENSION

Write the answers.

1. After they escaped the river, how did the travelers plan to get back to the Yellow Brick Road?

2. Why was the Stork able to carry the Scarecrow so easily?

3. Why couldn't the Tin Woodman and the Scarecrow lift the Lion?

4. How did the Scarecrow and the Tin Woodman work together to save Dorothy and Toto?

5. Why did the Scarecrow and the Tin Woodman put Dorothy and Toto beside the river?

E WRITING

Write a passage that answers this main question:

• Do you think the Lion is brave?

Use details from the novel to answer these other questions in your passage:

1. What brave things has the Lion done since the travelers met him?

2. What cowardly things has the Lion done?

3. Do you think the Lion could be braver? How?

Write at least five sentences.

END OF LESSON 20

A WORD LISTS

1 | Hard Words

1. harness
2. introduce
3. limb
4. majesty
5. rescue

2 | Word Practice

1. beast
2. exclaim
3. hereafter
4. manage
5. poisonous
6. under
7. underneath

3 | Vocabulary Review

1. curtsy
2. fond of
3. permit
4. shrill
5. therefore
6. timid

4 | Vocabulary Words

1. drawn
2. dwell
3. glitter
4. oats

5 | Vocabulary Words

1. presence
2. scamper off
3. stun
4. throne

B READING LITERATURE: Novel

Chapter 13

The Field Mice

"We cannot be far from the Yellow Brick Road now," remarked the Scarecrow as he stood beside Dorothy. "We have come nearly as far as the river carried us away."

The Tin Woodman was about to say something when he heard a low growl, and turning his head, he saw a strange beast come bounding over the grass toward them. It was, indeed, a great yellow wildcat. The Woodman thought it might be chasing something, for its ears were lying close to its head and its mouth was wide open, showing two rows of ugly teeth, while its red eyes glowed like balls of fire.

As the wildcat came nearer, the Tin Woodman saw that a little gray field mouse was running in front of the beast. Although the Woodman had no heart, he knew it was wrong for the wildcat to try to kill such a pretty, harmless creature. So the Woodman raised his axe, and as the wildcat ran by, he gave it a quick blow that stunned the beast, and it rolled over at his feet.

Now that the field mouse was freed from its enemy, it stopped. Coming slowly up to the Woodman, it said in a squeaky little voice, "Oh, thank you! Thank you ever so much for saving my life."

"Don't speak of it, please," replied the Woodman. "I have no heart, you know, so I am careful to help all those who may need a friend, even if it happens to be only a mouse."

"Only a mouse!" cried the little animal. "Why, I am a Queen—the Queen of all the field mice!"

"Oh, indeed," said the Woodman, making a bow.

The Queen continued, "Therefore you have done a great deed, as well as a brave one, in saving my life."

At that moment several mice came running up as fast as their little legs could carry them, and when they saw their Queen they exclaimed, "Oh, Your Majesty, we thought you would be killed! How did you manage to escape the great wildcat?" And they all bowed so low to the little Queen that they almost stood upon their heads.

"This funny tin man," she answered, "stunned the wildcat and saved my life. So hereafter you must all serve him and obey his wishes."

"We will!" cried all the mice, in their shrill voices. And then they scampered off in all directions, for Toto had awakened from his sleep. When Toto saw all these mice around him, he gave one bark of delight and jumped right into the middle of the group. Toto had always loved to chase mice.

But the Tin Woodman caught the dog in his arms and held him tightly while he called the mice, "Come back! Come back! Toto will not hurt you."

When the Woodman said this, the Queen of the Mice stuck her head out from underneath a clump of grass and asked, in a timid voice, "Are you sure he will not bite us?"

"I will not let him," said the Woodman. "Do not be afraid."

One by one the mice came creeping back, and Toto did not bark again, although he tried to get out of the Woodman's arms. Finally one of the biggest mice spoke. "Is there anything we can do," it asked, "to repay you for saving the life of our Queen?"

"I can't think of anything you could do," answered the Woodman.

The Scarecrow, who had been trying to think but could not because his head was stuffed with straw, said quickly, "Oh, yes. You can save our friend, the Cowardly Lion, who is asleep in the field."

"A lion!" cried the little Queen. "Why, he would eat us all up."

"Oh, no," declared the Scarecrow. "This lion is a coward."

"Really?" asked the Queen.

"He says so himself," answered the Scarecrow, "and he would never hurt anyone who is our friend. If you will help us to save him, I promise that he will treat you with kindness."

"Very well," said the Queen. "We will trust you. But what shall we do?"

The Scarecrow asked the Queen, "Are there many mice that are willing to obey you?"

"Oh, yes, there are thousands," she replied.

"Then ask them all to come here as soon as possible, and tell each one to bring a long piece of string." ♦

The Queen turned to the mice that were with her and told them to go at once and get all her mice. As soon as they heard her

orders, they ran away in every direction as fast as possible.

"Now," said the Scarecrow to the Tin Woodman, "you must go to those trees by the riverside and make a cart that will carry the Lion."

So the Woodman went to the trees and began to work. He cut down the limbs of some trees, and then he chopped away all their twigs and leaves. He made a cart out of the limbs and fastened it together with wooden pegs. Then he sliced four pieces from a big, round tree trunk and used the pieces for wheels. He worked so fast and well that by the time the mice began to arrive, the cart was all ready for them.

They came from all directions, and there were thousands of them—big mice and little mice and middle-sized mice. And each one brought a piece of string in its mouth.

It was about this time that Dorothy woke from her long sleep and opened her eyes. She was greatly astonished to find herself lying on the grass, with thousands of mice standing around and looking at her timidly. But the Scarecrow told her about everything, and turning to the Queen, he said, "Permit me to introduce you to Her Majesty, the Queen."

Dorothy nodded gravely, and the Queen made a curtsy, after which she became quite friendly with Dorothy.

The Scarecrow and the Woodman now began to fasten the mice to the cart, using the strings they had brought. One end of each string was tied around the neck of each mouse, and the other end to the cart. Of course, the cart was a thousand times heavier than any of the mice; but when all the mice had been harnessed, they were able to pull the cart quite easily. Even the

Scarecrow and the Tin Woodman could sit on the cart, and they were drawn swiftly by their strange little horses to the place where the Lion lay asleep.

After a great deal of hard work, they managed to get the Lion up on the cart. Then the Queen hurriedly gave her mice the order to start, for she feared that if the mice stayed among the flowers too long, they would also fall asleep.

At first, the little creatures could hardly move the heavy cart. But the Tin Woodman and the Scarecrow both pushed from behind, and they got along better. Soon they rolled the Lion out of the flower bed to the green fields, where he could breathe the sweet, fresh air again, instead of the poisonous odor of the flowers.

Dorothy came to meet them and thanked the little mice warmly for saving her companion from death. She had grown so fond of the big Lion that she was glad he had been rescued.

Then the mice were unharnessed from the cart, and they scampered away through the grass to their homes. The Queen of the Mice was the last to leave. She handed Dorothy a little whistle and said, "If ever you need us again, come out into the field and blow this whistle. We shall hear you and come to help you. Goodbye!"

"Goodbye!" they all answered, and away the Queen ran. Dorothy held Toto tightly so that he would not run after the Queen and frighten her.

After this, they sat down beside the Lion, waiting for him to wake up. The Scarecrow brought Dorothy some fruit from a tree nearby, which she ate for her dinner.

C COMPREHENSION

Write the answers.

1. Why did the Tin Woodman stun the wildcat instead of killing it?

2. Why did the Queen say that the mice had to obey the Tin Woodman's wishes?

3. Why did the mice have to work fast after the Lion was on the cart?

4. What was Dorothy supposed to do with the whistle that the Queen of the Mice gave her?

5. What lessons does this chapter give about teamwork? Explain your answer.

D WRITING

Write a passage that answers this main question:

- How did the characters work together to move the Lion in this chapter?

Use details from the novel to answer these other questions in your passage:

1. Who came up with a plan for moving the Lion?

2. What did each mouse have to bring?

3. Who made the cart?

4. How were the mice fastened to the cart?

5. Who pulled the cart to where the Lion was sleeping?

6. Who pulled and pushed the cart after the Lion was aboard?

Write at least five sentences.

END OF LESSON 21

A WORD LISTS

1 | Hard Words
1. apron
2. cereal
3. generously

2 | Word Practice
1. arched
2. ceiling
3. disturb
4. palace
5. scrambled

3 | Word Practice
1. shadow
2. silvery
3. starve
4. yawn

4 | Vocabulary Review
1. dwell
2. glitter
3. presence

5 | Vocabulary Words
1. admit
2. countless
3. studded
4. tint

B READING LITERATURE: Novel

Chapter 14

The Land of Oz

It was some time before the Cowardly Lion awakened, for he had slept among the flowers a long while, breathing in their deadly odor. When he did open his eyes and roll off the cart, he was very glad to find himself still alive.

"I ran as fast as I could," he said, sitting down and yawning. "But the flowers were too strong for me. How did you get me out?"

Then Dorothy and the others told the Lion about the field mice and how the mice had generously saved him from death.

The Cowardly Lion laughed and said, "I have always thought that I was very big

and terrible; yet such little things as flowers came near to killing me, and such small animals as mice have saved my life. How strange it all is! But, comrades, what shall we do now?"

"We must journey on until we find the Yellow Brick Road again," said Dorothy. "And then we can go on to the Emerald City."

So, when the Lion was fully refreshed and felt like himself again, they all started on the journey. They greatly enjoyed the walk through the soft, fresh grass, and it was not long before they reached the

Yellow Brick Road and turned again toward the Emerald City where the Great Oz dwelled.

The road was smooth and well-paved now, and the country was beautiful. The travelers were happy that the forest was far behind, and with it the many dangers they had met in its dark shadows. Once more they could see fences built beside the road; but these were painted green, not blue. They saw a small house, in which a farmer lived, and that was also painted green.

They passed by several of these houses during the afternoon, and sometimes people came to the doors and looked at them as if they would like to ask questions. But no one came near them nor spoke to them, for they were afraid of the great Lion. The people were all dressed in lovely emerald green clothing and wore green hats that were shaped like those of the Munchkins.

"This must be the Land of Oz," said Dorothy, "and we are surely getting near the Emerald City."

"Yes," answered the Scarecrow. "Everything is green here, while in the country of the Munchkins, blue was the favorite color. But the people do not seem to be as friendly as the Munchkins, and I'm afraid we shall be unable to find a place to spend the night."

"I would like something to eat besides fruit," said the girl, "and I'm sure Toto is nearly starved. Let's stop at the next house and talk to the people."

So when they came to a good-sized farmhouse, Dorothy walked boldly up to the door and knocked. A woman opened it just far enough to look out and said, "What do you want, child, and why is that great Lion with you?"

"We wish to pass the night with you if you will allow us," answered Dorothy.

"The Lion is my friend and comrade and would not hurt you for the world."

"Is he tame?" asked the woman, opening the door a little wider.

"Oh, yes," said the girl, "and he is a great coward, too. He will be more afraid of you than you are of him."

"Well," said the woman after thinking it over and taking another peek at the Lion, "if that is the case, you may come in, and I will give you some dinner and a place to sleep."

So they all entered the house. Inside were the woman, two children, and a man. The man had injured his leg and was lying on a couch in the corner. The people seemed greatly surprised to see so strange a party, and while the woman was busy setting the table, the man asked, "Where are you all going?"

"To the Emerald City," said Dorothy, "to see the Great Oz."

"Oh, indeed!" exclaimed the man. "Are you sure that Oz will see you?"

"Why not?" she replied.

"It is said that he never lets anyone come into his presence. I have been to the Emerald City many times, and it is a beautiful and wonderful place. But I have never been permitted to see the Great Oz, nor do I know of any living person who has seen him." ♦

"Does the Wizard never go out?" asked the Scarecrow.

"Never. He sits day after day in the great throne room of his palace, and even those who serve him do not see him face to face."

"What is he like?" asked Dorothy.

"That is hard to tell," said the man thoughtfully. "You see, Oz is a great wizard and can take on any form he wishes. Some say he looks like a bird, and some say he looks like an elephant, and some say he looks like a cat. To others, he appears as a beautiful princess or in any other form that pleases him. But no one knows who the real Oz is."

"That is very strange," said Dorothy. "But we must try to see him, or we shall have made our journey for nothing."

"Why do you wish to see the terrible Oz?" asked the man.

"I want him to give me some brains," said the Scarecrow eagerly.

"Oh, Oz could do that easily enough," declared the man. "He has more brains than he needs."

"And I want him to give me a heart," said the Tin Woodman.

"That will not trouble him," continued the man. "Oz has a large collection of hearts, of all sizes and shapes."

"And I want him to give me courage," said the Cowardly Lion.

"Oz keeps a great pot of courage in his throne room," said the man. "He covers the pot with a golden plate to keep it from running over. He will be glad to give you some."

"And I want him to send me back to Kansas," said Dorothy.

"Where is Kansas?" asked the man.

"I don't know," replied Dorothy sorrowfully. "But it is my home, and I'm sure it's somewhere."

"Oz can do anything, so I suppose he will find Kansas for you. But first you must get to see him, and that will be a hard task. The Great Wizard does not like to see anyone, and he usually has his own way."

Then the man turned to Toto and asked, "And what do you want?" But Toto only wagged his tail, for he could not speak.

The woman now told them that dinner was ready, so they gathered around the table. Dorothy ate some delicious hot cereal and a dish of scrambled eggs and a plate of nice white bread, and she enjoyed her meal. The Lion ate some of the hot cereal but did not care for it, saying it was made from oats, which is food for horses, not lions. The Scarecrow and the Tin Woodman ate nothing at all. Toto ate a little of everything and was glad to get a good dinner again.

The woman now gave Dorothy a bed to sleep in, and Toto lay down beside her, while the Lion guarded the door of her room so that Dorothy would not be disturbed. The Scarecrow and the Tin Woodman stood up in a corner and kept quiet all night, although of course they could not sleep.

The next morning, as soon as the sun was up, the travelers started on their way and soon saw a beautiful green glow in the sky just in front of them.

"That must be the Emerald City," said Dorothy.

As they walked on, the green glow became brighter and brighter, and it seemed that at last they were nearing the end of their travels. Yet it was afternoon before they came to the great wall that surrounded the city. The wall was high and thick and had a bright green color.

In front of them, at the end of the Yellow Brick Road, was a big gate, all studded with emeralds that glittered so much in the sun that even the painted eyes of the Scarecrow were dazzled by their brightness.

There was a button beside the gate, so Dorothy pushed the button and heard a silvery tinkling sound on the other side. Then the big gate swung slowly open. They all went through and found themselves in a room with a high arched ceiling. The walls of the room glistened with countless emeralds.

In front of them stood a little man about the size of a Munchkin. He was clothed all in green from his head to his feet, and even his skin had a greenish tint. At his side was a large green box.

C COMPREHENSION

Write the answers.

1. Why did the Lion think it was strange that flowers nearly killed him and the mice saved his life?

2. Name at least three ways that the road near the Emerald City was different from the road in the forest.

3. Why didn't the people come out and ask Dorothy and the others questions?

4. Why didn't the man with the injured leg know what Oz really looks like?

5. Why did the man with the injured leg think Oz could help the Scarecrow, the Tin Woodman, and the Lion?

D WRITING

- The travelers have seen just a small part of the Emerald City.

Write a passage that describes what you think the rest of the Emerald City will look like.

Use words that tell how the streets and buildings look and feel. Be sure your passage answers the following questions:

1. What color is everything?

2. What are the streets like?

3. What are the buildings like?

Write at least five sentences.

END OF LESSON 22

A WORD LISTS

1 | Compound Words

1. everything
2. scarecrow
3. sunshine
4. therefore
5. wildcat
6. woodman

2 | Word Practice

1. ceiling
2. cereal
3. fountain
4. furniture

3 | Word Practice

1. honest
2. lemonade
3. uniform
4. whistle

4 | Vocabulary Review

1. admit
2. prefer
3. studded

5 | Vocabulary Words

1. basin
2. guardian
3. marble
4. spectacles

B READING LITERATURE: Novel

Chapter 15

The Emerald City

When the little green man saw Dorothy and her companions, he asked, "What do you wish in the Emerald City?"

"We came here to see the Great Oz," said Dorothy.

The man was so surprised at this answer that he sat down to think it over.

"It has been many years since anyone asked me to see Oz," the green man said. "He is powerful and terrible, and if you come here for the foolish reason of bothering the wise thoughts of the great Wizard, he might be angry and destroy you all in an instant."

"But it is not a foolish reason," replied the Scarecrow. "It is important, and we have been told that Oz is a good Wizard."

So he is," said the green man. "And he rules the Emerald City wisely and well. But to those who are not honest or who approach him out of curiosity, he is most terrible, and few have ever asked to see his face. I am the Guardian of the Gates, and since you demand to see the Great Oz,

I must take you to his palace. But first you must put on these spectacles."

"Why?" asked Dorothy.

"Because if you did not wear spectacles, the brightness of the Emerald City would blind you. Even those who live in the City must wear spectacles night and day. The spectacles are all locked on, for Oz so ordered it when the city was first built, and I have the only key that will unlock them."

The green man opened the big green box, and Dorothy saw that it was filled with spectacles of every size and shape. All of them had green glass in them. The Guardian of the Gates found a pair that fit Dorothy and put them over her eyes.

The spectacles had two golden bands fastened to them that passed around the back of Dorothy's head. The Guardian of the Gates locked the bands together with a little key that was at the end of a chain that he wore around his neck. When the spectacles were on, Dorothy could not take them off. Of course, she did not wish to be blinded by the glare of the Emerald City, so she said nothing.

The Guardian of the Gates also put spectacles on the Scarecrow and the Tin Woodman and the Lion and even on little Toto. All were locked with the key. Then he put on his own glasses and told the travelers that he was ready to show them to the palace. Taking a big golden key from a peg on the wall, he opened another gate, and they all followed him through the gate and into the streets of the Emerald City.

Even with their eyes protected by the green spectacles, Dorothy and her friends were at first dazzled by the brightness of the wonderful city. The streets were lined with beautiful houses built of green marble and studded everywhere with sparkling emeralds. The party walked on a sidewalk made of the same green marble. All the

pieces of the marble were joined together by rows of emeralds that glittered in the brightness of the sun. The window panes were made of green glass. Even the sky above the city had a green tint, and the rays of the sun were green.

There were many men, women, and children walking around. These people were all dressed in green clothes and had greenish skin. They looked at Dorothy and her strange companions with wondering eyes. The children all ran away and hid behind their mothers when they saw the Lion, and no one spoke to the travelers.

The streets had many shops, and Dorothy saw that everything in them was green. Green candy and green popcorn were for sale, as well as green shoes, green hats, and green clothes of all sorts. At one place, a man was selling green lemonade, and when the children bought it, Dorothy could see that they paid for it with green pennies.

There seemed to be no horses. The men carried things around in little green carts, which they pushed in front of them. Everyone seemed happy and rich.

The Guardian of the Gates led the travelers through the streets until they came to a big building, exactly in the middle of the city, which was the Palace of Oz, the Great Wizard. There was a soldier in front of the door, dressed in a green uniform and with a long green beard.

"Here are some strangers," the Guardian of the Gates said to the soldier. "They demand to see the Great Oz."

"Step inside," answered the soldier, "and I will carry your message to him."

So they passed through the palace gates and were led to a big room with a green carpet and lovely green furniture studded with emeralds. The soldier made all of them wipe their feet on a green mat before he let them enter this room. When they were inside, he said politely, "Please make yourselves comfortable while I go to the door of the throne room and tell Oz you are here."

The party had to wait a long time before the soldier returned. When he finally came back, Dorothy asked, "Have you seen Oz?"

"Oh, no," replied the soldier. "I have never seen him. But I just spoke to him as he sat behind his screen and gave him your message. Oz said he will see you if you want, but each one of you must enter his presence alone, and he will admit only one each day. Therefore, since you will have to remain in the palace for several days, I will have someone take you to rooms where you may rest in comfort after your journey." ♦

"Thank you," replied Dorothy. "That is very kind of Oz."

The soldier now blew on a green whistle, and at once a young girl dressed in a pretty green silk gown entered the room. She had lovely green hair and green eyes, and she bowed low before Dorothy as she said, "Follow me."

So Dorothy said goodbye to all her friends except Toto. She took the dog in her arms and followed the green girl through seven hallways and up three flights of stairs until they came to a room at the front of the palace.

It was the sweetest little room in the world, with a soft, comfortable bed that had sheets of green silk and a green blanket. There was a tiny fountain in the middle of the room, which shot a spray of green perfume into the air, and the perfume fell back into a beautifully carved green marble basin. Beautiful green flowers stood in the windows, and there was a shelf with a row of little green books. When Dorothy had time to open these books she found them full of strange green pictures that made her laugh.

The closet had many green dresses, made of silk and satin and velvet, and all of them fit Dorothy exactly.

"Make yourself at home," said the green girl. "And if you want anything, ring the bell. Oz will send for you tomorrow morning."

Then the girl left Dorothy alone and went back to the others. She led each one to a different room in a pleasant part of the palace. Of course, this politeness was wasted on the Scarecrow; for when he found himself alone in his room, he stood in one spot, right next to the door. He had no need to lie down, and he could not close his eyes. So he stood up all night staring at a little spider weaving its web in a corner of the room. The spider didn't act as if it was in one of the most wonderful rooms in the world.

The Tin Woodman lay down on his bed, for he remembered what he had done when he was made of flesh. But since he was unable to sleep, he spent the night moving his legs and arms up and down to make sure that they were in good working order. The Lion would have preferred a bed of dried leaves in the forest and did not like being shut up in a room. But he had too much sense to let this worry him, so he sprang on the bed and rolled himself up like a house cat and fell asleep in a minute.

The next morning after breakfast, the green girl came to get Dorothy and helped

her dress in a pretty green satin gown. Then Dorothy put on a green silk apron and tied a green ribbon around Toto's neck, and the little party started for the throne room of the Great Oz.

First they came to a great hall in which many ladies and gentlemen were standing around, all dressed in fancy clothes. These people had nothing to do but talk to each other, but they always came to wait outside the throne room every morning, even though they were never permitted to see Oz. As Dorothy entered, they looked at her curiously, and one of them whispered, "Are you really going to look upon the face of Oz the Terrible?"

"Of course," answered Dorothy, "if he will see me."

"Oh, he will see you," said the soldier who had taken her message to the Wizard, "although he does not like to have people ask to see him. Indeed, at first he was angry and said I should send you back where you came from. Then he asked me what you looked like, and when I mentioned your silver shoes, he was very much interested. At last I told him about the mark on your forehead, and he decided he would admit you to his presence."

Just then a bell rang, and the green girl said to Dorothy, "That is the signal. You must go into the throne room alone."

C COMPREHENSION

Write the answers.

1. Why was the Guardian of the Gates so surprised when he heard the travelers' request?

2. Why do you think Oz made everyone in the Emerald City wear green spectacles?

3. What could the Emerald City look like if you weren't wearing green spectacles?

4. When the green girl gives the Scarecrow his own bedroom, the story says, "This politeness was wasted on the Scarecrow." What does that mean?

5. What made Oz change his mind about seeing Dorothy?

D WRITING

Write a passage that answers this main question:

• What would your life be like if you had to wear green spectacles all the time?

Use details from your own life to answer these questions in your passage:

1. What kinds of things would look green?

2. How could you tell the difference between objects if they're all one color?

3. How would you feel if you could see only one color?

4. What colors would you miss the most?

5. Would you get used to wearing green spectacles? Why or why not?

Write at least five sentences.

A WORD LISTS

1 | Hard Words

1. disappointed
2. dreadfully
3. giant
4. grindstone
5. rhinoceros

2 | Vocabulary Words

1. enormous
2. grant
3. meek
4. tremendous
5. weep
6. willingly

3 | Word Endings

1. anxious
2. enormous
3. gorgeous
4. tremendous

B READING LITERATURE: Novel

Chapter 6

The Wizard and Dorothy

Dorothy opened the door to the throne room and walked boldly through. She found herself in a wonderful place. It was a big round room with a high arched roof. The walls, ceiling, and floor were covered with large emeralds set closely together. In the center of the roof was a great light, as bright as the sun, which made the emeralds sparkle in a wonderful way.

But what interested Dorothy most was the big throne of green marble that stood in the middle of the room. It was shaped like a chair and sparkled with gems, as did everything else.

In the center of the chair was an enormous head, floating by itself, without a body, arms, or legs. There was no hair on the floating head, but it had eyes and a nose and a mouth and was much bigger than the head of the biggest giant.

As Dorothy gazed at the head in wonder and fear, the eyes turned slowly and looked at her sharply and steadily. Then the mouth moved, and Dorothy heard a voice say, "I am Oz, the Great and Terrible. Who are you, and why do you want to see me?"

Oz's voice was not as awful as Dorothy had expected, so she took courage and answered, "I am Dorothy, the Small and Meek. I have come to you for help."

The eyes looked at her thoughtfully for a full minute. Then Oz said, "Where did you get the silver shoes?"

"I got them from the Wicked Witch of the East when my house fell on her and killed her," she replied.

"Where did you get the mark on your forehead?" Oz continued.

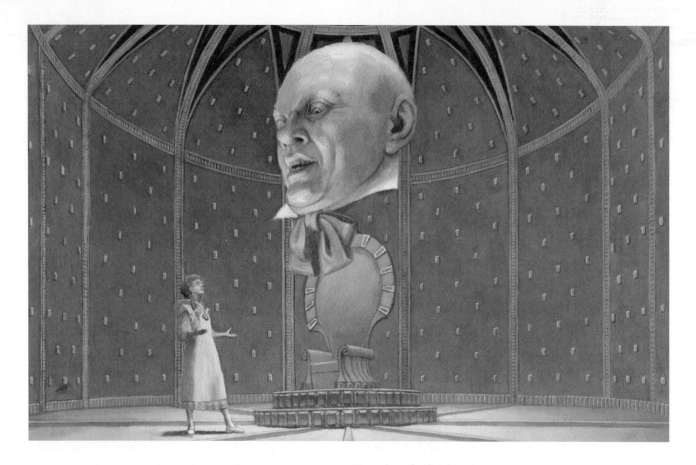

"That is where the Good Witch of the North kissed me when she said goodbye and sent me to you," said the girl.

Again the eyes looked at her sharply, and they saw that she was telling the truth. Then Oz asked, "What do you want me to do?"

"Send me back to Kansas, where Aunt Em and Uncle Henry live," she answered earnestly. "I don't like your country, although it is beautiful. And I am sure Aunt Em is dreadfully worried by my being away so long."

The eyes blinked three times. Then they turned up to the ceiling and down to the floor and rolled around so strangely that they seemed to see every part of the room. And at last they looked at Dorothy again.

"Why should I do this for you?" asked Oz.

"Because you are strong and I am weak; because you are a great wizard and I am only a small child."

"But you were strong enough to kill the Wicked Witch of the East," said Oz.

"That just happened," answered Dorothy. "I could not help it."

"Well," said Oz, "I will give you my answer. You have no right to expect me to send you back to Kansas unless you do something for me. In this country, people must pay for everything they get. If you want me to use my magic power to send you home again, you must do something for me first. Help me and I will help you."

"What must I do?" asked the girl.

"Kill the Wicked Witch of the West," answered Oz. ♦

"But I cannot!" exclaimed Dorothy, greatly surprised.

"You killed the Witch of the East, and you wear the silver shoes, which have a magic charm. There is now only one Wicked Witch left in all this land, and when you can tell me that she is dead, I will send you back to Kansas—but not before."

The girl was so disappointed that she began to weep. The eyes blinked again and looked at her anxiously, as if the great Oz felt that she could help him if she wanted to.

"I never killed anything willingly," she said. "And even if I wanted to, how could I kill the Wicked Witch? If you, who are great and terrible, cannot kill her yourself, how do you expect me to do it?"

"I do not know," said Oz. "But that is my answer, and until the Wicked Witch dies, you will not see your uncle and aunt again. Remember that the Witch is wicked—tremendously wicked—and must be killed. Now go and do not ask to see me again until you have done your task."

C FIRSTHAND ACCOUNTS

- A **firsthand account** is told by somebody who experienced an event. A firsthand account tells about **I** or **we**.

- Here's a firsthand account that tells about **I** or **we**: We went down the ladder from the spaceship and stood on the moon. We were the first humans to stand on the moon.

- Here's another account of the same event: In 1969, two astronauts climbed down the ladder of a spaceship and stood on the moon. They were the first humans to stand on the moon.

For each item, write *firsthand account* or *don't know.*

1. The grass had grown more than a foot since last week.

2. He looked at the other workers.

3. I didn't know that she was talking to us.

4. The fire started in a corner of the warehouse.

5. George helped me get up the hill.

6. Don told us that we were spending too much money.

D COMPREHENSION

Write the answers.

1. Do you think that Oz is really a floating head? Explain your answer.

2. Why did Dorothy call herself "Dorothy, the Small and Meek"?

3. Why do you think Oz was so interested in the silver shoes and the witch's kiss?

4. What did Oz mean when he told Dorothy, "Help me and I will help you"?

5. Why do you think Oz wants to kill the Wicked Witch of the West?

E WRITING

Write a passage that describes the throne room when Dorothy enters it.

Use details from the novel to answer these questions in your passage:

1. What shape is the room?

2. What is the room covered with?

3. How is the room lit?

4. What is in the room?

Write at least five sentences.

END OF LESSON 24

25

A WORD LISTS

1 | Hard Words

1. castle
2. daisies
3. telescope

2 | Word Practice

1. cackle
2. cackling
3. rhinoceros
4. single

3 | Vocabulary Review

1. enormous
2. grant
3. meek
4. tremendous

4 | Vocabulary Words

1. advance
2. grindstone
3. kingdom
4. pure

5 | Vocabulary Words

1. request
2. singe
3. slightest
4. terror

B READING LITERATURE: Novel

Chapter 17

The Wizard's Commands

Dorothy was very sad when she left the throne room. She went back to where the Lion and the Scarecrow and the Tin Woodman were waiting to hear what Oz had said to her.

"There is no hope for me," Dorothy said sadly. "Oz will not send me home until I have killed the Wicked Witch of the West, and I cannot do that."

Her friends were sorry, but they could do nothing to help her. So she went to her own room and lay down on the bed and went to sleep.

The next morning the soldier with the green whiskers came to the Scarecrow and said, "Come with me, for Oz has sent for you."

So the Scarecrow followed him and went into the great throne room, where he saw a most lovely lady sitting on the emerald throne. She was dressed in green silk and wore a crown of jewels upon her flowing green hair. Gorgeously colored wings were attached to her shoulders. The wings were so light that they fluttered if the slightest breath of air reached them.

The Scarecrow made a clumsy bow before this beautiful creature. She looked upon him sweetly and said, "I am Oz, the

Great and Terrible. Who are you, and why do you seek me?"

The Scarecrow, who had expected to see the great head Dorothy had told him about, was amazed that Oz was now a woman.

"I am only a Scarecrow, stuffed with straw. Therefore, I have no brains, and I come to you hoping that you will put brains in my head instead of straw so that I may become as much a man as any other in your kingdom."

"Why should I do this for you?" asked Oz.

"Because you are wise and powerful, and no one else can help me," answered the Scarecrow.

"In this country, people must pay for everything they get," said Oz. "If you will kill the Wicked Witch of the West for me, I will give you a great many brains—and such good brains that you will be the wisest man in all the Land of Oz."

"I thought you asked Dorothy to kill the witch," said the Scarecrow in surprise.

"So I did. I don't care who kills her. But until she is dead, I will not grant your wish. Now go, and do not ask to see me again until you have earned the brains you so greatly desire."

The Scarecrow went sorrowfully back to his friends and told them what Oz had said. Dorothy was surprised to find that the great Wizard was not a head, as she had seen him, but a lovely lady.

"All the same," said the Scarecrow, "she needs a heart as much as the Tin Woodman."

On the next morning, the soldier with green whiskers came to the Tin Woodman and said, "Oz has sent for you. Follow me."

So the Tin Woodman followed the soldier and came to the great throne room. He did not know whether Oz would be a lovely lady or a head, but he hoped Oz would be the lovely lady.

The Tin Woodman said to himself, "If it is the head, I am sure I will not be given a heart, for a head has no heart of its own and therefore cannot feel for me. But if it is the lovely lady, I will beg hard for a heart, for all ladies are supposed to be kindhearted."

But when the Tin Woodman entered the great throne room, he saw neither the head nor the lady, for Oz had taken the shape of a terrible beast. It was nearly as big as an elephant, and the green throne seemed barely strong enough to hold its weight.

The beast had a head like a rhinoceros, except that its face had five eyes. There were five long arms growing out of its body, and it also had five long, slim legs. Thick hair covered every part of it, and it was the most dreadful looking monster that the Tin Woodman had ever seen. It was fortunate that the Tin Woodman had no heart, for it would have beat loud and fast from terror. But because he had no heart, the Tin Woodman was not at all afraid. ♦

"I am Oz, the Great and Terrible," said the beast in a roaring voice. "Who are you, and why do you seek me?"

The Tin Woodman answered, "I am a Woodman and made of tin. Therefore, I have no heart and cannot love. I want you to give me a heart so that I may be like other men."

"Why should I do this?" demanded the beast.

"Because I ask it and because you alone can grant my request," answered the Tin Woodman.

Oz gave a low growl at this but said, "If you really want a heart, you must earn it."

"How?" asked the Tin Woodman.

"Help Dorothy kill the Wicked Witch of the West," replied the beast. "When the Witch is dead, come to me, and I will then give you the biggest and kindest and most loving heart in all the Land of Oz."

So the Tin Woodman was forced to return sorrowfully to his friends and tell them of the terrible beast he had seen. They were all amazed by how many forms the great Wizard could take, and the Lion said, "If he is a beast when I go to see him, I will roar my loudest and frighten him so much that he will grant all I ask. And if he is the lovely lady, I will pretend to spring at her and make her do what I want. And if he is the great head, I will roll him all around the room until he promises to give us what we desire. So be happy, my friends, for everything will go well."

The next morning the soldier with the green whiskers led the Lion to the great throne room.

The Lion at once passed through the door, glanced around, and saw to his surprise that a ball of fire was in front of the throne. The ball was so fierce and glowing that the Lion could scarcely bear to look at it. The Lion's first thought was that Oz had accidentally caught on fire and was burning up. But when the Lion tried to go nearer, the heat was so great that it singed his whiskers, and he crept back to a spot near the door.

Then a low, quiet voice came from the ball of fire and said, "I am Oz, the Great and Terrible. Who are you, and why do you seek me?"

The Lion answered, "I am a Cowardly Lion, afraid of everything. I come to you to beg that you give me courage so that I may become the King of Beasts."

"Why should I give you courage?" demanded Oz.

"Because, of all the Wizards, you are the greatest and because you alone have the power to grant my request," answered the Lion.

The ball of fire burned fiercely for a time, and then the voice said, "Help Dorothy kill the Wicked Witch of the West, and then I will give you courage. But as long as the Witch lives, you must remain a coward."

The Lion was angry at this speech but could say nothing in reply. While he stood silently gazing at the ball of fire, it became so unbearably hot that he turned around and rushed from the room. He was glad to find his friends waiting for him, and he told them about his terrible meeting with the Wizard.

"What shall we do now?" asked Dorothy sadly.

"There is only one thing we can do," answered the Lion, "and that is to go to the Land of the West, seek out the Wicked Witch, and destroy her."

"But suppose we cannot?" said the girl.

"Then I will never have courage," declared the Lion.

"And I will never have brains," added the Scarecrow.

"And I will never have a heart," said the Tin Woodman.

"And I will never see Aunt Em and Uncle Henry," said Dorothy.

Dorothy looked at her friends and said, "I suppose we must try it. But I am sure I do not want to kill anybody, even to see Aunt Em again."

"I will go with you," said the Lion. "But I'm too much of a coward to kill the Witch."

"I will go, too," declared the Scarecrow. "But I won't be much help to you because I am a fool without any brains."

"I haven't the heart to harm even a witch," remarked the Tin Woodman. "But if you go, I certainly must go with you."

Therefore, they decided to start their journey to the Land of the West the next morning. The Tin Woodman sharpened his axe on a green grindstone and had all his joints properly oiled. The Scarecrow stuffed himself with fresh straw, and Dorothy put new paint on his eyes so that he could see better. The green girl, who was very kind to them, filled Dorothy's basket with good things to eat and fastened a little green bell around Toto's neck with a green ribbon.

Dorothy, Toto, and the Lion went to bed quite early and slept soundly.

They were awakened by the crowing of a green rooster that lived in the backyard of the palace and by the cackling of a green hen that had laid a green egg. The travelers were ready to start on their journey to the west.

C FIRSTHAND ACCOUNTS

For each item, write *firsthand account* or *don't know*.

1. We thought he was telling the truth.

2. The witness swore to tell the truth.

3. Lying on the ground can be uncomfortable.

4. I thought she was too bossy.

5. They started talking to me.

6. Barack rubbed his eye and scratched his nose.

D COMPREHENSION

Write the answers.

1. After the Scarecrow saw the lovely lady, he said, "She needs a heart as much as the Tin Woodman." What did he mean by that?

2. Why did the Tin Woodman hope that Oz would be a lady?

3. Why do you think Oz appeared in a different form to each traveler?

4. Why did the travelers decide to kill the Wicked Witch?

E WRITING

• So far, Oz has appeared as a floating head, a lovely lady, a terrible beast, and a ball of fire.

Write a passage that describes what Oz might look like if you saw him.

Be sure your passage answers these questions:

1. What does he look like?

2. What does he sound like?

3. What does he smell like?

Write at least five sentences.

END OF LESSON 25

A | WORD LISTS

1 | Word Practice

1. buttercup
2. invisible
3. strange
4. struggle

2 | Related Words

1. daisy / daisies
2. desperate / desperately
3. hill / hillier

3 | Vocabulary Words

1. batter
2. bundle
3. castle
4. chatter
5. fate

4 | Vocabulary Words

1. fine
2. seize
3. spear
4. tempt
5. untilled

B | READING LITERATURE: Novel

Chapter 18

The Search for the Wicked Witch

The soldier with the green whiskers led Dorothy and her friends through the streets of the Emerald City until they reached the room where the Guardian of the Gates lived. The Guardian unlocked their spectacles and put them back in his green box, and then he politely opened the gate for the travelers.

"Which road leads to the Wicked Witch of the West?" asked Dorothy.

"There is no road," answered the Guardian of the Gates. "No one ever wishes to go that way."

"Then how can we find her?" inquired the girl.

"That will be easy," replied the man. "When she knows you are in the country of the Winkies, she will find you and make you all her slaves."

"Perhaps not," said the Scarecrow, "for we hope to destroy her."

"Oh, that is different," said the Guardian of the Gates. "No one has ever destroyed her before, so I naturally thought she would make slaves of you. But take care, for she is wicked and fierce and may try to destroy you first. Keep going west, where the sun sets, and you cannot fail to find her."

They thanked him and said goodbye and turned toward the west, walking over fields of soft grass dotted here and there with daisies and buttercups. Dorothy still wore the pretty silk dress she had put on in the palace; but now, to her surprise, she found that it was no longer green, but pure white. The ribbon around Toto's neck had also lost its green color and was as white as Dorothy's dress.

The Emerald City was soon far behind them. As they advanced, the ground became rougher and hillier, for there were no farms or houses in this country of the West, and the ground was untilled.

In the afternoon, the sun shone hot in their faces, and there were no trees to offer them shade. The sun made Dorothy and Toto and the Lion very tired, and before night, they lay down on the grass and fell asleep, with the Tin Woodman and the Scarecrow keeping watch.

Now the Wicked Witch of the West had only one eye, but it was as powerful as a telescope and could see everywhere. As she sat in the door of her yellow castle, she happened to see Dorothy lying asleep, with her friends all around her. They were a long way away, but the Wicked Witch was angry to find them in her country. So she called a dozen of her slaves, who were called the Winkies, gave them sharp yellow spears, and told them to go to the strangers and destroy them.

The Winkies were not a brave people, but they had to do as they were told, so they marched away until they came near Dorothy. Then the Lion gave a great roar and sprang toward them, and the poor Winkies were so frightened that they ran back to the castle as fast as they could.

When the Winkies returned to the Wicked Witch, she sent them back to their work. Then she sat down to think. She could not understand why her plan to destroy these strangers had failed. But she was a powerful Witch, as well as a wicked one, and she soon decided what to do next. ♦

Now, the Wicked Witch had a golden cap in her cupboard. The cap was studded with diamonds and rubies, and it had a special power. Whoever owned the cap could call upon the Winged Monkeys, who would obey any order they were given. But no one could command these strange creatures more than three times.

The Wicked Witch had already used the cap twice. The first time was when she had made the Winkies her slaves and become the ruler of their country. The Winged Monkeys had helped her do this. The second time was when she had fought against the great Oz and driven him out of the Land of the West. The monkeys had also helped her do this.

The Witch could use the golden cap only one more time, but she knew that it was the only way to destroy Dorothy and her friends. So she took the golden cap from her cupboard and placed it on her head. Then she stood on her left foot and said slowly, "Ep-pe, pep-pe, bep-pe!"

Next she stood on her right foot and said, "Hil-lo, hol-lo, hel-lo!"

After that she stood on both feet and cried in a loud voice, "Ziz-zy, zuz-zy, zik!"

Now the charm began to work. The sky was darkened, and a low rumbling sound came through the air. The Witch heard the flapping of many wings, and then a great chattering and laughing. When the sun came out of the dark sky, the Wicked Witch was surrounded by a crowd of monkeys. Each monkey had a pair of large and powerful wings on his shoulders.

One monkey, much bigger than the others, seemed to be the leader. He flew

close to the Witch and said, "You have called us for the third and last time. What do you command?"

"Go to the strangers who are within my land and destroy them all except the Lion," said the Wicked Witch. "Bring the beast to me, for I have a mind to harness him like a horse and make him work."

"Your commands shall be obeyed," said the leader. And then, with a great deal of chattering and noise, the Winged Monkeys flew away to the place where Dorothy and her friends were walking.

Some of the monkeys seized the Tin Woodman and carried him through the air until they were over a plain that was thickly covered with sharp rocks. Here they dropped the poor Tin Woodman, who fell a great distance to the rocks. He

became so battered and dented that he could neither move nor groan.

Other monkeys caught the Scarecrow and pulled all the straw out of his clothes and head with their long fingers. They made his hat and boots and clothes into a small bundle and threw the bundle into the top branches of a tall tree.

The remaining monkeys threw pieces of thick rope around the Lion and wound the rope around his body and head and legs until he was unable to bite or scratch or struggle in any way. Then they lifted him up and flew away with him to the Witch's castle, where he was placed in a small yard with a high iron fence around it so that he could not escape.

But they did not harm Dorothy at all. She stood, with Toto in her arms, watching the sad fate of her comrades and thinking it would soon be her turn. The leader of the Winged Monkeys flew up to her with his long, hairy arms stretched out and his ugly face grinning terribly. But when he saw the mark of the Good Witch's kiss on Dorothy's forehead, he stopped short and told the other monkeys not to touch her.

"We dare not harm this girl," he said to them, "for the mark on her forehead shows that she is protected by the Power of Good, and that is greater than the Power of Evil. All we can do is carry her to the castle of the Wicked Witch and leave her there."

So, carefully and gently, they lifted Dorothy in their arms and carried her swiftly through the air until they came to the yellow castle, where they set her down on the front doorstep. Then the leader said to the Witch, "We have obeyed you as far as we were able. The Tin Woodman and the Scarecrow are destroyed, and the Lion is tied up in your yard. We dare not harm the girl, nor the dog she carries in her arms. Your power over us is now ended."

Then all the Winged Monkeys, with much laughing and chattering and noise, flew into the air and were soon out of sight.

The Wicked Witch was both surprised and worried when she saw the mark on Dorothy's forehead, for she knew very well that she dare not hurt the girl in any way. She looked down at Dorothy's feet, and when she saw the silver shoes, she began to tremble with fear, for she knew what a powerful charm the shoes had.

At first the Witch was tempted to run away from Dorothy, but she happened to look into the girl's eyes and realized that the girl did not know of the wonderful power of the silver shoes. So the Witch laughed to herself and thought, "I can still make her my slave, for she does not know how to use her power."

Then she said to Dorothy, severely, "Come with me. And see that you obey me, for if you do not, I will make an end of you, as I did of the Tin Woodman and the Scarecrow."

Dorothy followed the Witch through many of the beautiful rooms in her castle until they came to the kitchen, where the Witch ordered her to clean the pots and kettles and sweep the floor and feed the fire with wood. The girl went to work meekly, with her mind made up to work as hard as she could, for she did not want the Wicked Witch to make an end of her.

C | POINT OF VIEW

- A **firsthand account** is told by somebody who experienced an event. A firsthand account tells about **I** or **we**.

For each item, write *firsthand account* or *don't know*.

1. Taylor and Digby are my best friends.
2. Taylor and Digby are brothers.
3. They live next door to me.
4. Digby has a dog that barks all the time.
5. We can hear that dog barking during the night.
6. I like Taylor more than Digby.
7. Who left that big package in our driveway?

D | COMPREHENSION

Write the answers.

1. Do you think the inside of the Emerald City was really green? Explain your answer.
2. Do you think the Tin Woodman is really dead? Explain your answer.
3. What do you think will happen to the Scarecrow? Explain your answer.
4. Why didn't the chief monkey dare to harm Dorothy?
5. Why did Dorothy decide to work as hard as she could for the Witch?

E | WRITING

- The Winged Monkeys have to obey whoever owns the golden cap.

Write a story that explains where the Winged Monkeys come from and why they have to obey the owner of the golden cap.

Use details from the novel to answer these questions in your story:

1. Where do the Winged Monkeys come from?
2. How did the Winged Monkeys get their wings?
3. Why did the Winged Monkeys fall under the power of the golden cap?
4. How do the Winged Monkeys feel about obeying the owner of the golden cap?
5. What do the Winged Monkeys hope will happen?

Write at least five sentences.

END OF LESSON 26

A WORD LISTS

1 Word Practice	2 Word Endings	3 Vocabulary Review	4 Vocabulary Words
1. bathe	1. anxious	1. fate	1. courtyard
2. bathing	2. enormous	2. seize	2. cruelty
3. despair	3. gorgeous	3. tempt	3. cunning
4. despairing	4. tremendous		4. desperately
5. desperate			5. feast
6. holiday			6. mend
7. invisible			7. tenderly
8. straightened			

B READING LITERATURE: Novel

Chapter 19

The Rescue

Now, the Wicked Witch desperately wanted to have Dorothy's silver shoes. She had used up all the power of the golden cap; but if she could only get hold of the silver shoes, they would give her more power than before. She watched Dorothy carefully to see if she ever took off her shoes. But Dorothy was so proud of her pretty shoes that she never took them off except at night and when she took her bath.

The Witch was too afraid of the dark to go into Dorothy's room at night to take the shoes.

And the Witch's fear of water was greater than her fear of the dark, so she never came near when Dorothy was bathing. Indeed, the old Witch never touched water, nor ever let water touch her in any way.

But the Witch was very cunning, and she finally thought of a trick that would give her what she wanted. She placed an iron bar in the middle of the kitchen floor, and then, using her magic arts, she made the bar invisible to human eyes. When Dorothy walked across the floor, she stumbled over the invisible bar and fell down. She was not hurt, but as she fell, one of the silver shoes came off. Before she could reach the shoe, the Witch seized it and put it on her own skinny foot.

The wicked woman was greatly pleased with the success of her trick. As long as she had one of the shoes, she owned half the power of their charm, and Dorothy could not use the magic against her, even if she had known how to do so.

The girl, seeing that she had lost one of her pretty shoes, grew angry and said to the Witch, "Give me back my shoe!"

"I will not," replied the Witch, "for it is now my shoe and not yours."

"You are a wicked creature!" said Dorothy. "You have no right to take my shoe from me."

"I will keep it, just the same," said the Witch, laughing at her, "and someday I will get the other one from you, too."

This made Dorothy so angry that she picked up the bucket of water that stood near and threw it over the Witch, soaking her from head to foot.

Instantly, the wicked woman gave a loud cry of fear, and then, as Dorothy looked at her in wonder, the Witch began to shrink and fall away.

"See what you have done!" the Witch screamed. "In a minute I will melt away."

"I'm very sorry," said Dorothy, who was truly frightened to see the Witch actually melting away before her eyes.

"Didn't you know that water would be the end of me?" asked the Witch in a wailing, despairing voice.

"Of course not," answered Dorothy. "How could I?"

"Well, in a few minutes I will be all melted, and you will have the castle to yourself. I have been wicked in my day, but I never thought a girl like you would ever be able to melt me and end my wicked deeds. Look out—here I go!"

With these words, the Witch fell down in a brown, melted, shapeless mass that began to spread over the kitchen floor.

Seeing that the Witch had really melted away to nothing, Dorothy got another bucket of water and threw it over the mess. Then she swept it all out the door. She picked up the silver shoe, which was all that was left of the old woman, cleaned and dried it with a cloth, and put it on her foot again. Free at last, she ran out to the courtyard to tell the Lion that the Wicked Witch had died and that they were no longer prisoners in a strange land. ♦

The Cowardly Lion was very pleased to hear that the Wicked Witch had been melted by a bucket of water, and Dorothy at once unlocked the gate of his yard and set him free. They went into the castle, where Dorothy called all the Winkies together and told them that they were no longer slaves.

There was great rejoicing among the yellow Winkies, for the Wicked Witch had made them work hard and had always treated them with great cruelty. The Winkies decided to make that day a holiday and began feasting and dancing.

"If only our friends, the Scarecrow and the Tin Woodman, were with us," said the Lion, "I would be quite happy."

"Don't you think we could rescue them?" asked the girl anxiously.

"We can try," answered the Lion.

So they called the yellow Winkies and asked for help to rescue their friends. The Winkies said that they would be delighted to do everything they could for Dorothy, who had set them free from bondage. Dorothy chose the Winkies who looked as if they knew the most, and they all started away.

They traveled that day and part of the next until they came to the rocky plain where the Tin Woodman lay, all battered and bent. His axe was near him, but the blade was rusted and the handle was broken.

The Winkies lifted him tenderly in their arms and carried him back to the yellow castle. Dorothy shed many tears at the sad fate of her old friend, and the Lion looked sober and sorry. When they reached the castle, Dorothy said to the Winkies, "Do you have any tinsmiths?"

"Oh, yes, we have some very good tinsmiths," they told her.

"Then bring them to me," she said. And when the tinsmiths came, bringing with them all their tools in baskets, Dorothy asked, "Can you straighten out those dents in the Tin Woodman and bend him back into shape again and put him back together?"

The tinsmiths looked the Tin Woodman over carefully and then answered that they thought they could mend him so he would be as good as ever. They set to work in one of the big yellow rooms of the castle and worked for three days and four nights, hammering and twisting and bending and polishing and pounding at the legs and body and head of the Tin Woodman. At last he was straightened out into his old form, and his joints worked as well as ever. To be sure, there were several patches on him, but the tinsmiths did a good job, and the Tin Woodman did not mind the patches at all.

When he walked into Dorothy's room at last and thanked her for rescuing him, he was so pleased that he wept tears of joy, and Dorothy had to wipe every tear carefully from his face with her apron so his joints would not be rusted. At the same time, her own tears fell thick and fast at the joy of meeting her old friend again, and these tears did not need to be wiped away. As for the Lion, he wiped his eyes so often with the tip of his tail that it became quite wet, and he had to go out into the courtyard and hold his tail in the sun until it dried.

"If we only had the Scarecrow with us again," said the Tin Woodman when Dorothy had finished telling him everything that had happened, "I would be quite happy."

"We must try to find him," said the girl.

So she called the Winkies to help her, and they walked all that day and part of the next until they came to the tall tree where the Winged Monkeys had tossed the Scarecrow's clothes.

It was a very tall tree, and the trunk was so smooth that no one could climb it. The Tin Woodman said at once, "I'll chop it down, and then we can get the Scarecrow's clothes."

Now, while the tinsmiths had been mending the Tin Woodman, another Winkie, who was a goldsmith, had made an axe handle of solid gold and fitted it on the Tin Woodman's axe in place of the old broken handle. Other Winkies had polished the blade until all the rust was removed, and it glistened like silver.

As soon as he had spoken, the Tin Woodman began to chop. In a short time, the tree fell over with a crash, and the Scarecrow's clothes fell out of the branches and dropped to the ground.

Dorothy picked them up and had the Winkies carry them back to the castle, where they were stuffed with nice, clean straw—and behold, here was the Scarecrow as good as ever, thanking them over and over again for saving him.

C COMPARING ACCOUNTS

Work the items.

- You know that a **firsthand account** is told by somebody who experienced an event. A firsthand account tells about **I** or **we.**

- A **secondhand account** is told by somebody who has information about the event but may not have experienced the event.

Here are two accounts of the same event:

Account A: We went down the ladder from the lunar module and stood on the moon. We were the first humans to stand on the moon.

Account B: In 1969, two astronauts climbed down the ladder from the lunar module and stood on the moon. They were the first humans to stand on the moon.

1. Which account is a firsthand account?

2. How do you know?

3. Which account is a secondhand account?

4. How do you know?

D COMPREHENSION

Write the answers.

1. Do you think it's strange that the Witch was afraid of the dark? Explain your answer.

2. Explain how the Witch made Dorothy trip on the kitchen floor.

3. Why did Dorothy throw the water over the Witch?

4. How were the tinsmiths able to bring the Tin Woodman back to life?

5. Do you think the Scarecrow will be different now that he is stuffed with new straw? Explain your answer.

E WRITING

Write a passage that answers this main question:

- Why do you think the water melted the Witch?

Use details from the novel to answer these other questions in your passage:

1. What kind of person was the Witch?

2. What do you think the Witch was made of?

3. Why was the water more powerful than the Witch?

Write at least five sentences.

END OF LESSON 27

A WORD LISTS

1	Hard Words
1.	discourage
2.	encourage
3.	tongue

2	Word Endings
1.	fortunately
2.	presently
3.	promptly
4.	solemnly

3	Vocabulary Words
1.	exclaim
2.	lining
3.	mischief
4.	patter
5.	reunite

B READING LITERATURE: Novel

Chapter 20

The Journey Back

Now that they were reunited, Dorothy and her friends spent a few happy days at the Witch's castle, where they found everything they needed to make themselves comfortable. But one day the girl thought of Aunt Em and said, "We must go back to Oz and claim his promise."

Then Dorothy went to the Witch's cupboard to fill her basket with food for the journey, and there she saw the golden cap. She tried it on her own head and found that it fit her exactly. She did not know anything about the charm of the cap, but she saw that it was pretty, so she made up her mind to wear the cap and carry her sunbonnet in the basket.

Then they all started for the Emerald City. The Winkies gave them three cheers and many good wishes to carry with them.

Now, you will remember there was no road—not even a pathway—between the castle of the Wicked Witch and the Emerald City. When the travelers had gone in search of the Witch, she had seen them coming and sent the Winged Monkeys for them. But it was much harder to find their way back through the big fields of buttercups and bright daisies. They knew, of course, that they had to go straight east, toward the rising sun, and they started off in the right way.

But then at noon, when the sun was over their heads, they did not know which was east and which was west, and they soon became lost in the great fields. They kept on walking, however, and at night the moon came out and shone brightly. So they lay down among the sweet-smelling flowers and slept soundly until morning—all but the Scarecrow and the Tin Woodman.

The next morning the sun was behind a cloud, but they started on as if they were quite sure which way they were going.

"If we walk far enough," said Dorothy, "we will soon come to some place, I am sure."

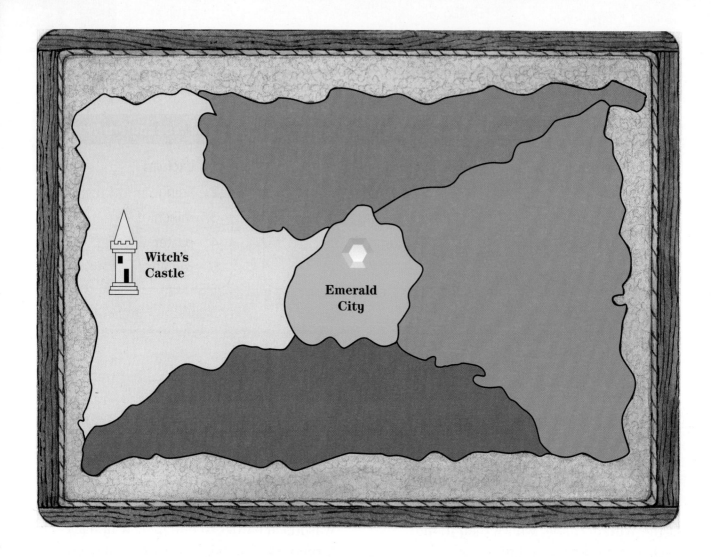

Witch's
Castle

Emerald
City

But day by day passed away, and they still saw nothing before them but the yellow fields.

Then Dorothy became discouraged. She sat down on the grass and looked at her companions, and they sat down and looked at her. Toto found that for the first time in his life he was too tired to chase a butterfly that flew past his head. So he put out his tongue and panted and looked at Dorothy as if to ask her what they should do next.

Dorothy and her friends sat in the fields for a long time. Then she said, "Why don't we call the field mice? They could probably tell us the way to the Emerald City."

"Why, of course they could," cried the Scarecrow. "Why didn't we think of that before?" ♦

Dorothy blew the little whistle she had always carried around her neck since the Queen of the Mice had given it to her. In a few minutes, they heard the pattering of tiny feet, and many of the small gray mice came running up to her. The Queen was among them, and she asked in her squeaky little voice, "What can I do for my friends?"

We have lost our way," said Dorothy. "Can you tell us where the Emerald City is?"

"Certainly," answered the Queen. "It is a great way off, for it has been behind you all this time." Then she noticed Dorothy's golden cap and said, "Why don't you use the charm of the cap and call the Winged Monkeys? They will carry you to the Emerald City in less than an hour."

"I don't know how to use the charm," answered Dorothy in surprise. "How do I make it work?"

"The directions for using the charm are written inside the golden cap," replied the Queen of the Mice. "But if you are going to call the Winged Monkeys, we must run away, for they are full of mischief and think it is great fun to chase us."

"Won't the Winged Monkeys hurt me?" asked the girl anxiously.

"Oh, no, they must obey the wearer of the cap. Goodbye!" And the Queen scampered out of sight, with all the mice hurrying after her.

Dorothy looked inside the golden cap and saw some words written on the lining. These, she thought, must be the charm, so she read the directions carefully and put the cap on her head.

"Ep-pe, pep-pe, bep-pe!" she said, standing on her left foot.

"Hil-lo, hol-lo, hel-lo!" she went on, standing this time on her right foot.

"Ziz-zy, zuz-zy, zik!" she said at last, standing on both feet.

Suddenly, the travelers heard a great chattering and flapping of wings as the band of Winged Monkeys flew up to them. The King bowed low before Dorothy and asked, "What is your command?"

"We want to go to the Emerald City," said the girl, "and we have lost our way."

"We will carry you," replied the King, and no sooner had he spoken than two of the monkeys caught Dorothy in their arms and flew away with her. Other monkeys

took the Scarecrow and the Tin Woodman and the Lion, and one little monkey seized Toto and flew after the others, although the dog tried hard to bite him.

The Scarecrow and the Tin Woodman were rather frightened at first, for they remembered how badly the Winged Monkeys had treated them before. But they soon saw that the monkeys were not going to hurt them, so they rode through the air quite cheerfully and had a fine time looking at the pretty gardens and woods far below.

Dorothy was carried by two of the biggest monkeys, and one of them was the King Monkey. They had made a chair out of their hands and were careful not to hurt her.

Less than an hour later, Dorothy looked down and saw the shining green walls of the Emerald City below them. She was amazed by how rapidly the monkeys had flown, but she was glad the journey was over.

The monkeys set the travelers down carefully in front of the gate of the city. Then the King bowed low to Dorothy before flying swiftly away, followed by all his band.

"That was a good ride," said the girl.

"Yes, and a quick way out of our troubles," replied the Lion. "How lucky it was that you took the wonderful cap!"

The travelers walked up to the great gate of the Emerald City and rang the bell. After several rings, the gate was opened by the same Guardian of the Gates they had met before.

"What! Are you back again?" he asked in surprise. "I thought you had gone to visit the Wicked Witch of the West."

"We did visit her," said the Scarecrow.

"And she let you go again?" asked the man in wonder.

"She could not help it, for she is melted," explained the Scarecrow.

"Melted! Well, that is good news, indeed," said the man. "Who melted her?"

"It was Dorothy," said the Lion solemnly.

"Good gracious!" exclaimed the man, and he bowed very low before her.

Then he led them into his little room and locked spectacles on their eyes, just as he had done before. Next they passed on through the gate into the Emerald City. When the people heard from the Guardian of the Gates that Dorothy and the others had melted the Wicked Witch of the West, they all gathered around the travelers and followed them in a great crowd to the palace of Oz.

The soldier with the green whiskers was still on guard before the door, but he let them in at once, and they were again met by the beautiful green girl, who showed each of them to their old rooms. She told them they could rest there until the Great Oz was ready to receive them.

The soldier sent a message to Oz that Dorothy and the other travelers had come back again, after destroying the Wicked Witch. But Oz made no reply.

Dorothy and the others thought the great wizard would send for them at once, but he did not. They had no word from him the next day nor the next nor the next. The waiting was tiresome, and at last they became angry with Oz for treating them so poorly after they had killed the Witch for him. So the Scarecrow asked the green girl to take another message to Oz, saying that if Oz did not let them in to see him at once, they would call the Winged Monkeys.

When Oz received this message, he was so frightened that he sent word for them to come to the throne room at nine o'clock the next morning. He had once been defeated by the Winged Monkeys in the Land of the West, and he did not want to meet them again.

The travelers spent a sleepless night, each thinking of the gift Oz had promised.

Dorothy fell asleep only once, and then she dreamed she was in Kansas, where Aunt Em was telling her how glad she was to have her home again.

C COMPARING ACCOUNTS

Work the items.

Account A

The Golden Gate Bridge took four years to build and opened in 1937. The bridge spans the Golden Gate Strait, a mile-wide stretch of water that links San Francisco Bay to the Pacific Ocean. The city of San Francisco is on the south end of the bridge and Marin County is on the north end. More than 100,000 cars cross the bridge each day, along with thousands of pedestrians and bicyclists.

The total length of the bridge is 1.7 miles. The highway on the bridge, Highway 101, is more than 200 feet above the water. The tops of the two towers that support the highway are about 750 feet above the water. The total weight of the bridge and towers is almost 420,000 tons.

Account B

Walking across the Golden Gate Bridge is a lot of fun. You can start on the north or south side of the bridge and walk on the sidewalk next to Highway 101. It's a 1.7-mile walk to the other side, which means you have to walk 3.4 miles for a round trip. Many people just walk halfway across the bridge and turn around.

I drive back and forth across the bridge almost every day, but I always seem to be too busy to walk across. But one spring day the sun was shining, and I had a little extra time, so I parked on the north side of the bridge and began walking. It was a beautiful day, and I could see dozens of sailboats on San Francisco Bay. The only problem was that the cars on the highway made a lot of noise.

1. Which account is a firsthand account?

2. Which account is a secondhand account?

3. How long is the Golden Gate Bridge?

4. Is item 3 answered by *account A* only; *account B* only; *both* accounts; or *neither* account?

5. How many cars cross the bridge each day?

6. Is item 5 answered by *account A* only; *account B* only; *both* accounts; or *neither* account?

7. Why is the bridge noisy during the day?

8. Is item 7 answered by *account A* only; *account B* only; *both* accounts; or *neither* account?

9. How big are the sailboats?

10. Is item 9 answered by *account A* only; *account B* only; *both* accounts; or *neither* account?

D COMPREHENSION

Write the answers.

1. Why did the travelers get lost on their way back to the Emerald City?

2. Why had the Queen of the Mice promised always to help the travelers?

3. Why were the Scarecrow and the Tin Woodman frightened of the Winged Monkeys at first?

4. Why do you think the Guardian of the Gates was so surprised to see the travelers again?

5. Why do you think Oz is treating the travelers so poorly?

E WRITING

• In this chapter, the travelers got lost because they lost track of the sun.

Write a story about someone who gets lost and then finds their way back home.

Use your own ideas to answer these questions in your story:

1. Who is the main character in your story?

2. How does the main character get lost?

3. How does the main character find their way back?

4. How does the story conclude?

Write at least five sentences.

END OF LESSON 28

A | WORD LISTS

1 | Word Endings

1. angrily
2. greatly
3. meekly
4. presently
5. solemnly
6. usually

2 | Vocabulary Words

1. bald
2. humbug
3. overhear
4. promptly

B | READING LITERATURE: Novel

Chapter 21

Another Meeting With Oz

Promptly at nine o'clock the next morning, the green-whiskered soldier came to the travelers. Four minutes later they all went into the throne room of the Great Oz.

Of course, each one of the travelers expected to see the Wizard in the shape he had taken before, and all were greatly surprised when they looked around and saw no one at all in the room. They kept close to the door and closer to one another, for the stillness of the empty room was more dreadful than any of the forms they had seen Oz take.

Presently they heard a voice that seemed to come from somewhere near the top of the great dome. The voice said solemnly, "I am Oz, the Great and Terrible. Why do you want to see me?"

They looked again in every part of the room, and then, seeing no one, Dorothy asked, "Where are you?"

"I am everywhere," answered the voice, "but to your eyes I am invisible. I will now seat myself upon the throne so that you may speak with me." The voice seemed to move toward the throne, so Dorothy and the others walked toward the throne and stood in a row. But Oz was still invisible.

Dorothy said, "We have come to claim your promise, great Oz."

"What promise?" asked Oz.

"You promised to send me back to Kansas when the Wicked Witch was destroyed," said the girl.

"And you promised to give me brains," said the Scarecrow.

"And you promised to give me a heart," said the Tin Woodman.

"And you promised to give me courage," said the Cowardly Lion.

"Is the Wicked Witch really destroyed?" asked the voice. Dorothy noticed that it trembled a little.

"Yes," Dorothy answered. "I melted her with a bucket of water."

"Dear me," said the voice. "Well, come to me tomorrow, for I must have time to think it over."

"You've had plenty of time already," said the Tin Woodman angrily.

"We won't wait a day longer," said the Scarecrow.

"You must keep your promises to us!" exclaimed Dorothy.

The Lion thought he might as well frighten the Wizard, so he gave a large, loud roar, which was so fierce and dreadful that Toto jumped away from him in alarm and tipped over a screen that stood in a corner of the throne room.

The travelers looked at the screen as it fell with a crash, and the next moment all of them were filled with wonder. They saw a little old man with a bald head and a wrinkled face. He was standing in the spot the screen had hidden, and he seemed to be as surprised as they were.

The Tin Woodman raised his axe and rushed toward the little man, crying out, "Who are you?"

"I am Oz, the Great and Terrible," said the little man in a trembling voice. "Don't strike me—please don't! I'll do anything you want me to."

Everybody looked at him in surprise. ♦

"I thought Oz was a great head," said Dorothy.

"And I thought Oz was a lovely lady," said the Scarecrow.

"And I thought Oz was a terrible beast," said the Tin Woodman.

"And I thought Oz was a ball of fire," exclaimed the Lion.

"No, you are all wrong," said the little man meekly. "I have been making believe."

"Making believe!" cried Dorothy. "Aren't you a great wizard?"

"Hush, my dear," he said. "Don't speak so loudly, or you will be overheard—and I will be ruined. I'm supposed to be a great wizard."

"And aren't you?" Dorothy asked.

"Not a bit, my dear, I'm just a common man."

"You're more than that," said the Scarecrow in a sad tone. "You're a humbug."

"Exactly so!" declared the little man. "I am a humbug."

"But this is terrible," said the Tin Woodman. "How will I ever get my heart?"

"Or I my courage?" asked the Lion.

"Or I my brains?" wailed the Scarecrow.

"But, my dear friends," said Oz, "think of me and the terrible trouble I'm in at being found out."

"Doesn't anyone else know you're a humbug?" asked Dorothy.

"No one knows it but you—and myself," replied Oz. "I have fooled everyone so long that I thought I would never be found out. It was a great mistake ever to let you into the throne room. Usually I will not even see the people I rule over, and so they believe that I am something terrible."

"But I don't understand," said Dorothy. "How was it that you appeared to me as a great head?"

"That was one of my tricks," answered Oz. "Step this way, please, and I will tell you all about it."

C VOCABULARY

For each word, write a sentence that uses the word.

1. terror
2. advanced
3. admit
4. desperately
5. cruelty
6. tenderly

D COMPREHENSION

Write the answers.

1. The novel says, "the stillness of the empty room was more dreadful than any of the forms they had seen Oz take." What does that mean?

2. How do you think Oz made his voice move around the room?

3. Why do you think Oz pretended to forget his promises to the travelers?

4. In what way was Oz a humbug?

5. Why did Oz hardly ever see the people he ruled?

E WRITING

Write a story that explains how the little old man became the Wizard of Oz.

Use your own ideas and evidence from the text to answer these questions in your story:

1. Where did the man come from?

2. What skills did the man have?

3. How did he travel to Oz?

4. How did he fool the people of the Emerald City into thinking he was a wizard?

Write at least five sentences.

END OF LESSON 29

A WORD LISTS

1 Hard Words	2 Word Endings	3 Vocabulary Words	4 Vocabulary Words
1. amuse	1. explanation	1. confidence	1. high spirits
2. balloonist	2. hesitation	2. consider	2. imitate
3. precious	3. imagination	3. experience	3. knowledge
4. ventriloquism	4. imitation	4. gradually	4. ventriloquist

B READING LITERATURE: Novel

Chapter 22

The Wizard's Story

Oz led Dorothy and the others to a small room in the rear of the throne room. He pointed to a corner of the small room, and there was the great head. It was made out of paper, and it had a carefully painted face.

"I hung this from the ceiling by a wire," said Oz. "I stood behind the screen and pulled a thread to make the eyes move and the mouth open."

"But how about the voice?" Dorothy inquired.

"Oh, I am a ventriloquist," said the little man. "I can throw the sound of my voice wherever I want. ✿ You thought my voice was coming out of the head. Here are the other things I used to trick you."

Then the little man showed the Scarecrow the dress and the mask he had worn when he seemed to be the lovely lady. And the Tin Woodman saw that his terrible beast was nothing but a lot of animal skins sewn together. As for the ball of fire, the false wizard had also hung that from the ceiling. It was really a ball of cotton, but when oil was poured on it, the ball had burned fiercely.

"Really," said the Scarecrow, "you ought to be ashamed of yourself for being such a humbug."

"I am—I certainly am," answered the little man sorrowfully. "But it was the only thing I could do. Sit down, please—there are plenty of chairs—and I will tell you my story."

Dorothy and the others sat down and listened while the Wizard told the following tale:

I was born near Kansas. When I grew up, I became a ventriloquist, and I was very well trained at that by a great master. I could imitate any kind of bird or beast.

After a time, I tired of ventriloquism and became a balloonist for a circus. I went up in my balloon on circus day and called down to people. Then I got them to go to the circus.

Well, one day I went up in a balloon and the ropes got twisted so that I couldn't come down again. The balloon went way up above the clouds. It went so far up that a current of air struck it and carried it many, many miles away. For a day and a night, I traveled through the air. On the morning of the second day, I awoke and found the balloon floating over a strange and beautiful country.

The balloon came down gradually, and I was not hurt a bit. But I found myself among strange people, who, when they saw me come from the clouds, thought I

was a great wizard. Of course, I let them think I was a wizard because they were afraid of me, and they promised to do anything I wanted.

Just to amuse myself and to keep the people busy, I ordered them to build this city and my palace; and they did it all willingly and well. Then I thought, because the country was so green and beautiful, that I would call the city the Emerald City; and to make the name fit better, I put green spectacles on all the people so that everything they saw was green.

The Emerald City is no greener than any other city. But when you wear green spectacles, everything you see looks green to you. It was built a great many years ago, for I was a young man when the balloon brought me here, and I am a very old man *now. But my people have worn green glasses on their eyes so long that most of them think it really is an Emerald City.*

And it certainly is a beautiful place, full of jewels and precious metals and every good thing that is needed to make people happy. I have been good to the people, and they like me; but ever since this palace was built, I have shut myself up and do not see any of them. ♦

One of my greatest fears was the witches, for I soon found out that they were really able to do powerful things. There were four of them in this country, and they ruled the people who live in the North and South and East and West. Fortunately, the witches of the North and South were good, and I knew they would do me no harm. But the witches of the East and West were terribly wicked. I knew that if they ever figured out that I was less powerful than they were, they would destroy me.

I lived in deadly fear of the wicked witches for many years, so you can imagine how pleased I was when I heard that Dorothy's house had fallen on the Wicked Witch of the East. When you came to me, I was willing to promise anything if you would only do away with the other wicked witch. But now that you have melted her, I am ashamed to say that I cannot keep my promises.

"I think you are a very bad man," said Dorothy after Oz had finished his story.

"Oh, no, my dear. I'm really a very good man; but I'm a very bad wizard, I must admit."

"Can't you give me brains?" asked the Scarecrow.

"You don't need them. You are learning something every day. A baby has brains, but it doesn't know much. Experience is

the only thing that brings knowledge, and the longer you are alive the more experience you are sure to get," replied Oz.

"That may all be true," said the Scarecrow, "but I shall be very unhappy unless you give me brains."

The false wizard looked at him carefully.

"Well," he said with a sigh, "I'm not much of a magician, but if you will come to me tomorrow morning, I will stuff your head with brains. I cannot tell you how to use them, however; you must find that out for yourself."

"Oh, thank you, thank you!" cried the Scarecrow. "I'll find a way to use them, never fear!"

"But how about my courage?" asked the Lion anxiously.

"You have plenty of courage, I am sure," answered Oz. "All you need is confidence in yourself. Every living thing is afraid when it faces danger; but if you have confidence, you can face danger even when you are afraid. You have plenty of that kind of courage."

"Perhaps I do, but I'm scared just the same," said the Lion. "I will really be very unhappy unless you give me the sort of courage that will make me less afraid."

"Very well. I will give you that sort of courage tomorrow," replied Oz.

"How about my heart?" asked the Tin Woodman.

"Why, as for that," answered Oz, "I think you are wrong to want a heart. It makes most people unhappy. If you only knew it, you are lucky not to have a heart."

"I don't agree," said the Tin Woodman. "I will bear all the unhappiness without a grumble."

"Very well," answered Oz meekly. "Come to me tomorrow and I will give you a heart. I have played wizard for so many years that I may as well continue the part a little longer."

"And now," said Dorothy, "how am I going to get back to Kansas?"

"We will have to think about that," replied the little man. "Give me two or three days to consider the matter, and I'll try to find a way to carry you over the desert. In the meantime, you will all be treated as my guests. While you live in the palace, my people will wait upon you and obey your slightest wish. There is only one thing I ask in return for my help—you must keep my secret and tell no one I am a humbug."

They agreed to say nothing of what they had learned and went back to their rooms in high spirits. Even Dorothy had hope that "The Great and Terrible Humbug," as she called him, would find a way to send her back to Kansas. And if he did, she was willing to forgive him for everything he had done.

C COMPREHENSION

Write the answers.

1. Why did the people think that Oz was a wizard when he first arrived?

2. Why do you think Oz wanted his people to see nothing but green?

3. Oz said that "Experience is the only thing that brings knowledge." Give an example that shows how experience brings knowledge.

4. Oz also said, "If you have confidence, you can face danger even when you are afraid." Give an example of how confidence can help you face danger.

5. What did Oz mean when he said that having a heart makes most people unhappy?

D WRITING

Write a passage that answers this main question:

• Do you think Oz is a bad man?

Use details from the novel to answer these other questions in your passage:

1. What bad things has Oz done?

2. What good things has Oz done?

3. What could Oz do to change your opinion?

Write at least five sentences.

END OF LESSON 30

A WORD LISTS

1 | Hard Words

1. bulged
2. liquid
3. uneasily

2 | Words Spelled the Same

1. content / content
2. excuse / excuse

3 | Word Endings

1. congratulation
2. explanation
3. hesitation
4. imagination
5. imitation

4 | Vocabulary Review

1. confidence
2. consider
3. imitate

5 | Vocabulary Words

1. congratulate
2. deceive
3. replace
4. sawdust
5. shears

B READING LITERATURE: Novel

Chapter 23

Brains, Heart, and Courage

The next morning, the Scarecrow said to his friends, "Congratulate me. I am going to Oz to get my brains at last. When I return, I will be like other men."

"I have always liked you as you are," said Dorothy.

"It is kind of you to like a scarecrow," he replied. "But surely you will think more of me when you hear the splendid thoughts my new brains are going to turn out."

Then he said goodbye to them in a cheerful voice and went to the throne room, where he knocked on the door.

"Come in," said Oz.

The Scarecrow went in and found the little man sitting by the window, thinking hard.

"I have come for my brains," remarked the Scarecrow, a little uneasily.

"Oh, yes. Sit down in that chair, please," replied Oz. "You must excuse me for taking your head off, but I will have to do it in order to put your brains in their proper place."

"That's all right," said the Scarecrow. "You are quite welcome to take my head off as long as it will be a better one when you put it on again."

So the Wizard unfastened the Scarecrow's head and emptied out the straw. Then he entered the back room and got hundreds of pins and needles. After shaking them together thoroughly, he filled the top of the Scarecrow's head with the mixture and stuffed the rest of the space with straw to hold the pins and needles in place.

When Oz had fastened the Scarecrow's head onto his body, the Wizard said to him, "I have filled your head with pins and needles. Now you have all the brains you need."

"I don't understand," replied the Scarecrow thoughtfully. "How can I have brains if I have nothing but straw, pins, and needles in my head?"

The Wizard replied, "People who have brains are very sharp. Anybody looking at the pins and needles sticking out of your head will know at once that you are very sharp."

The Wizard patted the Scarecrow on the back and continued, "From now on, you will be a great man, for I have given you new brains."

The Scarecrow was both pleased and proud to have new brains, and after thanking Oz warmly, he went back to his friends.

Dorothy looked at him curiously. His head bulged out at the top with brains.

"How do you feel?" she asked.

"I feel wise indeed," he answered earnestly. "When I get used to my brains, I will know everything."

Then the Tin Woodman said, "Well, I must go to Oz and get my heart." He walked to the throne room and knocked on the door.

"Come in," called Oz, and the Tin Woodman entered.

The Tin Woodman stood before Oz and said, "I have come for my heart."

"Very well," answered the little man. "But I will have to cut a hole in your chest so I can put your heart in the right place. I hope it won't hurt you."

"Oh, no," answered the Tin Woodman. "I won't feel it at all."

So Oz brought a pair of shears and cut a small, square hole in the left side of the Tin Woodman's chest. Then, Oz went to his cupboard and took out a pretty heart that was made entirely of silk and stuffed with sawdust.

"Isn't it a beauty?" Oz asked.

"It is, indeed!" replied the Tin Woodman, who was greatly pleased. "But is it a kind heart?"

"Oh, very!" answered Oz. Then he put the heart into the Tin Woodman's chest and replaced the square of tin.

"There," said Oz. "Now you have a heart that any man would be proud of. I'm sorry I had to put a patch on your chest, but it really couldn't be helped."

"Never mind the patch," exclaimed the happy Tin Woodman. "I am very grateful to you, and I will never forget your kindness."

"Don't mention it," replied Oz.

Then the Tin Woodman went back to his friends, who were very happy for him. ♦

The Lion now walked to the throne room and knocked on the door.

"Come in," said Oz.

"I have come for my courage," announced the Lion, entering the room.

"Very well," answered the little man, "I will get it for you."

He went to his cupboard, reached up to a high shelf, and took down a large green bottle. He poured the contents of the bottle into a beautifully carved dish. Then he placed the dish in front of the cowardly Lion, who sniffed at it as if he did not like it.

"What is it?" asked the Lion.

"Courage," replied the Wizard.

"Do I have to drink it?" asked the Lion.

"Of course," said Oz. "You know that courage is something inside you. If you don't drink it, you won't have courage inside you."

"But," said the Lion slowly, as he looked at the large dish of liquid. "Do I have to drink all of it?"

Oz replied, "You want to be full of courage, don't you?"

"Yes," said the Lion.

"Then you must drink it all. That is the only way you will be full of courage."

The Lion hesitated no longer and drank until the dish was empty.

"How do you feel now?" asked Oz.

"Full of courage," replied the Lion, who went joyfully back to his friends to tell them about his good fortune.

When Oz was alone, he smiled at his success in giving the Scarecrow and the Tin Woodman and the Lion exactly what they wanted. He said, "It was easy to make the Scarecrow and the Lion and the Tin Woodman happy because they imagined I could do anything. But it will take a lot more imagination to carry Dorothy back to Kansas, and I don't know how it can be done."

For three days, Dorothy heard nothing from Oz. These were sad days for the girl, although her friends were all quite happy and comfortable. The Scarecrow told them that there were wonderful thoughts in his head, but he would not say what they were because he knew no one could understand them but himself. When the Tin Woodman walked around, he felt his heart rattling in his chest, and he told Dorothy that it was a kinder and more tender heart than the one he had owned when he was made of flesh. The Lion declared he was afraid of nothing on earth and would gladly face an army of men or a dozen of the fierce Kalidahs.

Thus, each of the friends was satisfied except Dorothy, who wanted more than ever to get back to Kansas.

On the fourth day, Oz sent for Dorothy. When she entered the throne room, he said pleasantly, "Sit down, my dear. I think I have found the way to get you out of this country."

"And back to Kansas?" Dorothy asked eagerly.

"Well, I'm not sure about Kansas," said Oz, "for I haven't the faintest idea of how to get there. But the first thing to do is to cross the desert, and then it should be easy to find your way home."

"How can I cross the desert?" Dorothy inquired.

"Well, I'll tell you what I think," said the little man. "You see, I came to this country in a balloon. You also came through the air, carried by a cyclone. So I believe the best way to get across the desert will be

through the air. Now, it is quite beyond my powers to make a cyclone. But I've been thinking the matter over, and I believe I can make a balloon."

"How are you going to build a balloon?" asked Dorothy.

"As you know," said Oz, "a balloon is a large bag that floats when it is filled with gas. The balloon I had was made of silk, which was coated with glue to keep the gas from leaking out. I destroyed my old balloon, but I have plenty of silk in the palace, so it will be no trouble to make a new one. Unfortunately, in this whole country there is no gas that will make the balloon float."

"If it won't float," remarked Dorothy, "it will be of no use to me."

"True," answered Oz. "But there is another way to make the balloon float, which is to fill it with hot air. Hot air isn't as good as gas, for if the air were to get cold, the balloon would come down in the desert, and we would be lost."

"We!" exclaimed Dorothy. "Are you going with me?"

"Yes, of course," replied Oz. "I am tired of being such a humbug. If I were to leave this palace and walk through the city, my people would soon discover that I am not a wizard, and then they would be angry with me for having deceived them. So I have to stay shut up in these rooms all day, and it gets tiresome. I'd much rather go back to Kansas and be in a circus again."

"I will be glad to have your company," said Dorothy.

"Thank you," Oz answered. "Now if you will help me sew the silk together, we will begin to work on our balloon."

C COMPREHENSION

Write the answers.

1. Do you think the Scarecrow will change now that he has brains? Explain your answer.

2. Do you think the Tin Woodman will change now that he has a heart? Explain your answer.

3. Do you think the Lion will change now that he has courage? Explain your answer.

4. How could Oz get hot air into his balloon?

5. Do you think Dorothy and Oz can get back to Kansas in a balloon? Explain your answer.

D WRITING

• Oz and Dorothy are planning to cross the Great Desert in a balloon.

Write a report that compares toy balloons with balloons that carry people.

Use details from the novel and from your own research to answer the following questions in your report:

1. What materials are used to make toy balloons?

2. What materials are used to make balloons that carry people?

3. What is helium?

4. Why do balloons filled with helium rise in the air?

5. Why do toy balloons that you blow up by yourself fall to the ground?

Write at least five sentences.

A WORD LISTS

1 | Word Practice

1. collar
2. precious
3. thorough
4. through
5. towel
6. underneath
7. ventriloquism
8. vibrate

2 | Vocabulary Review

1. contents
2. deceive
3. gradually

3 | Vocabulary Words

1. dose
2. extend
3. farewell
4. hush
5. tug
6. utter

B READING LITERATURE: Novel

Chapter 24

The Witch of the South

Oz and Dorothy began working on the balloon right away. First Oz got some silk and cut it into strips. Then Dorothy took the strips and sewed them together with needle and thread. She began with a strip of light green silk, then a strip of dark green, and then a strip of emerald green— for Oz wanted to make the balloon in different shades of his favorite color.

It took three days to sew all the strips together, but when Dorothy was finished, they had a big bag of green silk more than twenty feet long.

Oz painted the inside of the bag with a coat of thin glue to make it airtight, and then he announced that the balloon was ready.

"But we must have a basket to ride in," Oz said. So he sent the soldier with the green whiskers for a big clothes basket, which he fastened to the bottom of the balloon with many ropes.

When it was all ready, Oz sent word to his people that he was going to make a visit to his great brother wizard who lived in the clouds. The news spread rapidly throughout the city, and everyone came to see him leave.

Oz ordered the balloon carried out in front of the palace, and the people gazed at it with much curiosity. The Tin Woodman chopped a big pile of wood and made a fire. Oz held the bottom of the balloon over the fire so that the hot air that rose from the fire would be caught in the bag. The balloon swelled and rose into the air, until finally the basket started to leave the ground.

Then Oz got into the basket and said to all the people in a loud voice, "I am now going away to make a visit. While I am gone, the Scarecrow will rule over you. I command you to obey him as you would me."

By this time, the balloon was tugging hard at the rope that held it to the ground. The air in the balloon was hot, and the heat made the inside air so much lighter than the outside air that the balloon started to rise.

"Come, Dorothy!" cried the Wizard. "Hurry up, or the balloon will fly away."

"I can't find Toto anywhere," replied Dorothy, who did not want to leave her little dog behind. Toto had run into the crowd to bark at a kitten, and Dorothy found him at last. She picked him up and ran toward the balloon.

Dorothy was within a few steps of the balloon, and Oz was holding out his hands to help her into the basket, when the ropes suddenly snapped, and the balloon rose into the air without her.

"Come back!" Dorothy screamed. "I want to go, too!"

"I can't come back, my dear," called Oz from the basket. "Goodbye!"

"Goodbye!" shouted everyone, and all eyes were turned upward to where the Wizard was riding in the basket, rising every moment farther and farther into the sky.

And that was the last any of them ever saw of Oz, the wonderful Wizard. He may have reached Kansas safely and be there now. But the people remembered him lovingly and said to one another, "Oz was always our friend. When he was here, he built this beautiful Emerald City for us,

and now he has left the wise Scarecrow to rule over us." ♦

Dorothy was sad after the Wizard left without her. The Tin Woodman came to her and said, "I feel sad also, for the Wizard was the man who gave me my lovely heart. I would like to cry a little because Oz is gone. Will you kindly wipe away my tears so that I will not rust?"

"With pleasure," she answered and brought a towel at once. Then the Tin Woodman wept for several minutes, and Dorothy watched the tears and wiped them away with the towel. When he had finished, he thanked her kindly and oiled himself thoroughly.

The Scarecrow was now the ruler of the Emerald City, and although he was not a wizard, the people were proud of him. They said, "There is not another city in all the world that is ruled by a stuffed man." And so far as they knew, they were quite right.

The morning after Oz left in the balloon, the four travelers met in the throne room and talked matters over. The Scarecrow sat on the big throne, and the others stood before him.

"We are not so unlucky," said the new ruler. "This palace and the Emerald City belong to us, and we can do whatever we want. Why, just a short time ago I was on a pole in a farmer's cornfield, and now I am the ruler of this beautiful city, so I am quite satisfied with my life."

The Lion said, "As for me, I am content to know that I am as brave as any beast that ever lived, if not braver."

The Tin Woodman said, "And as for me, I feel that my new heart is the kindest in the land."

"If Dorothy would be content to live in the Emerald City," said the Scarecrow, "we would all be happy together."

"But I don't want to live here," cried Dorothy. "I want to go to Kansas and live with Aunt Em and Uncle Henry."

"Well, then, what can we do?" inquired the Tin Woodman.

The Scarecrow decided to think, and he thought so hard that the pins and needles in his head began to vibrate. The others hushed while the Scarecrow thought. Finally the Scarecrow said, "Let us call in the soldier with the green whiskers and ask his advice."

So the soldier was called to the throne room. He entered timidly, for while Oz was ruler, he had been allowed to come no farther than the door.

The Scarecrow said to him, "Dorothy wants to cross the desert. How can she do so?"

"I do not know," answered the soldier. "Nobody has ever crossed the desert, other than Oz himself."

"Is there no one who can help me?" asked Dorothy earnestly.

"Glinda might," he suggested.

"Who is Glinda?" inquired the Scarecrow.

"The Witch of the South. She is the most powerful of all the witches, and she rules over the Quadlings. Glinda's castle stands on the edge of the desert, so she may know a way to cross it."

"Glinda is a good witch, isn't she?" asked Dorothy.

"The Quadlings think she is good," said the soldier, "and she is kind to everyone. I have heard that Glinda is a beautiful woman who knows how to keep young in spite of the many years she has lived."

"How can I get to her castle?" asked Dorothy.

"The road to the south is straight," the soldier answered, "but it is said to be dangerous to travelers. There are wild beasts in the woods and odd-looking men who can extend their arms and legs. For this reason, none of the Quadlings ever come to the Emerald City."

After the soldier left, the Scarecrow said, "It seems, in spite of dangers, that the best thing Dorothy can do is to travel to the Land of the South and ask Glinda to help her. For, of course, if Dorothy stays here, she will never get back to Kansas."

The Tin Woodman remarked to the Scarecrow, "You must have been thinking again."

"I have been," said the Scarecrow.

"I will go with Dorothy," declared the Lion, "for I am tired of your city and long for the woods and the country again. I need a dose of fresh air. Besides, Dorothy will need someone to protect her."

"That is true," agreed the Tin Woodman. "My axe may be of service to her, so I will also go with her to the Land of the South."

"When should we start?" asked the Scarecrow.

"Are you going?" they asked in surprise.

"Certainly. If it wasn't for Dorothy, I would never have gotten brains. She lifted me from the pole in the cornfield and brought me to the Emerald City. So my good luck is all due to her, and I will never leave her until she starts back to Kansas."

"Thank you," said Dorothy gratefully. "You are all very kind to me. I would like to start as soon as possible."

The Scarecrow said, "Why not call the Winged Monkeys and ask them to carry us to the Land of the South?"

"I never thought of that!" said Dorothy joyfully. "It's just the thing. I'll go at once for the golden cap."

She brought the cap into the throne room and uttered the magic words. Soon the band of Winged Monkeys flew in through the open window and stood beside her.

"This is the second time you have called us," said the King Monkey, bowing before Dorothy. "What do you want?"

"I want you to fly us to the Land of the South."

"It shall be done," said the king, and at once, the Winged Monkeys took the four travelers and Toto in their arms and flew away with them. After a long journey, they set the group down in the beautiful country of the Quadlings.

"Farewell, and thank you very much," said Dorothy. The monkeys rose into the air and were out of sight in a moment.

C COMPARING ACCOUNTS

Work the items.

Account A

A few years ago, a German friend of mine took me for a ride on the Autobahn. Like other freeways around the world, the Autobahn has at least four lanes. It also has speed limits—but only near cities or parts of the road that are being repaired. The rest of the Autobahn has no speed limit, and drivers sometimes go really fast.

The speed limit on American freeways is usually 65 or 70 miles per hour. On the Autobahn, some drivers go 150 miles per hour and even faster. Driving on the Autobahn can be frightening for tourists who aren't used to high speeds. If you're driving in the left lane, fast-moving drivers will come behind your car and start honking until you move over to the right lane.

My friend owned an Alpina sedan that could go up to 180 miles per hour. After we left the city, he quickly zoomed up to 150 miles per hour. I was pinned to my seat. I could barely lift my arms or turn my head. The cars we passed looked like they were standing still.

I was afraid we would crash into a slow-moving car, but nothing happened. My friend drove at high speed for two hours and then returned to the city. I thanked him for the ride but told him I'd take a train next time.

Account B

The Autobahn is the freeway system in Germany. Like freeways in the United States, it consists of multi-lane highways with only a few entrances and exits. Unlike American freeways, many sections of the Autobahn have no speed limit. On these sections, drivers go as fast as they want.

The total length of all sections of the Autobahn is almost 8,000 miles. In the United States, the total length of the freeways is about 45,000 miles.

The Autobahn was the first freeway in the world. Construction began in the 1930s and wasn't fully completed until the 1990s. During the Second World War in the early 1940s, Germany used the Autobahn to move troops and supplies. Dwight Eisenhower, the American general who led the invasion of Germany, greatly admired the Autobahn. When he became President of the United States in 1952, he guided efforts to build a freeway system that was similar to the Autobahn.

While the Autobahn is well designed, it is most famous for its lack of speed limits. In fact, the world record for the fastest car on a freeway was set on the Autobahn in 1938. A German driver in a racing car went 268 miles per hour on a stretch of road near the city of Frankfurt.

Fortunately, no other cars were on the road at the time.

1. What does *account A* focus on?

2. What does *account B* focus on?

3. What is the name of the famous freeway in Germany?

4. Is item 3 answered by *account A* only; *account B* only; *both* accounts; or *neither* account?

5. What is the total length of the Autobahn?

6. Is item 5 answered by *account A* only; *account B* only; *both* accounts; or *neither* account?

7. How many cars drive on the Autobahn each day?

8. Is item 7 answered by *account A* only; *account B* only; *both* accounts; or *neither* account?

9. When did construction begin on the Autobahn?

10. Is item 9 answered by *account A* only; *account B* only; *both* accounts; or *neither* account?

11. What is the Autobahn most famous for?

12. Is item 11 answered by *account A* only; *account B* only; *both* accounts; or *neither* account?

13. What is the speed record of a car on the Autobahn?

14. Is item 13 answered by *account A* only; *account B* only; *both* accounts; or *neither* account?

D COMPREHENSION

Write the answers.

1. How did Dorothy help Oz make the balloon?

2. Why did the balloon rise when Oz held it over the fire?

3. Why was the Scarecrow so happy with his life now?

4. Why might Glinda be able to help Dorothy?

5. Why did the travelers ask the Winged Monkeys to carry them to the Land of the South?

E WRITING

Write a story that answers this main question:

• What happened to Oz after he left the Emerald City?

Use your imagination and details from the novel to answer these questions in your story:

1. What happened to Oz during the balloon ride?

2. Where did the balloon land?

3. What happened to Oz after the balloon landed?

Write at least five sentences.

END OF LESSON 32

A WORD LISTS

1	Word Practice
1.	cackling
2.	crackling
3.	giant
4.	grant
5.	overhear
6.	singe
7.	timid
8.	timidly

2	Vocabulary Words
1.	chorus
2.	disgusting
3.	whisk

B READING LITERATURE: Novel

Chapter 25

The Silver Shoes

The Land of the Quadlings seemed rich and happy. There was field upon field of grain, with well-paved roads running between them. The fences and houses and bridges were all painted bright red, just as they had been painted yellow in the Land of the Winkies and blue in the Land of the Munchkins. The Quadlings were short and good-natured. They were dressed all in red, which looked bright against the green grass and the yellow grain.

Dorothy and the others walked up to a farmhouse and knocked on the door, and it was opened by the farmer's wife.

When Dorothy asked for something to eat, the woman gave the girl and the Lion a good dinner, with many fruits and nuts, and a bowl of milk for Toto.

"How far is it to Glinda's castle?" asked Dorothy.

"It is not a great way," answered the farmer's wife. "Take the road to the south and you will soon reach it."

They thanked the good woman and started walking by the fields and across the pretty red bridges until they saw a beautiful red castle before them. Three young girls, dressed in handsome red uniforms trimmed with gold braid, were in front of the gates. As Dorothy approached, one of them said to her, "Why have you come to the South Country?"

"To see the Good Witch who rules here," Dorothy answered. "Will you take me to her?"

"I will ask Glinda if she will see you," said the girl.

Dorothy and the others told her who they were, and the girl went into the castle. After a few moments, she came back to say that the travelers could see Glinda at once.

Before they went to see Glinda, however, they were taken to a room of the castle, where Dorothy washed her face and combed her hair. The Lion shook the dust out of his mane, the Scarecrow patted himself into his best shape, and the Tin Woodman polished his tin.

Then Dorothy and the others followed the girl soldier into a big room where the Witch Glinda sat on a throne of rubies. Glinda looked both beautiful and young to them. Her hair was a rich red and flowed over her shoulders. Her dress was pure white, and her eyes were blue.

Glinda looked at Dorothy in a kindly way and asked, "What can I do for you?"

So Dorothy told Glinda her story. She told how the cyclone had brought her to the Land of Oz and how she had found her companions and of the wonderful adventures they had had.

"My greatest wish now," she added, "is to get back to Kansas, for Aunt Em will surely think something dreadful has happened to me, and that will make her and my uncle very sad."

Glinda leaned forward and kissed Dorothy.

"Bless your heart," Glinda said. "If I tell you of a way to get back to Kansas, will you give me the golden cap?"

"Certainly!" exclaimed Dorothy. "I have it with me now, and when you have it, you can command the Winged Monkeys three times."

Glinda smiled and said, "I know just what to do with those three commands."

So Dorothy gave the golden cap to the witch. Then Glinda said to the Scarecrow, "What will you do when Dorothy has left us?"

"I will return to the Emerald City," the Scarecrow replied, "for Oz has made me its ruler, and the people like me. The only thing that worries me is how to return there, for the road to Oz is very dangerous."

"I will command the Winged Monkeys to carry you to the gates of the Emerald City," said Glinda.

Turning to the Tin Woodman, Glinda asked, "What will become of you when Dorothy leaves this country?"

He leaned on his axe and thought a moment. Then he said, "I became a Tin Woodman because I loved a Munchkin maiden. I would like to go back to the Land of the East and marry her." ♦

Glinda said to the Tin Woodman, "My second command to the Winged Monkeys will be to carry you safely to the Land of the East so that you may find your maiden."

Then Glinda looked at the big, shaggy Lion and asked, "When Dorothy has returned to her own home, what will become of you?"

The Lion answered, "There is a grand old forest where I used to live and be the king. If I could only get back to that forest, I would be very happy there."

Glinda said, "My third command to the Winged Monkeys will be to carry you to your forest. Then, since I will have used up the powers of the golden cap, I will give it to the King of the Monkeys so that he and his band may be free at last."

The Scarecrow and the Tin Woodman and the Lion thanked the good Witch Glinda earnestly for her kindness.

Dorothy exclaimed, "You are certainly as good as you are beautiful! But you have not yet told me how to get back to Kansas."

"Your silver shoes will carry you over the desert," replied Glinda. "If you had known their power, you could have gone back to your Aunt Em the very first day you came to this country."

"But then I would not have had my wonderful brains!" cried the Scarecrow. "I might have passed my whole life in the farmer's cornfield."

"And I would not have had my lovely heart," said the Tin Woodman. "I might have stood and rusted in the forest until the end of the world."

"And I would have been a coward forever," declared the Lion. "And no beast in all the forest would have had a good word to say to me."

"This is all true," said Dorothy. "But now that each of my friends has what he wanted most, I think I would like to go back to Kansas."

"The silver shoes," said the good witch, "have wonderful powers. One of the most curious things about them is that they can carry you to any place in the world in the wink of an eye. All you have to do is to knock the heels together three times and command the shoes to carry you wherever you want to go."

"If that is so," said Dorothy, "I will ask them to carry me back to Kansas at once."

She threw her arms around the Lion's neck and kissed him, patting his big head tenderly. Next she kissed the Tin Woodman, who was weeping in a way that was very dangerous to his joints. Then she hugged the soft, stuffed body of the Scarecrow in her arms. Dorothy felt very sad at the thought of leaving her good friends.

At last Dorothy picked up Toto and said one final goodbye to her companions. Then she clapped the heels of her shoes together three times, saying, "Take me home to Aunt Em and Uncle Henry!"

Instantly she was whirling through the air, so swiftly that all she could feel was the wind whistling past her ears. The next moment, she noticed that she was rolling on the ground. She sat up and looked around her.

"Oh, my!" she cried. She was sitting on the broad Kansas prairie, and just in front of her was the new farmhouse Uncle Henry had built after the cyclone carried away the old one. Uncle Henry was milking the cows in the barnyard.

Toto instantly jumped out of Dorothy's arms and ran toward the barn, whisking his tail from side to side.

Dorothy stood up and found she was in her stocking feet, for the silver shoes had fallen off through her flight through the air and were lost forever in the desert.

Aunt Em had just come out of the house to water the cabbages. She looked up and saw Dorothy running toward her.

"My darling child!" she cried, hugging Dorothy. "Where in the world did you come from?"

"From the Land of Oz," said Dorothy gravely. "And here is Toto, too. And oh, Aunt Em! I'm so glad to be home again!"

C COMPREHENSION

Write the answers.

1. Why did the Scarecrow want to return to the Emerald City?

2. Why did the Tin Woodman want to return to the Land of the East?

3. Why did the Lion want to return to the forest?

4. What was the power of the silver shoes?

5. How did Dorothy feel about leaving the Land of Oz?

D WRITING

Write a passage that answers this main question:

- What did Dorothy learn from her visit to the Land of Oz?

Use details from the novel to answer these other questions in your passage:

1. What did Dorothy learn about teamwork? Give an example.

2. What did Dorothy learn about how to defeat the Wicked Witch of the West?

3. What did Dorothy learn about who the Wizard of Oz really was?

4. What did Dorothy learn about her own power?

Write at least five sentences.

A WORD LISTS

1 | Vocabulary Words

1. cocoa
2. half nelson
3. latch onto
4. presentable

2 | Vocabulary Words

1. renaissance
2. roomer
3. stoop
4. suede

3 | Vocabulary Words

1. ain't
2. contact
3. frail
4. icebox
5. kitchenette
6. mistrust

B VOCABULARY DEFINITIONS

1. **cocoa**—*Cocoa* is a chocolate powder. A hot drink made with this powder is also called cocoa.

2. **half nelson**—If you wrestle with someone, you can make a *half nelson* by putting an arm under one of your opponent's armpits and pushing on their neck with your hand.

3. **latch onto**—When you grab something, you *latch onto* it.

• What's another way of saying *Roni grabbed the baseball?*

4. **presentable**—When you are clean and well dressed, you are *presentable*.

5. **renaissance**—When people have a renewed interest in something, that thing has a *renaissance*.

• What happens when people have a renewed interest in reading by candlelight?

6. **roomer**—A *roomer* is a person who lives in a rented room in a house.

• What kind of room does a roomer live in?

7. **stoop**—A porch with stairs in front of a house is called a *stoop*.

• What is a stoop?

8. **suede**—*Suede* is leather with a soft surface.

• What are some things made with suede?

C VOCABULARY FROM CONTEXT

1. You can go to the party, but I don't like those people, so **I ain't** going.

2. Kwan jerked her hand back after it **came into contact with** the hot stove.

3. The old teacup was so cracked and **frail** that nobody dared to touch it.

4. Doli put the milk in the **icebox** so it would stay cold.

5. The roomer liked to cook, but he had very little space, so he put a **kitchenette** in the corner.

6. People **mistrust** someone they think is lying.

D HYPHENS

Sometimes, words that appear at the end of a printed line are too long to fit on that line, so only the first part of the word appears on the line. That part is followed by a hyphen, which is a horizontal mark that looks like this: -

The rest of the word appears at the beginning of the next line. The following passage includes words that run from the end of one line to the beginning of the next line.

That morning Dorothy kissed the pretty green girl goodbye. Then the four travelers walked through the Emerald City toward the gate.

When the guard saw them approaching, he knew that they were planning to go on a new adventure. As he unlocked their green spectacles, he congratulated the Scarecrow, who was now the ruler of the city. The guard smiled and gladly shook the Scarecrow's hand.

E STORY BACKGROUND

Langston Hughes

In this lesson, you will read "Thank You, M'am," a short story by an African American writer named Langston Hughes. Hughes was born in Joplin, Missouri, in 1902. He moved several times while he was growing up, but he was always interested in writing. In 1921, he started living in the Harlem neighborhood in New York City. Many African American writers, musicians, and artists lived in Harlem, and Hughes was happy to join them.

Hughes soon became a leader in a movement in Harlem to bring African American traditions back to life through writing, music, and art. This movement was called the Harlem Renaissance. Hughes became well known for his poems, novels, short stories, and plays about the lives of African Americans. He kept writing until his death in 1967.

Even though Hughes published "Thank You, M'am" more than fifty years ago, the story's message still rings true today.

Thank You, M'am

Langston Hughes

She was a large woman with a large purse that had everything in it but a hammer and nails. It had a long strap, and she carried it slung across her shoulder. It was about eleven o'clock at night, dark, and she was walking alone, when a boy ran up behind her and tried to snatch her purse. The strap broke with the sudden single tug the boy gave it from behind. But the boy's weight and the weight of the purse combined caused him to lose his balance. Instead of taking off full blast as he had hoped, the boy fell on his back on the sidewalk, and his legs flew up. The large woman simply turned around and kicked him right square in his blue-jeaned sitter. Then she reached down, picked the boy up by his shirt front, and shook him until his teeth rattled.

After that the woman said, "Pick up my pocketbook, boy, and give it here."

She still held him tightly. But she bent down enough to permit him to stoop and pick up her purse. Then she said, "Now ain't you ashamed of yourself?"

Firmly gripped by his shirt front, the boy said, "Yes'm."

The woman said, "What did you want to do it for?"

The boy said, "I didn't aim to."

She said, "You a lie!"

By that time two or three people passed, stopped, turned to look, and some stood watching.

"If I turn you loose, will you run?" asked the woman.

"Yes'm," said the boy.

"Then I won't turn you loose," said the woman. She did not release him.

"Lady, I'm sorry," whispered the boy.

"Um-hum! Your face is dirty. I got a great mind to wash your face for you. Ain't you got nobody home to tell you to wash your face?"

"No'm," said the boy.

"Then it will get washed this evening," said the large woman, starting up the street, dragging the frightened boy behind her.

He looked as if he were fourteen or fifteen, frail and willow-wild, in tennis shoes and blue jeans.

The woman said, "You ought to be my son. I would teach you right from wrong. Least I can do right now is to wash your face. Are you hungry?"

"No'm," said the being-dragged boy. "I just want you to turn me loose."

"Was I bothering *you* when I turned that corner?" asked the woman.

"No'm."

"But you put yourself in contact with *me*," said the woman. "If you think that that contact is not going to last a while, you got another thing coming. When I get through with you, sir, you are going to remember Mrs. Luella Bates Washington Jones."

Sweat popped out on the boy's face, and he began to struggle. Mrs. Jones stopped, jerked him around in front of her, put a half nelson around his neck, and continued to drag him up the street. When she got to her door, she dragged the boy inside, down a hall, and into a large kitchenette-furnished room at the rear of the house. She switched on the light and left the door open. The boy could hear other roomers laughing and talking in the large house. Some of their doors were open, too, so he knew he and the woman were not alone. The woman still had him by the neck in the middle of her room.

She said, "What is your name?"

"Roger," answered the boy.

"Then, Roger, you go to that sink and wash your face," said the woman, whereupon she turned him loose—at last. Roger looked at the door—looked at the woman—looked at the door—and went to the sink.

"Let the water run until it gets warm," she said. "Here's a clean towel."

"You gonna take me to jail?" asked the boy, bending over the sink.

"Not with that face, I would not take you nowhere," said the woman. "Here I am trying to get home to cook me a bite to eat, and you snatch my pocketbook! Maybe you ain't been to your supper either, late as it be. Have you?"

"There's nobody home at my house," said the boy.

"Then we'll eat," said the woman. "I believe you're hungry—or been hungry—to try to snatch my pocketbook!"

"I want a pair of blue suede shoes," said the boy.

"Well, you didn't have to snatch my pocketbook to get some suede shoes," said Mrs. Luella Bates Washington Jones. "You could have asked me."

"M'am?"

The water dripping from his face, the boy looked at her. There was a long pause. A very long pause. After he had dried his face, and not knowing what else to do, dried it again, the boy turned around, wondering what next. The door was open. He could make a dash for it down the hall. He could run, run, run, *run!*

The woman was sitting on the daybed. After a while she said, "I were young once, and I wanted things I could not get."

There was another long pause. The boy's mouth opened. Then he frowned, not knowing he frowned.

The woman said, "Um-hum! You thought I was going to say *but*, didn't you? You thought I was going to say *but I didn't snatch people's pocketbooks*. Well, I wasn't going to say that." Pause. Silence. "I have done things, too, which I would not tell you, son—neither tell God, if He didn't already know. Everybody's got something in common. So you set down while I fix us something to eat. You might run that comb through your hair so you will look presentable."

In another corner of the room behind a screen was a gas plate and an icebox. Mrs. Jones got up and went behind the screen. The woman did not watch the boy to see if he was going to run now, nor did she watch her purse, which she left behind on the daybed. But the boy took care to sit on the far side of the room, away from the purse, where he thought she could easily see him out of the corner of her eye if she wanted to. He did not trust the woman *not* to trust him. And he did not want to be mistrusted now.

"Do you need somebody to go to the store," asked the boy, "maybe to get some milk or something?"

"Don't believe I do," said the woman, "unless you just want sweet milk yourself. I was going to make cocoa out of this canned milk I got here."

"That will be fine," said the boy.

She heated some lima beans and ham she had in the icebox, made the cocoa, and set the table. The woman did not ask the boy anything about where he lived, or his folks, or anything else that would embarrass him. Instead, as they ate, she told him about her job in a hotel beauty shop that stayed open late, what the work was like, and how all kinds of women came in and out, blondes, redheads, and Spanish. Then she cut him a half of her ten-cent cake.

"Eat some more, son," she said.

When they were finished eating, she got up and said, "Now here, take this ten dollars and buy yourself some blue suede shoes. And next time, do not make the mistake of latching onto *my* pocketbook *nor anybody else's*—because shoes got by devilish ways will burn your feet. I got to get my rest now. But from here on in, son, I hope you will behave yourself."

She led him down the hall to the front door and opened it. "Good night! Behave yourself, boy!" she said, looking out into the street as he went down the steps.

The boy wanted to say something other than, "Thank you, m'am," to Mrs. Luella Bates Washington Jones, but although his lips moved, he couldn't even say that as he turned at the foot of the barren stoop and looked up at the large woman in the door. Then she shut the door.

G COMPREHENSION

Write the answers.

1. What does Mrs. Jones mean when she tells Roger, "I have done things, too, which I would not tell you"?

2. What does Mrs. Jones mean when she tells Roger, "Everybody's got something in common"?

3. What does Mrs. Jones do to Roger instead of punishing him? Give examples from the story.

4. Why can't Roger say anything to Mrs. Jones at the end of the story?

5. Why do you think the story is called "Thank You, M'am"?

H WRITING

• When the story ends, Roger wants to say something other than "Thank you, m'am" to Mrs. Jones, but he can't even say that.

Pretend you are Roger. Write a speech that tells what you want to say to Mrs. Jones.

Be sure your speech answers these questions:

1. Why are you grateful to Mrs. Jones?

2. What are you sorry for?

3. What will you do with the money Mrs. Jones gave you?

4. How will you change after your meeting with Mrs. Jones?

Write at least five sentences.

END OF LESSON 34

A   WORD LISTS

1	Names
1.	Bandai
2.	Richter
3.	Tohoku

2	Vocabulary Words
1.	debris
2.	region
3.	sunburnt

B   VOCABULARY DEFINITIONS

1. **debris**—Scattered pieces of rock and other materials are called *debris*.

• What's another way of saying *The volcano exploded and sent scattered pieces of rock in all directions?*

2. **region**—A large area inside a country is called a *region*.

• What's another way of saying *Japan has many large areas?*

3. **sunburnt**—*Sunburnt* is another word for *sunburned*.

• What's another way of saying *You can get sunburned if you don't use sunscreen?*

C   HYPHENS

1. **Name this mark: -**

2. **Read the hyphenated words in the passage below.**

   The sun was bright as the friends slowly turned toward the Land of the Quadlings. They were all cheerful and chatted happily.

   Dorothy was almost certain she would get home, and the Woodman smiled at her. The Lion was wagging his tail back and forth. He was joyful to be outside again. Toto was chasing butterflies, jumping, and barking merrily all the time.

Open Range

Kathryn and Byron Jackson

Prairie goes to the mountain,
    Mountain goes to the sky.
The sky sweeps across to the
distant hills
And here, in the middle,
    Am I.

Hills crowd down to the river,
    River runs by the tree.
Tree throws its shadow on
sunburnt grass

And here, in the shadow,
    Is me.

Shadows creep up the mountain,
    Mountain goes black on the sky,
The sky bursts out with a million stars
And here, by the campfire,
    Am I.

E   COMPARING ACCOUNTS

Work the items.

Account A

Japan is a wonderful country to visit. Most tourists stay in the capital city, Tokyo, but some travel to different regions, such as the Tohoku region. In March 2011, our tour group took a bus from Tokyo to a volcano in the Tohoku region called Mount Bandai. We wondered if the volcano would erupt while we were visiting. Sure enough, the ground started shaking moments after we got off the bus at the base of the volcano. We looked up, but no smoke was coming out of the volcano. Then we realized that we were experiencing an earthquake. The ground shook for about five minutes, and we had to lie down and wait for the earthquake to end. We later learned that the earthquake had killed many people and caused major damage in the Tohoku region. We were lucky that nobody in our tour group was hurt.

Account B

Earthquakes usually start at fault lines that are several miles below the surface of the earth. Fault lines separate the giant sections of rock that make up the earth's crust. When one of these sections moves suddenly along a fault line, the movement causes an earthquake on the surface of the earth.

Earthquakes are frightening events. The ground shakes for a minute or more, sometimes making buildings and other structures collapse. Depending on how strong the earthquake is, thousands of people may be killed in just a few minutes.

The strength of an earthquake is measured on the Richter scale. Small earthquakes measure 3 or less on the Richter scale. Earthquakes that measure 7 or more on the scale can cause extensive damage. The March 2011 earthquake in the Tohoku region of Japan, which measured 9 on the Richter scale, killed almost 16,000 people and caused 127,000 buildings to collapse. More than a million other buildings were damaged.

1. What does *account A* focus on?

2. What does *account B* focus on?

3. In what year did the writer visit Mount Bandai?

4. Is item 3 answered by *account A* only; *account B* only; *both* accounts; or *neither* account?

5. How far below the surface of the earth do earthquakes begin?

6. Is item 5 answered by *account A* only; *account B* only; *both* accounts; or *neither* account?

7. In what year did the Tohoku earthquake occur?

8. Is item 7 answered by *account A* only; *account B* only; *both* accounts; or *neither* account?

9. How many thousand people died during the Tohoku earthquake?

10. Is item 9 answered by *account A* only; *account B* only; *both* accounts; or *neither* account?

11. What is the tallest volcano in Japan?

12. Is item 11 answered by *account A* only; *account B* only; *both* accounts; or *neither* account?

13. What's the name of the scale that measures the strength of an earthquake?

14. Is item 13 answered by *account A* only; *account B* only; *both* accounts; or *neither* account?

F WRITING

Write a poem that answers this main question:

- What is your favorite place and why?

Here are suggestions for writing your poem:

1. Use words that describe what your favorite place looks like.

2. Tell what sounds you hear in your favorite place.

3. Describe what you smell in your favorite place.

4. Tell how your favorite place makes you feel.

Write at least 10 lines. Your lines do not have to rhyme.

A WORD LISTS

1 Word Practice	2 Vocabulary Review	3 Vocabulary Words
1. blossom	1. chorus	1. bruise
2. duckling	2. disgusting	2. ease
3. swan	3. extend	3. echo
4. valley	4. hush	4. mock
5. worry	5. utter	5. reed

B VOCABULARY DEFINITIONS

1. **bruise**—An injury that changes the color of your skin but doesn't bleed is called a *bruise*. Bruises may look black and blue or purple.
- What do we call an injury that changes the color of your skin but doesn't bleed?

2. **ease**—When you do something with *ease*, you do it with little or no effort.
- What's another way of saying *She swam with little or no effort?*

3. **echo**—When a sound *echoes*, you can hear it again and again, but it gets softer.

Here's an echo: **HELLO** ... **hello** ... hello.
- What happens to a sound that echoes?

4. **mock**—When you make fun of someone, you *mock* them.
- What's another way of saying *Amad made fun of his sister?*

5. **reed**—Tall grasses that grow on the edge of water are called *reeds*.
- What are reeds?

C HYPHENS

1. **Name this mark: -**
2. **Read the hyphenated words in the passage below.**

In the morning, they traveled until they reached a forest. There was no way of going around it. It seemed to extend to the right and left farther than they could see. However, the Woodman and the Scarecrow left the group and soon discovered a way to enter the forest.

The Ugly Duckling

Hans Christian Andersen

Chapter 1

It was summer, and the valley was beautiful. The wheat was yellow, the oats were green, and the hay was golden. A river flowed through the valley, next to river-banks that were covered with tall reeds.

It was under those reeds that a mother duck had built herself a warm nest and was now sitting all day on six eggs. Five of them were white, but the sixth, which was larger than the others, was an ugly gray color. The duck was puzzled about the egg and couldn't understand why it was so different from the rest. She often wondered if another bird had slipped the egg in while she was swimming in the river. But ducks are neither clever nor good at counting. So this duck did not worry herself about the egg but just made sure that it was as warm as the rest.

Because this set of eggs was the first one the duck had ever laid, she was very pleased and proud, even though she was tired of sitting in her nest. However, she knew that if she left her eggs, the ducklings inside them might die. So she stayed in her nest, getting off the eggs several times a day only to see if the shells were cracking.

The mother duck had looked at the eggs at least a hundred and fifty times when to her joy she saw tiny cracks on two of them. She quickly drew the eggs closer to each other. Then she sat on them for the rest of the day.

The next morning, she noticed cracks in all the white eggs, and by midday, two little heads were poking out from the shells. She broke the shells with her bill so that the little ducklings could get out of them. Then she sat steadily for a whole night upon the others. Before the sun arose, the five white eggs were empty, and five pairs of eyes were gazing out upon the green world.

The mother duck felt delighted to have some other ducks to talk to until the last egg hatched. But day after day went by, and the big egg showed no signs of cracking. The duck grew more and more impatient.

"This egg is a real problem," the duck grumbled to her neighbor one day. "Why, I could have hatched ten eggs in the time that this one has taken."

"Let me look at it," said the neighbor. "Ah, I thought so; it's a turkey egg. Once, when I was young, I was tricked into sitting on a nest of turkey eggs, and when they were hatched, the birds were so stupid that I could not even teach them how to swim." ♦

"Well, I will give this big egg another chance," sighed the mother duck, "but if the duckling does not come out of its shell in another twenty-four hours, I will just leave it alone and teach the rest of my ducklings how to swim properly and how to find their own food. I really can't be expected to do two things at once." And with a fluff of her feathers, she pushed the egg into the middle of the nest.

All through the next day she sat on the big egg, even giving up her morning bath for fear that a blast of cold air might strike the egg. In the evening, when she looked at the egg, she thought she saw a tiny crack in the upper part of the shell. She was so filled with hope that she could hardly sleep all night. When the sun rose, she felt something stirring under her. Yes, there it was at last, and as she moved, a big awkward bird tumbled headfirst onto the ground.

The duckling was quite ugly. The mother looked with surprise at his long clumsy neck and the dull brown feathers that covered his back. He did not look at all like the little yellow ducklings who were playing in the nest.

The old neighbor came over the next day to look at the new duckling. "No, it is not a young turkey," she said to the mother.

"It is skinny and brown, but there is something rather beautiful about it, and it holds its head up well."

"It is very kind of you to say so," answered the mother. "Of course, when you see the duckling by itself, it seems all right. But when I compare it with the others, I can see how different it is. However, I cannot expect all my children to be beautiful."

Later that day, the mother and her ducklings went down to a clearing by the river. Some full-grown ducks were swimming in the river, and others were waddling around and quacking in chorus.

One large duck quacked much louder than the rest, and when he saw the ugly duckling, he said, in a voice that seemed to echo, "I have never seen anything as ugly as that great tall duckling. He is a disgrace.

I shall go and chase him away." And he ran up to the brown duckling and bit his neck, making a small bruise.

The ugly duckling gave out a loud quack because this was the first time he had felt any pain. His mother turned around quickly.

"Leave him alone," she said fiercely to the loud duck. "What has he done to you?"

"Nothing," answered the duck. "He is just so disgusting that I can't stand him!"

Although the ugly duckling did not understand the meaning of the loud duck's words, he felt he was being blamed for something. He became even more uncomfortable when the loud duck said, "It certainly is a great shame that he is so different from the rest of us. Too bad he can't be hatched over again."

The poor little fellow dropped his head and did not know what to do, but he was comforted when his mother answered, "He may not be quite as handsome as the others, but he swims with ease, and he is very strong. I am sure he will make his way in the world as well as anybody."

"I doubt it," said the loud duck as he waddled off.

Life was very hard for the duckling after that day. He was snapped at by the big ducks when they thought his mother was not looking. Even his brothers and sisters mocked him. Yet they would not have noticed how different he was if they hadn't heard the loud duck's complaints.

The ugly duckling became sadder and sadder. At last he could bear it no longer and decided to run away. So one night when the other ducks were asleep, he slipped quietly out of the nest and made his way through the reeds.

E   COMPREHENSION

Write the answers.

1. Use details from the story to name at least three ways the ugly duckling was different from the other ducklings.

2. What did the mother duck mean when she said, "When you see the duckling by itself, it seems all right"?

3. Use details from the story to explain why the loud duck wanted to chase the ugly duckling away.

4. Use details from the story to explain why the other ducks thought the duckling was ugly.

5. Use details from the story to explain why the duckling decided to run away.

F   WRITING

• Pretend that the ugly duckling's mother convinces him to stay instead of running away.

Write the conversation that shows how the ugly duckling's mother convinces him to stay with the other ducks.

Use details from the story and your own ideas to answer these questions in the conversation:

1. What feelings does the ugly duckling express to his mother about the other ducks?

2. How does the ugly duckling's mother respond when he tells her about his feelings?

3. What questions does the ugly duckling ask about why he is different from the other ducks?

4. How does the ugly duckling's mother explain why he is different from the other ducks?

5. What does the ugly duckling say about running away?

6. What does the ugly duckling's mother say that convinces him to stay with the other ducks?

Write at least six sentences.

Use this format for your conversation:

Ugly Duckling: (Write what the ugly duckling says.)

Mother: (Write what the ugly duckling's mother says.)

END OF LESSON 36

A WORD LISTS

1 | Word Practice

1. blow
2. bowl
3. scratch
4. strangle
5. stretch
6. struggle

2 | Vocabulary Words

1. bill
2. eventually
3. glorious
4. moss
5. reflection

B VOCABULARY DEFINITIONS

1. **bill**—The beak at the front of a bird's face can also be called a *bill*.
- What's another word for *beak?*

2. **eventually**—*Eventually* is another way of saying *after a while*.
- What's another way of saying *The rain stopped after a while?*

3. **glorious**—*Glorious* is another word for *delightful* or *beautiful*.
- What's another way of saying *The sunshine was delightful?*

4. **moss**—*Moss* is a tiny green plant that grows well in the shade. Sometimes moss grows on the shady trunks of trees.

5. **reflection**—Your *reflection* is the image of yourself that you see in a mirror.
- What do we call the image of yourself that you see in a mirror?

C READING LITERATURE: Fable

The Ugly Duckling
Chapter 2

The ugly duckling walked for a long time that night. At last he reached a wide plain, full of soft, mossy places where the reeds grew. Here he rested, but he was too tired and too frightened to fall asleep. The reeds began to move when the sun rose, and the duckling saw that he had accidentally ventured into a group of wild geese.

"It does not matter to us what you look like," said the wild geese after they had looked him over. "You are welcome to stay here."

So for two whole days the duckling lay quietly among the reeds, eating what food he could find and drinking the marsh water until he felt strong again. He wanted to stay where he was forever because he was so comfortable and happy away from the other ducks with nobody to bite him and tell him how ugly he was.

He was thinking about how contented he was when two young geese saw him. They were having their evening splash among the reeds, looking for their supper.

"We are tired of this place," they said. "Tomorrow we will fly to another place, where the lakes are larger and the food is better. Will you come with us?"

"Is it nicer than this place?" asked the duckling doubtfully. The words were hardly out of his mouth when two shots rang out, and the two geese were stretched dead before him.

At the sound of the gun, the rest of the wild geese flew into the air. For a few minutes, the firing continued. While the shooting was going on, the ugly duckling, who could not fly, waddled along through the shallow water. He had gone just a few feet when he noticed a dog standing on the bank gazing at him, with a long, red tongue hanging out of its mouth. The duckling grew cold with terror and tried to hide his head beneath his little wings. But the dog sniffed at him and trotted away.

"I am so ugly that dogs won't eat me," the duckling said to himself. Then he hid in some tall reeds and curled up in the soft grass until the shots died away in the distance. ♦

The duckling stayed in the reeds for several months. For a while, he was quite happy and content, but winter was approaching. Snow began to fall, and everything became wet and uncomfortable.

One day in late fall, the sun was setting like a great scarlet globe, and the river, to the duckling's amazement, was getting hard and slippery. The duckling heard a sound of whirring wings. High up in the air a flock of swans flew by. They were as white as the snow that had fallen during the night, and their long necks with yellow bills were stretched toward the south. They were going to a land that was warm in the winter. Oh, if only the duckling could have gone with them! But that was not possible, of course. Besides, what sort of companion would an ugly duckling like him be to those beautiful swans?

Every morning grew colder and colder, and the duckling had to work hard to keep himself warm. Soon, he was never warm.

After one bitterly cold night, he discovered that he could not move his legs and that his feathers were frozen to his body. The duckling's life might have ended that day, but a man walked through the reeds and saw what had happened. He picked up the duckling and tucked him under his sheepskin coat, where the bird's frozen feathers began to thaw a little.

Instead of going on to his work, the man turned back and took the duckling to his children, who gave the bird something to eat. Then they put him in a box by the fire before they went to school. When the children returned from school, the duckling was much more comfortable than he had been in a long time. They were kind children and wanted to play with him, but the duckling had never played in his life. He thought the children were trying to tease him, so he ran straight out the door and hid himself in the snow among the bushes at the back of the house.

He never could remember exactly how he spent the rest of the winter. He only knew that he was very cold and that he never had enough to eat. But eventually things grew better. The earth became softer, and the sun felt hotter. The birds sang, and the flowers once more appeared in the grass. When the duckling stood up, he felt different than he had ever felt before. His body seemed larger and his wings stronger. Something pink looked at him from the side of a hill. He thought he would fly toward it and see what it was. He spread his wings, and in a moment, he was flying.

Oh, how glorious it felt to be rushing through the air, wheeling first one way and then the other! He had never thought that flying could be like that! The duckling was almost sorry when he drew near the pink thing and found that it was only a small apple tree covered with pink blossoms. The apple tree was beside a cottage. Behind the cottage, a garden ran down to the banks of a river.

The duckling fluttered slowly to the ground and paused for a few minutes near the river. As he was gazing around, a group of swans walked slowly by. The duckling remembered the swans he had seen so many months ago. He watched them with great interest. One by one, they stepped into the river and floated quietly upon the water as if they were a part of it.

"I will follow them," said the duckling to himself. "As ugly as I am, I would rather be killed by the swans than suffer all I have

suffered from the cold and from the ducks who have treated me so poorly." And he flew quickly down to the water and swam after them as fast as he could.

It did not take him long to reach the swans, for they had stopped to rest in a green pool shaded by a tree. As soon as they saw him coming, some of the younger swans swam out to meet him with cries of welcome. The duckling hardly understood these cries. He approached the swans gladly, yet he was trembling.

The duckling turned to one of the older birds and said, "If I am to die, I would rather have you kill me. I don't know why I was ever hatched, for I am too ugly to live." And as he spoke, he bowed his head and looked down into the water.

Reflected in the still pool he saw many white shapes with long necks and golden bills. He looked for his dull brown body and his awkward skinny neck. But no such body was there. Instead, he saw a beautiful white swan beneath him. With great amazement, he spread his wings and looked at his reflection in the water.

Just then, some children ran up to the river, and they threw bread into the water. "Look at that pretty new swan," one of them said. "He is the most beautiful of them all."

And when the duckling had seen his true self at last, he felt that all his suffering had been worth it. Otherwise, he would never have known what it was like to be really happy.

D COMPREHENSION

Write the answers.

1. Use details from the story to explain why the duckling would have been happy to stay with the wild geese.

2. Find the sentence in the story that describes what the duckling wanted to do when he saw the swans flying south for the winter. Then write the sentence.

3. Even before he saw his reflection, the duckling noticed that he had changed. In what ways had he changed?

4. How else could the duckling have discovered that he was really a swan?

5. At the end of the story, why did the duckling feel that all his suffering had been worth it?

E WRITING

Write a story that is like "The Ugly Duckling," except make the main character a boy or a girl.

Your story should answer these questions:

1. How is the boy or girl different from everyone else?

2. How does the boy or girl feel about being different?

3. What does the boy or girl do to change the situation?

4. What happens in the end?

Write at least five sentences.

A WORD LISTS

1 Hard Words
1. amusement
2. exposition
3. schedule
4. structure
5. technology

2 Word Practice
1. axle
2. convince
3. electric
4. enlist
5. organizer

3 Names
1. Chicago
2. Columbian
3. Eiffel
4. Ferris
5. Paris

4 Vocabulary Words
1. achievement
2. attraction
3. confirm
4. engineer
5. foundation
6. revolve
7. suspend

B VOCABULARY DEFINITIONS

1. **achievement**—An *achievement* is something you do successfully. Successfully climbing a mountain or training a dog is an achievement. Doing well in school is an achievement.

2. **attraction**—An interesting thing or place that draws visitors is called an *attraction*. The first Ferris wheel was an attraction because people had never seen one before.

3. **engineer**—A person who designs and builds engines and other machines is called an *engineer*.

4. **foundation**—The *foundation* of a building is the part that's at the bottom of the building. A good foundation ensures that the building stays in place.

5. **suspend**—When you hold something in the air, you *suspend* it. When a flag is suspended, a pole holds the flag in the air.

C VOCABULARY FROM CONTEXT

1. Like a bicycle wheel, the Ferris wheel has a metal rim that **revolves** around an axle.

2. Ferris spent many months convincing the organizers that his wheel would be successful. He enlisted the support of other engineers, who **confirmed** that the wheel would work and that it would be safe.

George's Giant Wheel

Eiffel Tower at 1889 world's fair in Paris, France

Ferris wheel at 1891 world's fair in Chicago, Illinois

A Giant Idea

In 1891, the city of Chicago was getting ready to hold a world's fair called the Columbian Exposition. The fair was designed to show the huge advances the United States had made in science and technology. New inventions such as electric lights would be displayed.

There would be games and rides. The organizers also wanted to build a gigantic attraction that would astonish the world. Two years earlier, the world's fair in Paris, France, had featured the Eiffel Tower. People were amazed by the 1,063-foot tower made of steel and iron.

The organizers for the Chicago fair wanted something even better. They challenged people to come up with ideas for a unique attraction. An engineer named George Ferris had an idea. He wanted to build a giant passenger wheel that people could ride on. The wheel would not roll on the ground; it would just revolve around an axle as people rode on it.

Ferris didn't know it, but his invention would become one of the most popular rides of all time—the Ferris wheel.

Building the wheel would be a great achievement. According to one story, George Ferris created the plans for his passenger wheel when he was having dinner with some other engineers. Ferris sketched out the details of the wheel on a napkin.

Small passenger wheels had been around at fairs for a long time, but Ferris's wheel would be much bigger. He wanted to build a steel structure that was over 260 feet tall and could carry more than 2,000 people at one time! The wheel would be as tall as a 26-story building.

Ferris's wheel would be similar to a bicycle wheel. Like a bicycle wheel, the Ferris wheel would have metal rims that revolved around an axle. It would also have long metal spokes that connected the axle to the rims.

The passenger cars would hang between the rims. As the wheel turned, the passenger cars would travel to the top of the wheel and back down again. The view of Chicago would be amazing!

A Tough Sell

At first, people thought that Ferris's idea was crazy. When he showed his plan to the fair organizers, they rejected it. Some people laughed at his idea and called him the "man with wheels in his head." Others thought the wheel would be too heavy and might even fall over. Someone said that people would be afraid to ride on it. Why wouldn't the passenger cars just fly off into the air?

But George Ferris understood the science behind his idea because he was an engineer. He had been building railroad bridges and tunnels for many years. He was

spokes

rim

axle

support tower

passenger car

Ferris wheel diagram

an expert in making strong structures from steel. Ferris knew his idea would work.

Ferris spent many months convincing the organizers that his idea would be successful. He enlisted the support of other engineers, who confirmed that the wheel would work and that it would be safe. Finally, at the end of 1892, Ferris received permission to build his wheel. ♦

The Work Begins

Work began on the Ferris wheel only five months before the fair was scheduled to open. There wasn't much time to build the wheel.

Ferris's monster wheel would be very heavy, so the first job was to make a solid base to build it on. First concrete foundations were poured. Then two towers were built on top of the foundations, and a huge steel axle was suspended between the two towers.

Next the rims of the wheel were attached to the axle with the long steel spokes. Then the passenger cars were connected to the rims of the wheel. Two powerful steam engines were built to move the wheel. The engines turned a chain that turned the wheel.

The wheel needed another force to stop its movement. Ferris used a special air brake to stop the wheel from turning. ✶

An Exciting Ride

Ferris's giant wheel was finished in June 1893. On June 21, the fair organizers and the workers gathered to see the wheel in action. Ferris's wife handed him a golden whistle. He blew the whistle, and his giant wheel started turning.

The wheel was very popular with the fairgoers. The tickets cost 50 cents, and each ride was about 20 minutes long. As the wheel slowly turned, riders had an amazing

View of Columbian Exhibition from Ferris wheel

view of the fair below. The photograph shows what the view looked like.

At night, the wheel was lit by almost 3,000 light bulbs. Nearly one and a half million people enjoyed the thrilling ride during the Columbian Exposition. George Ferris had created an attraction to rival the Eiffel Tower.

Sadly, Ferris didn't live to see the impact his invention would have on the world. He died three years after the exposition, and his wheel was torn down in 1906. But his design was later used throughout the world. People still enjoy riding Ferris wheels at amusement parks, fairs, and other places.

E COMPREHENSION

Write the answers.

1. Why did the Chicago fair organizers want to build something different from the Eiffel Tower?

2. How is a Ferris wheel similar to a bicycle wheel?

3. How is a Ferris wheel different from a bicycle wheel?

4. Name at least two reasons people thought that Ferris's wheel wouldn't work.

5. Why was Ferris convinced that his idea would work?

F WRITING

- The world is full of attractions, from Ferris wheels to tall skyscrapers, giant shopping malls, amusement parks, zoos, museums, and national parks.

Write a passage that answers this main question:

- What is your favorite attraction?

Use your memory or reference materials to answer these other questions in your passage:

1. Where is your attraction located?

2. What are the main features of the attraction?

3. Why do you like that attraction better than other attractions?

Write at least six sentences.

A WORD LISTS

1 | Hard Words

1. appreciate
2. conclude
3. opinion

2 | Related Words

1. belief / disbelief
2. expensive / inexpensive
3. express / expression
4. suggest / suggestion

3 | Names

1. Derick
2. England
3. London
4. Tara

4 | Vocabulary Words

1. alert
2. develop
3. nag
4. nudge
5. pasture
6. plod
7. Thoroughbred

B VOCABULARY DEFINITIONS

1. **alert**—A person or animal who is quick to notice things is *alert*.
- What's another way of saying *The watchdog was quick to notice things?*

2. **develop**—*Develop* is another word for *grow*.
- What's another way of saying *Her skills grew?*

3. **nag**—A horse that is old or in poor shape is called a *nag*.
- What is an old horse called?

4. **nudge**—When you gently push something, you *nudge* it.

- What's another way of saying *The horse gently pushed the gate?*

5. **pasture**—A field for farm animals is called a *pasture*.
- What do we call a field for farm animals?

6. **plod**—When you *plod,* you move at a slow, tired pace.
- Everybody, what are you doing when you move at a slow, tired pace?

7. **Thoroughbred**—A *Thoroughbred* is a special breed of horse that is used for racing.
- What do we call a special breed of horse that is used for racing?

A Horse to Remember

Luisa Miller

Chapter 1

Nobody knows exactly how Nellie developed her bad habit, but she developed it. And nothing that Mr. Briggs or Tara did seemed to break her of the habit. The Briggs family lived in England on a small farm about fifty miles from London.

The farm was too small to keep Mr. Briggs and his family busy all the time, so Mr. Briggs had a full-time job on the railroad, and Mrs. Briggs worked for the telephone company. They took care of the farm in their spare time. Tara, their eleven-year-old daughter, also helped them.

Because the farm was so small, the Briggs family didn't own a tractor. Instead, they used horses to plow the fields in the spring. That's why they had Nellie. They had bought Nellie when she was three years old. She wasn't a very good-looking horse. She was a large gray horse with tiny black spots. Her legs were heavy, and she was swaybacked.

When Nellie was only three, she already looked like a ten-year-old horse. But the Briggses thought she would be well-suited to their needs. Nellie was gentle. She loved to have somebody ride her. She was a good worker, and in most situations, she obeyed well.

During the planting season, Mr. Briggs or Tara would harness Nellie to the plow with their other horse, Derick. He was a large brown horse who looked handsome when he stood alone in the fields or rested in the small barn next to the house. He looked at least twice as handsome when he was hitched to the plow with Nellie. Derick looked straight and tall and alert, but Nellie looked like an old swaybacked nag.

Although Nellie behaved well in most situations, she had her bad habit. That habit was jumping fences.

The first time the Briggses found out about this habit was during a thunderstorm

that occurred one summer night. Nellie was four years old at the time. Tara was looking out the kitchen window at the bending trees and the driving rain. From time to time, a brilliant flash of lightning would streak through the sky and make things appear to be as bright as day. Following each flash would come a terrible crash of thunder.

It was during one of these flashes that Tara noticed Nellie standing right outside the house. She was eating flowers from the flower garden next to the kitchen door. Tara called to her mother, "Nellie got out of the pasture!"

"You must have left the gate open," her mother replied.

Tara put on her raincoat, went outside, and led Nellie back to the small pasture that surrounded the barn. But when Tara approached the gate, she noticed that it was firmly bolted. She led Nellie through the pasture, then walked around the entire pasture, checking the fence to make sure it had not blown down.

The fence was in perfect condition. It was over four feet high, and it was made of strong wire mesh. When Tara went back inside, she reported to her mother the condition of the gate and the fence. Then she added, "I don't know how she got out, Mom. The only possible way would be to jump over the fence, but ..."

Tara's voice trailed off. The idea of Nellie jumping a fence was ridiculous.

Mr. and Mrs. Briggs didn't think that Nellie could jump that high either—until a few minutes later, when they saw Nellie once more nibbling on flowers in the garden next to the kitchen door. Tara's father asked, "Are you sure you checked the entire fence, Tara?"

"Every part of it," Tara replied.

Mr. Briggs shook his head gravely. His expression was one of disbelief. "Perhaps I'd better have a look at it myself," he said and reached for his raincoat. Mrs. Briggs

was also curious about Nellie's strange escapes, so she went outside with her husband and Tara.

Mr. Briggs led Nellie back through the pasture, bolted the gate carefully, and walked around the entire pasture, shining a flashlight on every part of the fence. It was in perfect condition. He shook his head and said, "If this isn't the strangest thing ..."

Before Mr. Briggs could finish his statement, a brilliant bolt of lightning brightened the sky. The bolt was followed by another and another. To the wonder of the Briggs family, they saw how Nellie had escaped from the pasture. There she was, in a moment of dazzling bright light, looking as if she was frozen in midair, easily jumping over the top of the fence.

"I don't believe it!" Mr. Briggs exclaimed. Tara said nothing. She was still staring into the darkness at the spot where Nellie had been caught in the light. Two things amazed Tara. The first was that Nellie—plodding, swaybacked Nellie—could jump like that. Tara had never seen any horse jump so high, not even the mayor's horse, which was a handsome Thoroughbred that looked shimmering red-brown when he stood in the sunlight.

The other thing that amazed Tara was that when she saw Nellie frozen in the air, Nellie didn't look like an old plow horse. She looked very graceful, with her front legs tucked up under her head and her back legs extended. She looked beautiful. ♦

Mr. Briggs didn't seem to appreciate Nellie's beauty. He said, "We've got a serious problem, I'm afraid." He called Nellie and led her back through the pasture, then into the barn, where he put her in a stall and attached a rope to her so she couldn't get out.

"I think the thunder frightens her," he explained. "Whenever it looks like rain, we're going to have to tie her up in the barn."

The plan worked for a while, until one stormy day when Nellie figured out how to bite through the rope. The side door of the barn didn't close well. A few moments after biting through the rope, Nellie nudged the door open, trotted into the pasture, jumped the fence, and went straight to the flower garden.

At first, Nellie jumped the fence only during thunderstorms. But within two months of her first escape, she began jumping fences whenever she was alone for more than a few minutes. One time she jumped the pasture fence and the fence next to the road. She then jumped four fences on the neighboring farm and three fences on the next farm, finally stopping to eat in Mr. Fanning's vegetable garden. ★

After Tara rode Nellie back, put her in the barn, and tied her up, Tara's father said sternly, "I know you like Nellie. So do I, and so does your mother. But Nellie is becoming far too much of a problem. Unless we can figure out some inexpensive way of keeping her inside, we're going to have to get rid of her."

"Couldn't we make the fence higher?" Tara asked.

"It would be very expensive," her father explained. "The top wire of the fence is attached to the fence posts, but the posts don't go up more than a few inches beyond the top wire. So we'd have to put in new posts all the way around the pasture. I can't afford to do that."

Tara came up with other suggestions, but her father didn't approve of them. Then Mr. Briggs concluded, "Well, I hope we can come up with a solution. If we can't, Nellie must go."

D COMPREHENSION

Write the answers.

1. Use details from the story to explain how Nellie's body was different from the bodies of good-looking horses.

2. The story says, "The idea of Nellie jumping a four-foot fence was ridiculous." Why was it ridiculous?

3. When Tara saw Nellie jumping, she was amazed by two things. What were those things?

4. How was Mr. Briggs's opinion of Nellie different from Tara's opinion?

5. In what ways is Nellie like the ugly duckling?

E WRITING

Write a passage that answers this main question:

- How do you think Tara could solve the problem with Nellie?

Use your experience or reference materials to answer these other questions in your passage:

1. How will your plan prevent Nellie from jumping fences?

2. How much will your plan cost?

3. Why do you think your plan will work?

Write at least five sentences.

END OF LESSON 39

A | WORD LISTS

1 | Hard Words

1. Arabian
2. attitude
3. encyclopedia
4. exhaustion
5. requirement
6. sizzle
7. steeplechase

2 | Word Sounds

1. grouch
2. ground
3. loudly
4. mound
5. mounted
6. sound

3 | Vocabulary Review

1. alert
2. develop
3. nudge

4 | Vocabulary Words

1. barrier
2. endurance
3. exhausted
4. obstacle
5. stall

5 | Vocabulary Phrases

1. blurt out
2. cock your head
3. resist the impulse

B | VOCABULARY DEFINITIONS

1. **barrier**—Something that blocks your way is called a *barrier*. A fence is a barrier.
   - What are some other barriers?

2. **endurance**—A person or animal who has a lot of *endurance* can keep on going.
   A horse that can keep on going has a lot of endurance.
   - A runner who can keep on going has a lot of something. What is that something?

3. **exhausted**—When you're *exhausted*, you're very tired.
   - What's another way of saying *She was very tired?*

4. **obstacle**—*Obstacle* is another word for *barrier*.
   - What's another way of saying *The fallen tree was a barrier in the road?*

5. **stall**—Small rooms for horses and other animals inside a barn are called *stalls*.

1. **blurt out**—When you *blurt out,* you say something suddenly.
- What do you do when you say something suddenly?

2. **cock your head**—When you *cock your head,* you tilt it to one side.

3. **resist the impulse**—When you *resist the impulse* to do something, you don't do something that you really want to do. If you don't buy toys you really want, you resist the impulse to buy toys.
- What do you do if you don't buy candy you really want?

D READING LITERATURE: Short Story

A Horse to Remember
Chapter 2

Tara's father had told her that the Briggs family might have to get rid of Nellie. As Tara prepared for bed that night, she felt discouraged. She kept thinking about possible ideas for keeping Nellie inside the pasture, but all the ideas cost money. Nellie couldn't stay tied up in her stall all day, but if Nellie was left alone in the pasture ...

Tara got into bed and tried to sleep, but Nellie kept popping into her mind. And every time she thought about Nellie, Tara remembered the instant she first saw her leaping the fence. ✿ Nellie was not a Thoroughbred, but she looked beautiful when she jumped.

Tara punched her pillow, rolled over angrily, and told herself that she had to come up with a solution to the problem. Suddenly, she sat upright in bed with a smile. An idea came to her with such force that she wondered why she hadn't thought of it before. "No horse can jump like that," she said aloud. "She's probably the greatest jumping horse in the world."

Tara had to resist the impulse to jump out of bed and tell her parents of the plan that was forming in her mind. She controlled herself, thinking, "I'll get all the facts first, and then I'll tell them about it."

The morning after Tara got her marvelous idea, she woke up early, when the sky was still dark, with just a hint of light along the horizon to the east. Tara was up early because she wanted to find out about jumping horses. Tara didn't own a cell phone or a tablet, but her family did have a computer in the kitchen. She clicked on the computer's search engine and typed in "jumping horses." She got lots of links for the results of her search. The first link was for an online encyclopedia article about jumping horses, so she clicked that one.

The article said that horses jump in different kinds of sports, such as horse trials, show jumps, and steeplechases. The word *steeplechase* was highlighted in the article, so Tara clicked on the word and was taken to another encyclopedia article just about steeplechases. She learned that a steeplechase is a race where horses run around a long track while jumping over different kinds of obstacles, such as fences, hedges, ditches, pools of water, and banks. A bank is like a stair step, but it's several feet high. Sometimes horses jump up the bank, and sometimes they jump down the bank.

The article explained that the obstacles—which are also called *jumps*—can be combined. A pool of water, for example, can be placed in front of a fence, or a ditch can be placed after a hedge. The fences and hedges can be four or five feet high.

Tara also learned that younger horses are not permitted to compete in steeplechases because their leg bones are still growing. If they break a leg bone, they might never be able to run again.

As Tara read more about steeplechases, she began to have serious doubts about whether her idea was as good as she thought. The passage that gave her the most doubt was about the Grand National, a steeplechase that is held once a year in Liverpool, a large city in northern England. The article said that about 40 horses enter the Grand National, but usually less than half are able to finish the race. Some horses fall from exhaustion. Some fail to make one of the 30 jumps in the four-and-a-half-mile course. Some throw their riders and continue without them.

The article did provide Tara with some good news. Horses that run in steeplechases do not have to be Thoroughbreds. Usually, the only requirement is that a horse must be at least four years old. According to the article, "The horses that win this event are usually large horses with tremendous endurance." The article also pointed out that Thoroughbreds are sometimes entered in steeplechases, but the most successful horses are only part Thoroughbred. The other part may be Arabian. ◆

Tara looked out the window after reading the steeplechase articles. The

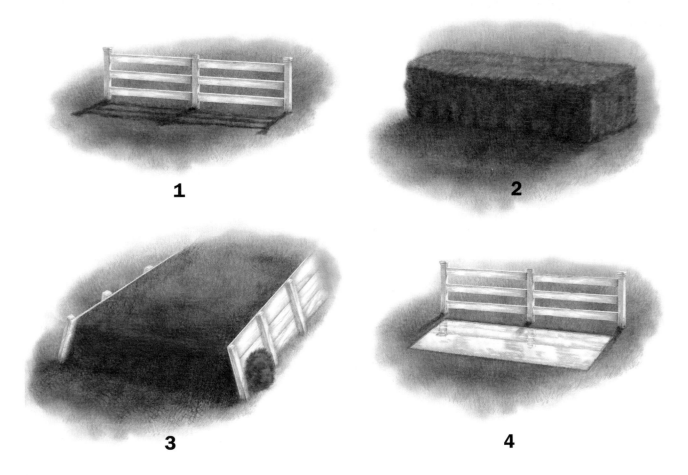

1

2

3

4

eastern sky was now bright, and the roosters in the barn were beginning to crow loudly. She was just about ready to forget the idea of training Nellie to be a jumping horse when Mrs. Briggs padded down the stairs in her bare feet.

"What are you reading so early in the morning?" she asked.

As Tara explained her plan, her mother smiled and cocked her head. "I've never seen a horse that could jump like Nellie, but I'm sure there are lots of them. Some very rich people do nothing but raise horses for steeplechases. It wouldn't surprise me if a lot of them could outjump our old Nellie."

"She's not that old," Tara objected. "She's only four years old."

"I know," her mother said thoughtfully. Then she snapped her fingers and said, "Why don't you talk to Mr. Jones, the blacksmith? He used to make shoes for steeplechase horses when he lived in Liverpool. I'm sure he could tell you a lot about the chances that Nellie might have as a jumping horse."

• • •

Tara had never talked much with Mr. Jones because he seemed to be a grouchy person who always complained about things. But after she had finished her chores, she rode Nellie down the road to the village. She knew that Mr. Jones was making horseshoes in his blacksmith's shop because she could hear the ringing of his hammer on red-hot metal from several blocks away.

When Tara arrived at the large open door of the blacksmith's shop, she stayed on Nellie's back and waited for Mr. Jones to look up. Then Tara blurted out, "I want to know what I'd have to do to make Nellie a jumping horse and if she's good enough to compete in steeplechases." ★

Mr. Jones had been hammering on a red-hot horseshoe that he held with a long pair of tongs. He dipped the shoe into a bucket of water and waited until the sizzling sound stopped. Then he took an old rag from his pocket and wiped the sweat from his face. He studied Nellie for a few moments, then smiled. "Why would you want to make her a jumping horse?" he asked at last.

Before Tara could answer, Mr. Jones continued, "She's a plow horse, not the kind of horse that is used in steeplechases."

"But she can jump like no horse I've ever seen," Tara said.

"Oh, can she now?" Mr. Jones asked in a doubting tone. He wiped his hands on the old rag and said, "I'll tell you what I'll do. If you show me that she can jump, I'll help you train her. But I'm not going to be responsible for any injuries."

Mr. Jones began looking around for a pole that he could use as a jumping barrier. He talked to himself as he searched through his workshop. "I'll have to make it about four feet high," he said.

Tara answered, "Your fence out back is about that high. Why don't we just have Nellie jump that fence?"

"No," Mr. Jones replied firmly. "I'm having no part of that poor old nag getting torn up on my fence."

"Here," Tara said, getting down from Nellie's back. "She won't get hurt. Let me show you." Before Mr. Jones could object, Tara climbed over the fence and ran into the field beyond. Then she turned and called, "Come on, Nellie."

The horse looked up quickly and trotted toward the fence. Just as Mr. Jones started to say, "But she can't ...," Nellie cleared the fence with a foot to spare.

Tara smiled and patted Nellie on the nose, but Mr. Jones didn't smile. He stood there with his mouth hanging open and his dirty rag in his hand. His eyes were wide open. "I don't believe it," he said.

E) MAIN IDEA

Write a main-idea sentence for each picture.

Picture 1: Mary

Picture 2: Tom

Picture 3: Maria

F) COMPREHENSION

Write the answers.

1. Use details from the story to explain why Tara wanted to get all the facts before she told her parents about her plan for Nellie.

2. Use details from the story to explain two ways that steeplechases are different from regular horse races.

3. After Tara read about the Grand National, she began to have doubts about her idea. Why did she have doubts?

4. Use details from the story to describe Mr. Jones's attitude toward Nellie when he first saw her.

5. Why did Mr. Jones change his attitude toward Nellie at the end of the chapter?

G) WRITING

Write a passage that answers this main question:

- Do you think Nellie would be a good steeplechase horse?

Use details from the story to answer these other questions in your passage:

1. What skills does Nellie have that would make her a good steeplechase horse?

2. What problems does Nellie have that might not be good for steeplechases?

3. What would Nellie have to learn and do to become a good steeplechase horse?

Write at least six sentences.

END OF LESSON 40

A WORD LISTS

1 Word Practice	2 Word Practice	3 Vocabulary Review	4 Vocabulary Words
1. anvil	1. demonstrate	1. barrier	1. abruptly
2. competition	2. encyclopedia	2. blurt out	2. brace your-self
3. county	3. mayor	3. endurance	3. dilapidated
4. country	4. select	4. exhausted	4. gallop
5. customer	5. thirty	5. obstacle	5. marvel
		6. resist the impulse	6. spectator

B VOCABULARY DEFINITIONS

1. **abruptly**—*Abruptly* is another word for *suddenly.*
- What's another way of saying *She stopped suddenly?*

2. **brace yourself**—When you prepare for something difficult, you *brace yourself.*
- If you get ready for a big jolt by tightening your muscles, you're bracing yourself for the jolt.

3. **dilapidated**—When something is *dilapidated,* it is really broken down and in bad shape.
- What do we call a house that is really broken down and in bad shape?

4. **gallop**—When horses *gallop,* they run almost as fast as they can.
- What are horses doing when they run almost as fast as they can?

5. **marvel**—When you *marvel* at something, you think that thing is marvelous.
- Here's another way of saying *They thought the weather was marvelous: They marveled at the weather.*

6. **spectator**—*Spectators* are people who watch an event, such as a horse race.
- What do we call people who watch an event?

A Horse to Remember
Chapter 3

"A deal is a deal," Mr. Jones said after Tara demonstrated two more times that Nellie could clear the fence with ease. "I told you I would help you train her if she could jump. And train her I will."

"You don't really have to," Tara said. "I ..."

Mr. Jones interrupted. "I'll also have to train a rider, you know. And I suppose that rider will be you."

"I'd love to be her rider," Tara said. "But you don't have to ..."

"It's not a chore, Tara," the old man said. "When I worked with steeplechase horses, I always dreamed of having one of my own. I never did, of course, but I dreamed. And now I have a chance to do something more interesting than standing over an anvil, hammering out horseshoes and fixing wheels."

"If you could train Nellie and me, I'd be very grateful," Tara said.

Mr. Jones grunted and then pointed at the horse. "You know, that horse is not what she seems to be when you first look at her. Her swayback makes you think she's a broken-down nag. But when you take a good look, she's as strong as an ox. Her legs are good—maybe a little heavy, but good. And her color makes me think she may be part Arabian."

Later that day, Tara told her parents that Mr. Jones would help her work with Nellie each day. The rest of the time, Nellie would be tied up in the pasture or in the barn.

During the weeks that followed, Tara and Nellie spent a lot of time with Mr. Jones. Tara discovered that although Mr. Jones talked like a grouch, he was a very fine person.

Mr. Jones laid out a little course in the pasture behind his shop. He made four jumps, and each one was a little less than three feet high. He explained to Tara, "When you can stay on her as she goes over these jumps, we'll make them higher."

The jumps stayed at the same height for three weeks. During those weeks, Tara fell off Nellie and landed on the soft grass of the pasture more than twenty times. At first, she lost her balance when Nellie took off. Nellie seemed to fly upward suddenly. To stay on her, Tara had to lean far forward, with her head right against Nellie's neck. Tara found out about leaning forward the hard way. Four times, she didn't lean forward far enough, and when Nellie took off, Tara fell backward.

After Tara learned about leaning forward for Nellie's takeoff, she learned about bracing herself for the landing. The first time that she didn't fall off on the takeoff, she fell on the landing. She flew right over Nellie's head when Nellie landed, and Nellie almost stepped on her.

By the third day of practice, however, Tara was able to make most of the jumps without falling. But just about the time that Tara thought she had mastered the art of jumping, Nellie would fool her by jumping a little higher than Tara expected or by coming down a little more abruptly.

Several times, Tara had the wind knocked out of her. One time she hurt so

much that she couldn't keep the tears from forming in her eyes. As she lay on her back after that fall, seeing spots in front of her eyes, Tara wondered whether she really wanted to become the rider of a jumping horse.

• • •

Before the first month of training had gone by, Mr. Jones raised the poles on the barriers half a foot. Two weeks later, they went up another half foot. Then the training moved from the pasture to a stream south of the village.

The banks of the stream were steep. In most places, the streambed was three or four feet lower than the banks. The stream covered only part of the streambed. The rest of the streambed was dry, flat, sandy land.

Mr. Jones selected a place where there was a wide, flat area below the banks. The streambed here was nearly thirty feet wide. The stream ran slowly next to one of the banks. The other bank was perfect for jumping. The sand below the perfect bank was soft, but not so soft that Nellie would sink into it when she landed.

First, Nellie jumped off the bank without a rider. Then Tara mounted her and got ready for jumping her first bank. "Remember," Mr. Jones told her, "you'll have to lean way, way back when you land, or you'll go flying right over her head." ♦

Tara's heart was beating so loudly that she could hear it in her ears. "Come on, Nellie," she said and nudged her heels into the horse's sides. Nellie broke into a gentle run, took off at the edge of the bank, and sailed gracefully to the sand below. Tara stayed on. "Good horse!" Tara shouted, and she felt very proud. When Nellie jumped, Tara felt like part of her. She seemed to know exactly where Nellie would land and how it would feel.

Mr. Jones was smiling. Then his expression quickly became serious. "Now try it with a fast run," he said.

Tara got off and led Nellie back up the bank. Then she got on again, rode Nellie about a hundred feet from the bank, and turned around. A few seconds later, she bent forward, gave Nellie a sharp nudge with her heels, and shouted, "Go, Nellie, go!"

Within two steps, Nellie was at a full gallop, going much faster than Tara had intended. Tara leaned forward, grabbed a handful of Nellie's mane with her right hand, and hung on. Nellie took one great leap

from the bank, sailed over the entire streambed, and landed on the other bank.

Somehow, Tara managed to stay on until Nellie abruptly stopped after landing. Nellie stopped right in front of a row of thick bushes, and Tara went sailing into them.

As Tara walked away from the bushes, brushing herself off, Mr. Jones came toward her in a waddling run. "Tara, are you all right?" he asked. ✦

Tara nodded her head. In an angry tone, Mr. Jones shook his finger at Nellie and hollered, "You! You are the most amazing horse I have ever seen in my life. You are the greatest jumping horse that ever lived!" Then Mr. Jones's face broke into a broad, wrinkled smile. "Amazing!" he shouted. "Amazing!"

When Nellie, Tara, and Mr. Jones returned to the blacksmith shop, an angry

customer met them. It was the mayor. Mr. Jones had promised to have the mayor's tractor wheel repaired that day. "I'm sorry," Mr. Jones said flatly. "But I won't get it done until next week. I'm busy training Nellie here to be a steeplechase champion."

The mayor laughed and said, "You've been working around hot fires too much, Elmer, if you think you'll ever make anything out of that nag."

"Is that so?" Mr. Jones said as he approached the mayor. "Well, I've just about decided to have Tara enter Nellie in the county steeplechase next month."

"Are you quite serious?" the mayor demanded. "There will be some fine horses in that race. In fact, I'm entering one of my own. You couldn't possibly think that poor old Nellie could stand a chance in that competition."

"Tell you what I'll do," Mr. Jones said. "If Nellie loses, I'll fix your tractor wheel for free."

The mayor laughed and shook his head. "If you're fool enough to repair the wheel for nothing, I'm not going to argue with you."

Mr. Jones turned to Tara and stared at her with a stern expression. Suddenly, he winked.

D MAIN IDEA

Write a main-idea sentence for each row of pictures.

Albert

Row 1

Patty

Row 2

Don

Row 3

E | COMPREHENSION

Write the answers.

1. Use details from the story to explain what reasons Mr. Jones had for helping Tara train Nellie.

2. At the beginning of the training, the jumps were less than three feet high. What did Tara have to show before Mr. Jones raised the jumps?

3. During training, Tara wondered if she really wanted to become a rider of a jumping horse. Use details from the story to explain why she felt that way.

4. Why did Mr. Jones think that Nellie was the greatest jumping horse ever?

5. At the end of the chapter, Mr. Jones made a deal with the mayor. Do you think that was a good deal for Mr. Jones? Why or why not?

F | WRITING

Write a passage that describes how Tara jumped Nellie across the stream.

Use details from the story to answer these questions in your passage:

1. How did Tara prepare for the jump?

2. How did Tara start Nellie running?

3. How did Tara hang on during the jump?

4. What happened after Nellie landed?

Write at least five sentences.

END OF LESSON 41

A WORD LISTS

1 | Hard Words
1. decorate
2. hooves
3. reins
4. Rudy

2 | Related Words
1. circle / circular
2. rectangle / rectangular
3. triangle / triangular

3 | Vocabulary Review
1. abruptly
2. brace yourself
3. dilapidated
4. gallop
5. marvel
6. spectators

4 | Vocabulary Words
1. ability
2. applaud
3. encourage
4. mount a horse
5. numb
6. official
7. shabby

B VOCABULARY DEFINITIONS

1. **ability**—When you are able to do something, you have the *ability* to do that thing.
- Here's another way of saying *Nellie was able to jump the fence: Nellie had the ability to jump the fence.*

2. **applaud**—When you clap your hands because you like something, you *applaud.*
- What's another way of saying *The spectators clapped their hands because they liked something?*

3. **encourage**—When you give somebody courage or hope, you *encourage* them.

- Here's another way of saying *The coach gave Thelma the courage to finish the race: The coach encouraged Thelma to finish the race.*

4. **mount a horse**—When you *mount a horse,* you get on the horse.
- What are you doing when you get on a horse?

5. **numb**—When part of your body is *numb,* you have no feeling in that part. When a dentist gives your mouth a shot before fixing your teeth, the shot makes your mouth numb.
- What happens to your mouth after a dentist gives it a shot?

6. **official**—Someone who makes sure that people and animals follow the rules in sports is called an *official*.

Officials at a horse race make sure that the horses and riders follow the rules.

7. **shabby**—When something is in poor condition, it looks *shabby*.
- How do clothes look when they are in poor condition?

C ▶ READING LITERATURE: Short Story

A Horse to Remember
Chapter 4

The county racetrack was about 20 miles from the Briggs's farm. Mr. Jones pulled Nellie's horse trailer with his dilapidated truck. He drove as Tara sat next to him. Tara's mother and father followed in their car, along with two boys from Tara's school. A third vehicle followed the Briggs's car. It was packed with seven neighbors. All of them had seen Nellie jump, and they had marveled over her ability.

Before they left, one of the neighbors shouted, "You'll hear some cheers for old Nellie even if she doesn't win."

Mr. Jones responded coldly, "She'll win."

The steeplechase at the county racetrack was a colorful affair. Just before the contest was to begin, Tara became so nervous that she didn't think she'd be able to ride. She was confused, and her mind seemed to go numb. Officials for the race examined the horse, asked Tara questions, and had Mr. Jones and Tara's father fill out some forms. Then one official said, "Well, she's a strong horse. She might even finish the race."

Tara didn't answer the official. She smiled politely, feeling embarrassed. She was wearing a shiny green shirt and a pair of riding boots that were too big for her. She wore a helmet and motorcycle goggles that she had found in Mr. Jones's shop. Her outfit looked shabby compared to the ones the other riders wore.

Nellie looked even shabbier compared to the other horses. Some of them were so beautiful that they gave Tara chills. One great horse was as white as snow. Another was as black as night. That horse was probably the most beautiful. When it moved, it glistened, and every muscle in its fine body seemed to ripple with power.

Tara tried to keep Nellie away from the other horses that were prancing about. From time to time, one of the riders would look over at Nellie and smile.

Before leaving the farm, Tara had decorated Nellie's mane with ribbons of green silk. When she put the ribbons on, she thought that Nellie looked pretty. But now she thought Nellie looked silly. "We'll show them," she said softly to her horse, but she knew that Nellie must have looked strange in the company of these other horses.

There were about a thousand spectators, most of them gathered near the starting line. As handlers led the horses to the starting line, an announcement came over the loudspeakers. "Ladies and gentlemen," the announcer said, "welcome to the county steeplechase. As you know, this is a one-mile

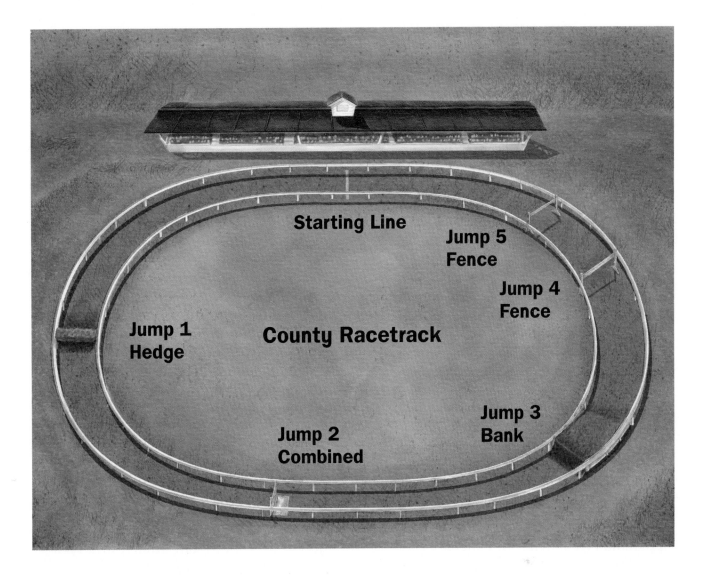

County Racetrack

Starting Line

Jump 5
Fence

Jump 4
Fence

Jump 1
Hedge

Jump 3
Bank

Jump 2
Combined

circular course with five jumps. The horses go around the course three times."

The announcer continued, "For a horse to finish, it must be successful in clearing all fifteen jumps and must still have a rider at the end of the course. A rider who falls may remount and continue running the course. The hardest parts of the course are the two fence jumps. Both fences are about five feet high, and they are spaced close together. The horse must clear the first and within a few strides get ready for the second. In a few moments, the race will begin."

A handler led Nellie to the starting line and stood next to her. Tara judged that there were more than twenty-five horses in the race. She put on her motorcycle goggles and looked at the other horses. She could

see the mayor's horse with the mayor's oldest son on its back. The mayor's son shouted to Tara, "You'll need those goggles. Rudy here is going to throw a lot of mud in your face." He patted Rudy on the neck.

Tara was still trying to organize her thoughts when a very loud bell sounded. ♦

When the bell sounded, Nellie jumped in the air and threw Tara to the ground. The other horses pounded across the soft ground, throwing chunks of grass and dirt into the air. Fortunately, Tara managed to hold on to the reins when she fell. Nellie wanted to run after the other horses, but Tara shouted, "Stop, Nellie! Stop!"

Nellie pulled Tara along the ground for a few steps; then she stopped calmly, waiting for Tara to mount her. Some of the spectators shouted mock encouragement to Tara. "You can still win!" one of them yelled, and a few people broke into loud laughter.

By the time Tara told Nellie, "Go Nellie! Run fast!" the other horses were so far ahead that Tara could no longer hear the pounding of their hooves. She bent forward and let Nellie run, but not as fast as Nellie wanted to run. Tara remembered what Mr. Jones had told her. "It's a long, tiring race, so you hold Nellie in. Don't let her go at full speed."

Tara followed Mr. Jones's directions, but it seemed hopeless. The first jump was the hedge jump. One horse had fallen trying to go over this jump, and the rider was walking slowly back toward the starting line.

The other horses were already approaching the third jump when Nellie was clearing the first jump. For an instant, Tara's attention was drawn to the crowd near the first jump. Almost in one voice, they said "Ooooo" as Nellie cleared it. Now Tara could hear the people near the first jump applauding Nellie's performance.

At the second jump there was more applause. Two more horses were out of the race—one of them standing next to the jump, holding one of its front hooves off the ground. "I hope he's all right," Tara said to herself.

Then she heard part of an announcement over the loudspeakers. She couldn't hear it very well above the sound of squeaking leather, pounding hooves, and heavy breathing. From what she could hear, she gathered that the announcer was talking about Nellie. ★

Here's what Tara heard: "... call your attention to ... She's worth watching ... a long way behind, but possibly the best jumper in ..."

The two fence jumps were at the end of the circle, jumps four and five. The crowd cheered wildly as Nellie sailed over these jumps. Three other horses hadn't cleared them.

Tara's mind was starting to clear now, and she was becoming more confident. As she started around the course the second time, she figured that there were only about ten horses left in the race. She was already almost catching some of them, including the mayor's horse and the brilliant white horse. But far ahead of these horses was the black horse. It was at least three jumps ahead of Nellie. She hadn't gained on that horse at all.

During the second round of the course, Nellie caught up to the mayor's horse at the second jump. Tara could see that the mayor's horse was tiring and straining, but Nellie was still running easily.

The second jump was a combined jump about ten feet across. Nellie and the mayor's horse took off for the jump at exactly the same time. Nellie cleared the jump with at least five feet to spare. The mayor's horse got off to a poor jump, landed with its front hooves in the water, stumbled, and fell forward, tossing the mayor's son from the saddle. Tara looked back. The mayor's son was sitting in the water. The horse was standing up.

Tara heard the loudspeakers. "Her name is Nellie," the announcer was saying, "and she jumps as if she has rockets in her feet."

Loud shouts of "Come on, Nellie!" came from the crowd.

Tara finished the second round of the course and started the third round. Nellie was starting to breathe very hard now, and Tara could feel her tug a little with each stride. She was tiring. But still the black horse was three jumps ahead of her.

MAIN IDEA

Write a main-idea sentence for each picture or row of pictures.

Picture 1

Picture 2

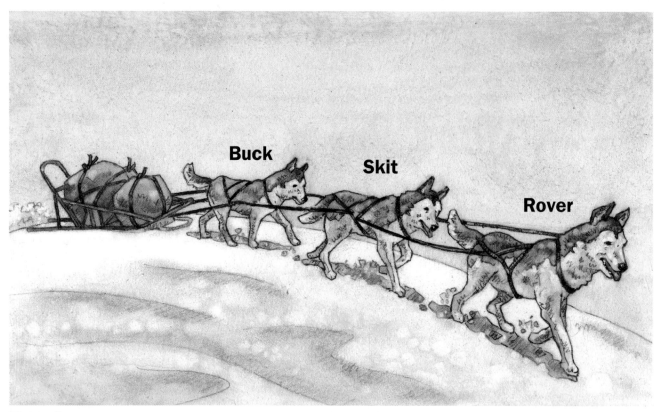

Picture 3

Picture 4

E COMPREHENSION

Write the answers.

1. Before the race began, what did Tara mean when she told Nellie, "We'll show them"?

2. Before the race began, which horse did the mayor's son think was better: Nellie or Rudy? How do you know?

3. Why did the spectators say "Ooooo" when Nellie cleared the first jump?

4. Why didn't Tara tell Nellie to run as fast as she wanted to?

5. Why will it be difficult for Nellie to win the race?

F WRITING

- Pretend you are the announcer who is describing the county steeplechase for the spectators.

Write how you describe Nellie and Tara during the first part of the race.

Use the announcer's words from the story and your own words to answer these questions in your description:

1. What happened to Tara and Nellie at the beginning of the race?

2. What happened when Tara and Nellie cleared the first jump?

3. What do you say after the second jump?

Write at least five sentences.

END OF LESSON 42

43

A WORD LISTS

1	Hard Words
	1. camera
	2. concentrate
	3. idiot
	4. photographer
	5. statue

2	Names
	1. Kelvin
	2. Liverpool
	3. Nighthawk

3	Vocabulary Words
	1. caution
	2. magnificent
	3. pound
	4. turf

4	Vocabulary Phrases
	1. hold a horse in
	2. let a horse out
	3. push a horse too hard

B VOCABULARY DEFINITIONS

1. **caution**—When you *caution* somebody, you warn them.
* What's another way of saying *He warned his brother about using the car?*

2. **magnificent**—*Magnificent* is another word for *wonderful* or *marvelous*.
* What's another way of saying *It was a marvelous race?*

3. **pound**—In England, the main unit of money is called a *pound*.
* What is the main unit of money in the United States called?

4. **turf**—Grass and the soil underneath the grass is called *turf*.
* What do we call grass and the soil underneath the grass?

C VOCABULARY PHRASES

1. **hold a horse in**—When you *hold a horse in*, you don't let it run faster, even though it wants to run faster.
* What are you doing when you don't let a horse run faster, even though it wants to run faster?

2. **let a horse out**—When you *let a horse out*, you let it run faster when it wants to run faster.
* What are you doing when you let a horse run faster when it wants to run faster?

3. **push a horse too hard**—When you *push a horse too hard*, you try to make the horse go too fast.
* What are you doing when you try to make a horse go too fast?

A Horse to Remember
Chapter 5

Tara didn't want to push Nellie too hard, but she wanted her to win. Oh, how she wanted her to win! As Tara cleared the first jump on the third round, she heard a familiar voice above the cheering crowd. "Let her out, Tara!" said the voice. "Let her out!" It was Mr. Jones's voice.

"Okay," Tara thought, and she bent forward. "A little faster, Nellie," she said. She nudged Nellie with her heels, and the horse responded by running a little faster.

Tara cleared the second jump and then looked ahead. She had now passed all the horses except one—the black horse—which was approaching the fourth jump. Nellie was gaining on the black horse, but all the black horse had to do to finish the race was to clear jumps four and five and then run to the finish line. Tara didn't think Nellie could make up the distance.

But Tara decided to try. She put her head right against Nellie's neck, out of the wind. She was concentrating on the third jump when she heard a loud roar from the crowd. After completing the jump, she looked toward the finish line. The black horse was approaching the finish line, but it couldn't win the race without a rider. The

rider had fallen off at the fifth jump, and the brave horse had continued alone to the finish line.

Now the crowd was cheering wildly. Tara looked behind to see if any horses were gaining on Nellie. None were even near, so Tara held Nellie in a little bit. Nellie cleared the last two jumps with two easy leaps. The crowd roared with delight as Nellie—swaybacked Nellie—ran easily across the finish line.

Photographers pointed cameras at Tara and Nellie. Flashes went off. Hundreds of people crowded around the tired horse. A wrinkled, smiling face pushed through the crowd. "I knew she could do it," Mr. Jones hollered, giving Nellie a big hug. Tara jumped down and gave Nellie a big hug, too. Then Mr. Jones grabbed the reins, shouted at the crowd to move back, and began walking the horse back to his truck, with Tara at his side.

Tara couldn't stop smiling, no matter how hard she tried and how many times she told herself she must look like a grinning idiot. She smiled and smiled and smiled.

Tara smiled all the way home. In her lap, she held the large first-place trophy. It was golden, topped with a statue of a handsome horse leaping over a jump. Tara thought the horse on the trophy looked much more handsome than Nellie, but that didn't matter. Nellie was the greatest horse in the world.

Tara stopped smiling when Mr. Jones's truck pulled up in front of the blacksmith shop. A long, black, expensive-looking car was parked in front of the shop, and a tall man in a dark suit was standing next to the car. As Tara and Mr. Jones got out of the truck, the man approached them. "I'm Kelvin Longly," he said in a pleasant voice. "I own Nighthawk, the black horse that would have beaten Nellie if he hadn't thrown his rider."

"That's a beautiful horse," Tara said. "I'm sorry for you that he didn't win."

Mr. Longly said, "I'll come right to the point. If you hadn't fallen at the starting line, you might have beaten Nighthawk. I don't like that kind of doubt. I bought Nighthawk because I thought he was a winner. That's what I want, a winner. Because your horse may be the real winner, I want to buy her."

"I'm sorry," Tara said. "We couldn't sell her."

By now, the cars that had followed Mr. Jones's truck from the racetrack were parked, and everybody who had been riding in them was standing behind Tara and Mr. Jones. Tara's father said, "How much are you prepared to pay for Nellie?"

Tara was shocked, and she looked at her father. "But, Dad, ..." she started to say.

"Tara," her father interrupted. "Let's hear what Mr. Longly has to say." ♦

Mr. Longly looked at Tara's father and said, "I paid fifty thousand pounds for Nighthawk, and I'm willing to pay the same amount for Nellie."

Tara's father earned less than twenty thousand pounds a year working for the railroad. The farm brought in another ten thousand pounds a year, but no more. So you can understand why Mrs. Briggs gasped when Mr. Longly made his offer for Nellie. She said, "Fifty thousand pounds is more money than we'll earn in ..."

Mr. Briggs interrupted. "Well," he said. Then he faced Mr. Longly, and Tara noticed her father's hands were trembling. "Well," Mr. Briggs repeated. "I think we have to talk this over with Tara. Would it be all right if I gave you a call later?"

"Certainly," Mr. Longly said. He handed Tara's father a card with his phone number on it. "Call me any time," he said pleasantly. Then he said farewell and got into the back seat of his car. Tara heard him tell the driver to go to Longly Place in London.

Tara was no longer smiling. She was stunned. As soon as the black car pulled away, she turned to her father and said, "But, Dad, you can't sell Nellie. She's the best ..."

Mr. Briggs interrupted quietly. "Tara," he said, "we'll talk about it at home."

Mr. Jones pointed at Nellie and said, "I think Tara's right. That horse may be the best jumping horse that has ever lived."

"I respect your opinion," Mr. Briggs said, "but I'm not sure that we should try to keep a horse as valuable as Nellie. If she's worth fifty thousand pounds, she should have an owner who can afford horses that are worth that much. I'm just a poor farmer."

"Oh, Dad, you can't ..."

"Tara, we'll talk about it at home." ✦

The thought of losing Nellie hurt so much that it almost broke Tara's heart. She ached with far more pain than she had experienced when she had fallen from Nellie's back. She couldn't believe her father would even think of selling Nellie.

Tara drove to the farm with Mr. Jones, who was silent during the trip. She just stared straight ahead as the old truck bounced down the road. Once Tara said, "He can't do that. It's not fair."

Without taking his eyes from the road, Mr. Jones said, "He's your father. You listen to what he says."

"I'll try," Tara said, almost choking. "I'll try."

When Mr. Jones pulled up in back of the house, he said, "You take care of Nellie. I'm going to say a few things to your father."

Tara led Nellie from the trailer, unbolted the gate, and stopped. She could hear Mr. Jones speaking loudly inside the house.

"Nellie is worth much more than fifty thousand pounds," Mr. Jones told Tara's father. "People pay that much for a steeple-chase horse that has a chance of winning. Nellie has a lot more than a chance. She *will* win. I've seen horses sell for one hundred thousand pounds that couldn't stay within three jumps of Nellie. If you want to sell her, give her a chance to show what she can do. Then you can name your own price."

Tara could hear other voices, but she couldn't hear what they were saying. Slowly, she led Nellie into her stall. She gave Nellie a big hug and said, "You're the most beautiful horse in the world."

When she looked up, her father and Mr. Jones were standing at the barn door, smiling. Tara's father said, "Well, I guess we're going to have to keep old Nellie for a while."

Tara started smiling again.

E MAIN IDEA

Write a main-idea sentence for each picture or row of pictures.

Row 1

Picture 2

Picture 3

F COMPREHENSION

Write the answers.

1. What evidence from the story shows that Mr. Longly is probably rich?

2. Why does Mr. Longly want to buy Nellie?

3. What reasons did Tara's father have for selling Nellie?

4. How does Tara feel about selling Nellie? Why? Use details from the story to support your answer.

5. What reasons did Mr. Jones give for keeping Nellie?

G WRITING

Write a passage that answers this main question:

- Why do you think Mr. Briggs decided to keep Nellie?

Use evidence from the story to answer these other questions in your passage:

1. What was the main reason for selling Nellie to Mr. Longly?

2. What was the main reason that Mr. Jones gave for keeping Nellie?

3. How would Tara feel if Mr. Briggs sold Nellie?

Write at least six sentences.

END OF LESSON 43

A | WORD LISTS

1 | Word Practice

1. concentrate
2. incredible
3. microphone
4. photograph
5. photographer
6. urge

2 | Related Words

1. eighteen / eighteenth
2. twenty / twentieth
3. thirty / thirtieth

3 | Word Endings

1. hedge
2. ledge
3. nudge
4. sledge

4 | Vocabulary Review

1. caution
2. magnificent
3. pound
4. turf

5 | Vocabulary Words

1. dangle
2. frantic
3. lag
4. prance
5. strain

B | VOCABULARY DEFINITIONS

1. **dangle**—When something hangs loosely, it *dangles*.
- What's another way of saying *The string was hanging loosely?*

2. **frantic**—When people act in a wild and nervous way, they are *frantic*. People who are frantic act frantically.
- What's another way of saying *The crowd yelled wildly?*

3. **lag**—When you fall behind, you *lag*. You are lagging behind.
- What's another way of saying *The slow horse was falling behind in the race?*

4. **prance**—When a horse *prances*, it takes high steps.
- What is a horse doing when it takes high steps?

5. **strain**—When you make your body work as hard as it can, you *strain* your body.
- What are you doing when you make your body work as hard as it can?

A Horse to Remember

Chapter 6

The Grand National is run on one of the most demanding steeplechase courses in the world. The course is triangular, and it has sixteen jumps. The distance around the course is a little over two miles, and the horses must go around the course twice. The first time around, the horses must go over all sixteen jumps. The second time around, the horses go over only fourteen jumps. Altogether, the horses must run about four and a half miles and make thirty jumps.

Only those horses with incredible endurance can finish this demanding event, but a lot of horses try each year. They come from all over the world—from the United States, France, Australia, Japan, and many other countries. Many horses that enter the competition are worth a lot of money. These horses are big and strong and have a great deal of endurance.

The Grand National takes place near the large city of Liverpool, which is about two hundred miles northwest of London.

By the time Nellie, Tara, Mr. Jones, and more than twenty neighbors from Tara's village made the long trip to Liverpool, people were no longer laughing at Nellie.

Nellie had entered two steeplechases after winning the county steeplechase. She won first place in one of those contests. In the other contest, she was the first horse to cross the finish line, but she had thrown Tara on a hedge jump. Tara had tumbled to the ground without holding on to the reins, and Nellie had continued to the finish line without her. But when she had thrown Tara, Nellie

was ahead of the other horses and was clearly the best jumping horse in the field.

Shortly before the trip to Liverpool, Mr. Longly had visited the Briggses and made another offer for Nellie. This time, he offered seventy thousand pounds, and he cautioned Tara, "You may be making a great mistake. Nellie is very good on these shorter courses, but Nighthawk has tremendous endurance. The rider was holding him in near the end of the county race when you were gaining on him.

I know Nighthawk can run the four and a half miles in the Grand National. I honestly don't think your Nellie will be able to stay with him." ♦

The words Mr. Longly had said kept popping into Tara's mind as she rode to Liverpool in the cab of the truck. Tara had already practiced running a four-mile course with Nellie, and Nellie had done very well; but the practice course was not as difficult as the Grand National course. Some of the jumps at Liverpool were over five feet high, and there were many jumps.

When Tara and Mr. Jones arrived at the Grand National, they walked Nellie to the starting line. This time, Tara was ready for the starting bell. She wore a smart green jacket and riding boots that fit. Nellie wore handsome green ribbons and the number 31. At the starting line, more than forty horses lined up side by side. ✦

On one side of Nellie was a handsome Arabian horse that was almost white, with just a hint of gray spots on its legs. On the other side was Nighthawk. Even in this field of magnificent horses, Nighthawk was still the most beautiful. He pranced and stomped at the turf with his front hooves as he shook his head and snorted.

Tara lowered the goggles that were attached to her new helmet, patted Nellie on the neck, and listened to the announcements. The announcer introduced each horse, told where it was from, and gave some information about it. When the announcer said, "And number thirty-one ..." a tremendous roar went up from the crowd. The announcer told about Nellie's record in jumping contests and then

said, "Nellie is one of the horses you should keep your eye on during this competition." The announcer then continued, "Another great horse you should watch is Nighthawk."

At last the announcer stopped. The thousands of people who had gathered to watch the competition became silent, the riders got ready and ... the race began.

Write a main-idea sentence for each picture or row of pictures.

Fred

Row 1

Donna

Row 2

Picture 3

<table>
<tr><td>**E** **COMPREHENSION**</td><td>**F** **WRITING**</td></tr>
</table>

E **COMPREHENSION**

Write the answers.

1. Use details from the story to explain what qualities a horse must have to win the Grand National.

2. How had Nellie proved that she might be able to win the Grand National?

3. Why did Mr. Longly visit the Briggs family again?

4. Why do you think Mr. Longly said that Nellie had less endurance than Nighthawk?

5. What details from the story help explain why Tara might be worried about Nighthawk?

F **WRITING**

Write a passage that answers this main question:

• Do you think Tara and Nellie can win the Grand National?

Use evidence from the story to answer these other questions in your passage:

1. How has Nellie performed in the other races she's run?

2. What are Nellie's strengths and weaknesses?

3. What are Tara's strengths and weaknesses?

Write at least six sentences.

A WORD LISTS

1	Hard Words	2	Place Names	3	Vocabulary Review	4	Vocabulary Words
	1. archbishop		1. Europe		1. dangle		1. continent
	2. audience		2. Austria		2. frantically		2. emperor
	3. available		3. Vienna		3. lagging behind		3. retire
	4. celebration		4. Salzburg		4. prance		
	5. funeral				5. strain		
	6. particular						

B VOCABULARY DEFINITIONS

1. **continent**—A *continent* is a large area of the world that may include several countries. The continents are Africa, Antarctica, Asia, Australia, Europe, North America, and South America. Some people say that Europe and Asia are one continent: Eurasia.
- In which continent is the United States located?

2. **emperor**—An *emperor* is more powerful than a king and rules over several countries.
- What is an emperor?

3. **retire**—When you get old and decide to stop working, you *retire*.
- What's another way of saying *The principal got old and decided to stop working?*

C READING LITERATURE: Short Story

A Horse to Remember
Chapter 7

The horses snorted and grunted when they started the race. Some of the riders shouted as they urged their horses to go fast. In the distance was a deafening roar from the crowd. Tara was aware of all these things, but her mind was concentrating on Nellie. She put Nellie into a slow, easy run and noticed the way she was moving. Tara checked to make sure that she was sitting forward in the saddle and moving easily with Nellie.

Some of the other horses shot away from the starting line. When Tara looked at them pulling far ahead of Nellie, she felt anxious, but she remembered what Mr. Jones had told her. "The idea is not to be the winner when you reach the first jump or even the fifth jump. The idea is to be the winner at the finish line. Hold Nellie in until there are only three or four jumps left in the race. Then let her out if you have to."

Tara looked around to see which horses were near Nellie. About three-fourths of the horses were ahead of her. A few were lagging behind. But right next to Nellie was the magnificent Nighthawk, matching Nellie stride for stride. The two horses were running almost as if they were one horse. They approached the first jump together, in step. They both cleared the jump at the same instant, traveling almost the same height and landing almost together. "This is incredible," Tara said to herself as a thunderous roar went up from the crowd.

Now came the second jump, a great hedge that was at least five feet high. Five riders failed to make this jump. The crowd gasped loudly as one of the horses directly in front of Nellie charged up to the hedge and then stopped abruptly, tossing its rider over the hedge. For a moment, Nellie got off stride with Nighthawk. She had to turn a little to the right to avoid the horse standing in front of the hedge. But Nellie and Nighthawk once more pleased the crowd by jumping over the hedge together and landing at almost the same instant. "Two incredible horses," the announcer said. "If they continue this way, we'll have two winners."

Now came a short fence followed by a bank. Nighthawk and Nellie cleared the fence and landed on the lower side of the bank together, but Tara wasn't prepared for the jolt of the landing. She fell forward and grabbed onto Nellie's neck. She was out of

the saddle, with one leg dangling near Nellie's front shoulder. Somehow, she managed to get back into the saddle. As she scolded herself for being careless, she heard a large cheer from the crowd.

By the time Nellie and Nighthawk had gone around the course one time, only about a dozen horses were left in the race. Horses and riders were scattered on the ground near every jump. Some horses had been seriously injured. Tara tried not to think about Nellie getting injured. She told herself, "Nellie will win if I can stay on her." But as Nighthawk and Nellie started on their second time around the course, Tara thought about what Mr. Longly had said about Nighthawk.

Tara glanced over at Nighthawk. His mouth was open, and he tossed his head from time to time. But he was running with ease. Only three horses were ahead of Tara now, the white Arabian and two brown horses. They seemed to be straining. Nighthawk and Nellie, still running stride for stride, caught the Arabian horse at the eighteenth jump. They passed the other two horses before the twentieth jump. "There are only ten more jumps to go," Tara said to herself. But a moment after having that thought, Tara noticed that Nighthawk was moving ahead.

Tara's first impulse was to stay with Nighthawk. But then she remembered what Mr. Jones had told her. Tara held Nellie at an easy run and watched nervously as Nighthawk pulled away, by ten feet, by twenty feet, now by thirty feet. When Nellie had cleared the twenty-sixth jump, Nighthawk was at least fifty feet ahead. ◆

"Go, Nellie!" Tara shouted as she nudged the horse. "Go!" Nellie bounded forward with such speed that Tara was amazed. The horse was covered with sweat and breathing hard. But she ran with the kind of power you would expect from a horse that was just starting a race.

The crowd screamed and cheered. The announcer shouted, "She's not out of this race yet. Look at her go."

Nellie caught up to Nighthawk two steps before the twenty-seventh jump. The horses jumped together again, but this time they didn't land together. Nellie landed at least five feet ahead of Nighthawk, and that was as close as Nighthawk ever came to Nellie for the rest of the race. Nellie moved away from Nighthawk so fast that Tara could hardly believe what was happening. Nellie cleared the rest of the jumps with ease and reached the finish line at least three hundred feet ahead of Nighthawk.

Above the frantic crowd and the thunderous applause, Tara could hear the announcer "... a new track record ... the greatest steeplechase horse that has ever run on this course ..."

There were pictures, questions from reporters, and prizes for winning the race. Tara made a brief victory speech. As a reporter held a microphone in front of her face and people with television cameras crowded close, she said, "I knew she could do it if I could stay on her. She's incredible."

The trip home was a very pleasant one. Imagine winning the Grand National with a horse that everybody called an old nag! Tara polished the first-place trophy with the sleeve of her jacket as she rode in the cab of the truck. ✦

After arriving at the farm, Tara took care of Nellie and gave her a special dinner and an extra special brushing. Then Tara, Mr. Jones, Tara's parents, and all the neighbors gathered at the Briggs's farmhouse for a celebration dinner.

During dinner, the phone kept ringing. Reporters wanted to talk to Tara. Other people called to congratulate her. Mr. Longly called and made a new offer of two hundred thousand pounds, but Mr. Briggs turned him down. After the seventh call, Mr. Briggs turned off the phone so callers wouldn't disturb the celebration.

After dinner, Mr. Briggs announced, "I was worried about having enough money to keep Nellie, but now we have enough money to keep her forever."

Mr. Jones shook his finger and said, "You have enough money to keep ten horses forever." Everybody laughed.

● ● ●

Nellie's story continued. She ran the Grand National two more times, and she won each time. She became the most photographed, most talked about steeplechase horse that ever lived.

When Nellie was nine years old, she gave birth to a magnificent male colt. The colt's father was a famous black horse. After Nellie was ten years old, she retired from racing, but she had two more colts. Nellie lived until Tara was a grown woman with a family of her own.

The day Nellie died was a very sad day, but Tara has fond memories and something else to remind her of Nellie—one of Nellie's colts.

D MAIN IDEA

Write the main idea for each passage.

1. Roses grow in the summer.
   Pansies grow in the summer.
   Buttercups grow in the summer.

2. Flowers produce oxygen.
   Trees produce oxygen.
   Grass produces oxygen.

3. Trucks need gasoline.
   Cars need gasoline.
   Motorcycles need gasoline.

E MAIN IDEA

Write the main idea for each picture or row of pictures.

Picture 1

Rhonda

Row 2

COMPREHENSION

Write the answers.

1. What did Mr. Jones mean when he said, "The idea is to be the winner at the finish line"?

2. Why didn't Tara try to catch up with Nighthawk when he first pulled away?

3. Why did Tara let Nellie out at the twenty-sixth jump?

4. Why were the Briggses able to keep Nellie for the rest of her life?

5. If you had a horse, would you want to race in the Grand National? Why or why not?

G **WRITING**

• The story shows just part of Tara's victory speech.

Pretend you are Tara. Write your entire victory speech.

Use Tara's statements in the story and other details to answer these questions in your speech:

1. How do you feel about winning the race?

2. What made the race challenging?

3. When did you know that you could win?

4. Who do you want to thank?

Write at least six sentences.

END OF LESSON 45

A WORD LISTS

1 Word Practice
1. archbishop
2. audience
3. available
4. celebration
5. funeral
6. particular

2 Music Words
1. classical
2. composer
3. concerto
4. opera
5. orchestra
6. symphony

3 Names
1. Constanze Weber
2. Don Giovanni
3. Mozart

4 Vocabulary Words
1. outstanding
2. prodigy
3. salary

B VOCABULARY DEFINITIONS

1. **outstanding**—When something stands out because it is really good, that thing is *outstanding*.
   A really good basketball player who stands out from the rest of the team is an outstanding basketball player.
   - What do we call a really good singer who stands out from other singers?

2. **prodigy**—A *prodigy* is a young person who has outstanding talent. A child with outstanding talent in music is a *musical prodigy*.
   - What's another way of saying *A child with outstanding talent in music?*

3. **salary**—A *salary* is the amount of money workers get paid for their jobs. Workers usually get paid once or twice a month.
   - If a worker earns $1,000 a month for a part-time job, what is her salary for the entire year?

Austria

Today you will read about a famous composer named Mozart. He was born in Salzburg, a small city in the country of Austria. Austria is one of many countries in the continent of Europe. The map shows where Austria is located.

Austria is surrounded by other countries and doesn't border a sea or ocean. The biggest city in Austria is Vienna. It's in the eastern part of the country, which is hilly. Salzburg is in the western part of Austria, which has some of the tallest mountains in Europe.

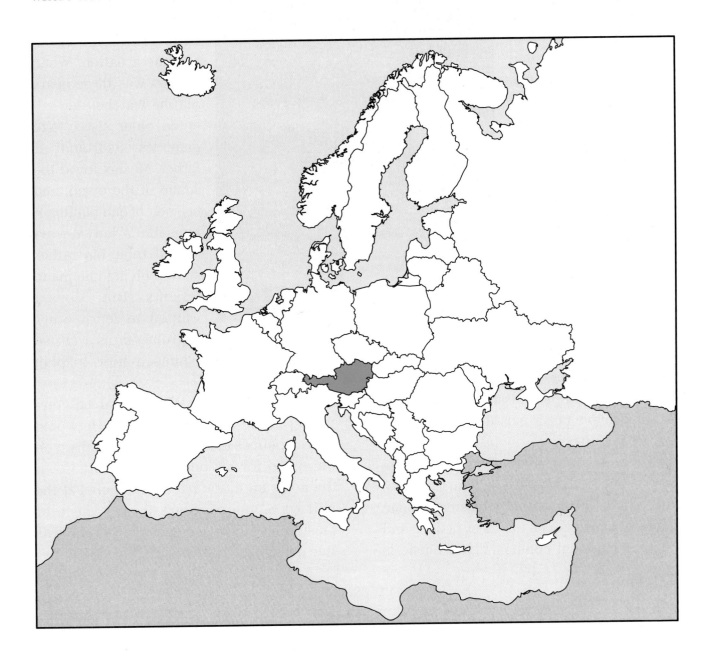

Mozart, the Musical Prodigy

Music is in your cell phone, your home, your car, your school, the places you eat, the places you shop, the movies you see. Music also comes in many styles, such as rock, Latin, jazz, blues, country, hip hop, soul, gospel, and heavy metal. Many of those styles are recent, but one style has been around for more than a thousand years—classical music.

Other styles of music are more popular these days, but many people still prefer classical music. One reason is that classical pieces are so complicated and beautiful that people discover something new every time they hear a particular piece. Classical pieces are not like simple pop songs that people may get tired of after a few months.

There are thousands of classical composers. Some of them lived a long time ago, and others are writing classical music today. Mozart may be the most famous and popular classical composer. His music is

Mozart as a child standing in front of a piano

played all over the world.

Early Years

Mozart was born in Salzburg, Austria, in 1756, which was 20 years before the United States became a nation. When Mozart was three years old, he watched his talented older sister take piano lessons from their father. Mozart loved the sound of the piano, and he soon began playing it himself. When Mozart turned four, his father started giving him piano lessons. But Mozart wanted to learn other instruments as well, so he began teaching himself how to play the violin.

Still not satisfied, Mozart started composing music when he was five. He would make up tunes in his head and play them on the piano for his father, who wrote down the notes on music paper. The notes at the bottom of the page are from a piece of music that Mozart composed when he was five years old.

Mozart's father realized that his son was a musical prodigy—a child with outstanding talent for music. In 1762, when Mozart was only six, his father decided to take him and his sister on a tour of Europe so they could show off their talents and make some money. Over the next three years, Mozart and his sister performed in almost every important city in Europe. The audiences loved Mozart. They were amazed by his piano playing and by the music he wrote for piano and other instruments.

The painting on the previous page shows Mozart standing next to a piano when he was six years old.

Mozart returned home for one year andthen set off on another tour. He kept touring for seven more years. During this time, he met many other composers. They were astonished by his playing and his music, but they were even more astonished when Mozart listened to a long, complicated piece of music by another composer and then wrote down every note from memory.

The Archbishop of Salzburg

By the time Mozart finished his last tour, he was 17 years old, and he was no longer considered a child prodigy. He was now an adult who had to make a living as a composer and performer. His first job was working for the ruler of Salzburg, who was called the Archbishop of Salzburg. The archbishop hired Mozart in 1773 to write music for the archbishop's orchestra. An **orchestra** is a musical group that includes dozens of musicians playing different musical instruments.

Mozart wrote many different kinds of classical music for orchestra, including symphonies, concertos, and operas.

Symphonies are long pieces that feature the orchestra by itself.

In a **concerto,** one or more musicians play at the front of the stage while the orchestra plays in the background.

An **opera** is a type of play that uses music to tell a story. Actors in an opera sing on a stage while the orchestra plays below the front of the stage. ♦

Mozart didn't get along with the archbishop, who paid him a very low salary. In 1777, Mozart quit his job, but the archbishop hired him back two years later and increased his salary. Mozart continued to write music for the archbishop and other people. In 1781, the archbishop ordered Mozart to join him in Vienna, the biggest city in Austria. The archbishop was in Vienna to celebrate the country's new ruler: Emperor Joseph.

Mozart, who was now 25 years old, was happy to be in Vienna because it was much bigger than Salzburg and had better musicians. But he was still unhappy with the archbishop, who treated him like a servant and refused to let him play a concert for the emperor. Mozart quit his job once again and made his living by writing and performing his own music.

The Last Ten Years

In 1781 Vienna was the musical center of Europe. Many composers lived there, and the city's residents and visitors flocked to concerts and operas. During Mozart's first year in Vienna, he played a concert for Emperor Joseph, and he composed a popular opera about a kidnapping, along with many other pieces. The next year he married Constanze Weber, a wonderful singer. He was happy and successful.

Over the next few years, Mozart became even more famous as a composer and performer. He was most well known for his 27 piano concertos. He performed them in sold-out concert halls, and he also conducted the orchestra. If a concert hall wasn't available, he rented large rooms in other buildings and sold even more tickets. Mozart earned lots of money from these concerts, but he spent it foolishly instead of saving it. Meanwhile, Constanze gave birth to their son Karl in 1784. ✦

By 1786, Mozart was only 30 years old, but he was tired of writing piano concertos, so he decided to compose more operas. The first one was performed later that year. It was about a wedding, and it was a big hit. Mozart wrote an even bigger hit, *Don Giovanni,* the next year. It became one of the most famous operas of all time. Later that year, Emperor Joseph hired Mozart to compose music for the dance parties in the emperor's palace, but the job didn't pay well.

Even though Mozart was still popular and worked for the emperor, he didn't have much money left. He started asking his friends for loans, which he promised to repay when his income increased. He also traveled to other cities, hoping to find a better-paying job. But he couldn't find a good job, and he and his family became very poor. They had a hard life. All the money Mozart had earned as a composer and performer was gone.

In 1791, Mozart's life began to improve. He was still a young man, and he had lots of ideas. Rich people began paying him to write new music, and his new opera, *The Magic Flute,* was a huge success. His second son, Franz, was born that summer. Mozart was happy again, but only for a short period. In September 1791, he got a deadly illness that nobody could cure.

Although Mozart realized that he was dying, he kept writing music. Over the next few months, he composed a piece for a choir to sing at someone else's funeral. Mozart felt that he was writing the piece for himself, and it was the last thing he wrote. His final

Mozart as an adult

words were, "The taste of death is upon my lips. I feel something that is not of this earth."

Mozart was only 35 years old when he died in December 1791, but his music has lived on for more than two centuries, and it will probably survive for many more centuries.

E MAIN IDEA

Write the main idea for each passage.

1. Wild deer live in the jungle.
   Wild tigers live in the jungle.
   Wild apes live in the jungle.

2. Vanessa dug a hole.
   Then Vanessa picked up a tree.
   Vanessa put the tree into the hole.

3. Maria goes to Lincoln School every day.
   Henry goes to Lincoln School every day.
   Lisa goes to Lincoln School every day.

F COMPREHENSION

Write the answers.

1. Why did Mozart's father decide to take him and his sister on a tour of Europe?

2. What astonishing thing was Mozart able to do after hearing a long and complicated piece by another composer?

3. Use evidence from the article to show why Mozart was unhappy with the Archbishop of Salzburg.

4. How did Mozart earn his living in Vienna?

5. Why did Mozart think he was writing his last piece of music for himself?

G WRITING

Write a brief report on the different instruments that musicians play in orchestras.

Use at least two reference sources to answer the following questions in your report:

1. What are the four families of instruments in an orchestra?

2. What are the main instruments in each family?

3. How are the families arranged on the stage?

4. Who leads the orchestra, and what does that person do?

5. What orchestra or orchestras play near where you live?

Write at least six sentences.

END OF LESSON 46

A

ability When you are able to do something, you have the *ability* to do that thing.

abruptly *Abruptly* is another word for *suddenly*.

accept When you agree to receive something, you *accept* that thing.

achievement An *achievement* is something you do successfully.

acknowledge When you agree that something is true, you *acknowledge* that it is true.

admit When you allow someone to enter a place, you *admit* that person to the place.

advance When you *advance*, you move forward.

affection *Affection* is another word for *love*.

aggressive People and animals who are *aggressive* are ready to argue or fight.

ain't *Ain't* is another way of saying *am not*.

alert A person or animal who is quick to notice things is *alert*.

amused *Amused* is another word for *entertained*.

ancestor A person in your family who lived before your grandparents is your *ancestor*.

apparent When something is *apparent*, it is easy to see or understand.

applaud When you clap your hands because you like something, you *applaud*.

approach *Approach* is another way of saying *come close to*.

approve *Approve* is another word for *like*.

arise When something begins to exist, it *arises*.

arouse *Arouse* is another word for *awaken*.

assignment A task that a teacher or boss gives you is an *assignment*.

astonished *Astonished* is another word for *surprised*.

attic An *attic* is a room just below the roof of a house.

attraction An interesting thing or place that draws visitors is called an *attraction*.

awkward *Awkward* is another word for *clumsy*.

B

balanced When something won't tip over, it is *balanced*.

bald A person who is *bald* doesn't have any hair on top of their head.

barrier Something that blocks your way is called a *barrier*.

basin *Basin* is another word for *sink*.

batter When you hit something again and again, you *batter* it.

behavior The way you act is your *behavior*.

bewildered *Bewildered* is another word for *confused*.

bill The beak at the front of a bird's face can also be called a *bill*.

blurt out When you *blurt out*, you say something suddenly.

bondage *Bondage* is another word for *slavery*.

boulder A *boulder* is a large rock. Some boulders are as big as cars.

bounding *Bounding* is another word for *running*.

brace yourself When you prepare for something difficult, you *brace yourself*.

brilliant *Brilliant* is another word for *bright*.

brisk *Brisk* is another word for *fast*.

brook A *brook* is a small stream.

bruise An injury that changes the color of your skin but doesn't cause bleeding is called a *bruise*.

budge *Budge* is another word for *move*.

bundle A group of objects that are wrapped together is called a *bundle* of objects.

C

candidate A person who is running for office is a *candidate* for that office.

cashier A *cashier* is someone who takes payments at a store.

castle A large building where an important person lives is sometimes called a *castle*.

caution When you *caution* somebody, you warn them.

celebration *Celebration* is another word for *party*.

charm *Charm* is another way of saying *magic power*.

chatter When something *chatters*, it makes a series of quick sounds.

cheering When something is *cheering* to you, it cheers you up.

chorus A group of singers is called a *chorus*.

civilized A *civilized* person is polite and well-mannered.

clumsiness *Clumsiness* is another word for *awkwardness*.

cluster A *cluster* is a group.

cock your head When you *cock your head*, you tilt it to one side.

cocoa Chocolate powder is called *cocoa*. A hot drink made with this powder is also called *cocoa*.

come into contact When you touch something, you *come into contact* with it.

comforted *Comforted* is another word for *calm*.

companion An animal or person who spends a lot of time with you is called your *companion*.

comrade *Comrade* is another word for *friend*.

confidence When you feel sure that you can do something, you have *confidence* that you can do the thing.

confirm When people agree that something is true, they *confirm* that it is true.

congratulate When you give someone praise or good wishes, you *congratulate* them.

consider When you think over whether you should do something, you *consider* whether you should do it.

continent A *continent* is a large area of the world that may include several countries.

countless *Countless* is another way of saying *too many to be counted*.

courage When you have *courage*, you are brave.

courtyard An open space surrounded by one or more buildings is called a *courtyard*.

coward A fearful person is a *coward*.

cozy *Cozy* is another way of saying *very comfortable*.

cradle A bed for babies is called a *cradle*.

crops *Crops* are plant foods that are raised on a farm.

crouch When you *crouch*, you bend your legs and get ready to spring forward.

cruelty When you do something in a mean way, you do it with *cruelty*.

cunning When you are clever but dishonest, you are *cunning*.

cupboard *Cupboard* is another word for *cabinet*.

current *Current* is another way of saying *flow of water*.

curtsy When you *curtsy*, you bend your knees and place one foot in front of the other.

customary *Customary* is another word for *usual*.

cyclone A *cyclone* is a powerful storm with winds that spin around.

D

dangerous *Dangerous* is another way of saying *not safe*.

dangle When something hangs loosely, it *dangles*.

dazzle When a bright light almost blinds you, it *dazzles* you.

deaf When you are *deaf*, you are unable to hear.

debris Scattered pieces of rock and other materials are called *debris*.

deceive When you *deceive* somebody, you trick that person into believing something that is not true.

declared *Declared* is another word for *said*.

delightful *Delightful* is another word for *wonderful*.

desert [dee-ZERT] When you *desert* people, you leave them when they need you.

desperately When you very much want something, you want it *desperately*.

develop *Develop* is another word for *grow*.

dilapidated When something is *dilapidated*, it is really broken down and in bad shape.

disappeared *Disappeared* is another word for *vanished*.

disgusting When something is *disgusting*, it is really horrible.

dismally *Dismally* is another word for *sadly*.

dome A *dome* is a kind of roof that looks like a round hat.

dominance An animal that has more *dominance* has more power over other animals.

dominant The most powerful animal in a group is the *dominant* animal.

dose A *dose* of something is a certain amount of that thing.

drawn If something is *drawn* by a horse, it is pulled by the horse.

dreadful *Dreadful* is another word for *horrible*.

dreary *Dreary* is another word for *dull*.

dwell When you *dwell* in a place, you live in that place.

E

earnestly *Earnestly* is another word for *sincerely*.

ease When you do something with *ease*, you do it with little or no effort.

echo When a sound *echoes*, you can hear it again and again, but it gets softer.

emperor An *emperor* is more powerful than a king and rules over several countries.

encourage When you give somebody courage or hope, you *encourage* them.

endurance A person or animal who has a lot of *endurance* can keep on going.

engineer A person who designs and builds engines and other machines is called an *engineer.*

enormous *Enormous* is another word for *huge.*

eventually *Eventually* is another way of saying *after a while.*

exclaim When you *exclaim,* you say something forcefully.

exhausted When you're *exhausted,* you're very tired.

expectant When you feel that something is about to happen, you look and feel *expectant.*

expecting When you are *expecting* an event, you think that event will probably happen.

experience Every time you do something, you have an *experience* with that thing.

express You *express* feelings and ideas by what you do or say.

extended When something is *extended,* it is stretched out very far.

F

farewell *Farewell* is another word for *goodbye.*

fate *Fate* is another word for things that happen to you.

feast A large meal is called a *feast.*

fiddler A *fiddler* is someone who plays the violin. Fiddlers call their violins *fiddles.*

field of grain A *field of grain* is a field that is filled with plants like wheat and corn.

fine The word *fine* sometimes means *very small.*

flustered When you are *flustered,* you are confused and nervous.

fond of When you are *fond of* something, you like that thing.

for Sometimes the word *for* is used in the same way as the word *because.*

fortunate *Fortunate* is another word for *lucky.*

foundation The *foundation* of a building is the part that's at the bottom of the building.

frail When something is *frail,* it is weak, delicate, or easy to break.

frantic When people act in a wild and nervous way, they are *frantic.* People who are frantic act *frantically.*

fret *Fret* is another word for *worry.*

G

gallop When horses *gallop,* they run almost as fast as they can.

gingham *Gingham* is a kind of cotton that usually has a checkered pattern.

glare *Glare* is another word for *brightness.*

glitter *Glitter* is another word for *glisten* or *sparkle.*

gloomy *Gloomy* is another word for *dismal.*

glorious *Glorious* is another word for *delightful* or *beautiful.*

gorgeous *Gorgeous* is another way of saying *very pretty.*

gradually *Gradually* is another word for *slowly.*

grant When you *grant* a person's wish, you give that person what he or she wishes.

grim *Grim* is another word for *serious.*

grindstone A *grindstone* is a large circular stone that is used to sharpen knives, scissors, and other sharp objects.

guardian The *guardian* of a castle is the person who guards the castle.

half nelson If you wrestle with someone, you can make a *half nelson* by putting an arm under one of your opponent's armpits and pushing on their neck with your hand.

hearty *Hearty* is another word for *large*.

high spirits When people have *high spirits,* they are happy and excited.

hold a horse in When you *hold a horse in,* you don't let it run faster, even though it wants to run faster.

horizon The *horizon* is the line where the sky meets the land.

humbug A *humbug* is a person who pretends to be something that he or she is not.

hush *Hush* is another way of saying *stop talking.*

husky *Husky* is another way of saying *deep* or *thick.*

icebox *Icebox* is an old-fashioned word for *refrigerator.*

ignore *Ignore* is another way of saying *pay no attention to.*

imitate When you *imitate* somebody, you do just what that person does.

improvise When you *improvise,* you do not prepare what you're doing ahead of time—you just do it.

in spite of *In spite of* is another way of saying *although there is.*

inconvenient If something is *inconvenient,* it causes trouble.

inherit When you are born with certain qualities, you *inherit* those qualities from your parents and other ancestors.

injured *Injured* is another word for *hurt.*

inquire *Inquire* is another word for *ask.*

instead Let's say you have to choose between watching TV and reading a book. You might choose to read the book *instead* of watching TV.

intention Something you plan to do is your *intention.*

jagged Something that is sharp and uneven is *jagged.*

journey *Journey* is another word for *trip.*

kayak A *kayak* is a small canoe that usually holds only one person.

kayaking When you paddle a kayak, you are *kayaking.*

kingdom A country that is ruled by a king or a queen is called a *kingdom.*

kitchenette A *kitchenette* is a small kitchen.

knowledge A person's *knowledge* is all the things that person knows.

lack When you *lack* something, you don't have that thing.

lag When you fall behind, you *lag.* You are lagging behind.

latch onto When you grab something, you *latch onto* it.

leather *Leather* is a tough material that is used to make boots, belts, jackets, and pants.

let a horse out When you *let a horse out,* you let it run faster when it wants to run faster.

lining The *lining* of something is the material on the inside.

magnificent *Magnificent* is another word for *wonderful* or *marvelous.*

maiden *Maiden* is an old-fashioned word for a young woman who isn't married.

manager *Manager* is another word for *boss.*

marble *Marble* is a beautiful rock that has wavy colored patterns in it.

marvel When you *marvel* at something, you think that thing is marvelous.

mass An area with no shape is called a *mass.*

meadow A piece of land that's covered with grass and flowers is called a *meadow.*

meek *Meek* is another word for *timid.*

mend When you fix something that is torn or broken, you *mend* it.

messenger A person who delivers messages is called a *messenger.*

mischief Naughty behavior is called *mischief.*

misfortune *Misfortune* is another way of saying *bad luck.*

mistress A woman who is the guardian or owner of a pet is the pet's *mistress.*

mistrust When you *mistrust* someone, you don't trust or believe them.

mock When you make fun of someone, you *mock* them.

moss *Moss* is a tiny green plant that grows well in the shade.

motionless *Motionless* is another way of saying *without movement.*

mount a horse When you *mount a horse,* you get on the horse.

moved When you are *moved* by something you see or hear, that thing gives you a strong feeling.

mystery A strange thing that you don't understand is a *mystery.*

nag A horse that is old or in poor shape is called a *nag.*

notice When you *notice* something, you become aware of it.

nudge When you gently push something, you *nudge* it.

numb When part of your body is *numb,* you have no feeling in that part.

oats *Oats* are a kind of grain. Oats are used to make oatmeal and other foods.

obstacle *Obstacle* is another word for *barrier.*

odor An *odor* is a smell.

official Someone who makes sure that people and animals follow the rules in sports is called an *official.*

outstanding When something stands out because it is really good, that thing is *outstanding.*

ovation When people give an *ovation,* they clap and cheer loudly for a long time.

overhear When somebody doesn't know that you hear them, you *overhear* them.

P

passage *Passage* is another word for *path*.

pasture A field for farm animals is called a *pasture.*

patter When something makes a tapping sound over and over, it *patters.*

pave When you *pave* a road, you cover it with bricks, asphalt, or other hard materials.

peculiar *Peculiar* is another word for *strange.*

people of flesh and blood *People of flesh and blood* is another way of saying *real people.*

permit [per-MIT] When you let somebody do something, you *permit* that person to do it.

philosophical If you feel *philosophical* about something that happened, you accept what happened, even though you're not happy about it.

plod When you *plod,* you move at a slow, tired pace.

podium Speakers sometimes stand behind a piece of furniture called a *podium.*

poster *Posters* are large pieces of paper that use words and pictures to advertise things.

potential When you realize your *potential,* you become all that you can be.

pound In England, the main unit of money is called a *pound.*

prance When a horse *prances,* it takes high steps.

presence When you're in somebody's *presence,* you're where that person can see you.

presentable When you are clean and well dressed, you are *presentable.*

prodigy A *prodigy* is a young person who has outstanding talent.

promptly When you do something *promptly,* you do it on time.

pure A thing that is not mixed with anything else is *pure.*

push a horse too hard When you *push a horse too hard,* you try to make the horse go too fast.

R

raft A flat boat with no sides is called a *raft.*

rapids *Rapids* are places in a river where the water flows quickly.

ray of sunshine A *ray of sunshine* is the streak of light that sunshine makes when it comes through a window or a cloud.

reed Tall grasses that grow on the edge of water are called *reeds.*

reflection Your *reflection* is the image of yourself that you see in a mirror.

refreshed *Refreshed* is another way of saying *full of energy.*

region A large area inside a country is called a *region.*

remarkable *Remarkable* is another word for *amazing.*

renaissance When people have a renewed interest in something, that thing has a *renaissance.*

replace When you put something back where you found it, you *replace* that thing.

represented *Represented* is another way of saying *looked like.*

request When you *request* something, you ask for that thing.

resist the impulse When you *resist the impulse* to do something, you don't do something that you really want to do.

resolve When you *resolve* to do something, you make up your mind to do it. **respect** When someone treats you seriously, they treat you with *respect*.

retire When you decide to stop working, you *retire*.

reunite When things come together, they *unite*. When they come together again, they *reunite*.

revolve When something spins or moves in a circle, it *revolves*.

ripples Small waves are called *ripples*.

roomer A *roomer* is a person who lives in a rented room in a house.

S

salary A *salary* is the amount of money workers get paid for their jobs. Workers usually get paid once or twice a month.

satisfaction When you're pleased about something you do, you feel *satisfaction* about that thing.

sawdust *Sawdust* consists of small pieces of wood that fall off during sawing.

scamper off When you *scamper off,* you run away quickly.

scarcely If you can *scarcely* do something, you can hardly do it.

scarlet *Scarlet* is another way of saying *bright red*.

scent *Scent* is another word for *smell*.

seize When you grab something and hang onto it, you *seize* that thing.

shabby When something is in poor condition, it looks *shabby*.

shears *Shears* are large scissors.

shiver *Shiver* is another word for *tremble*.

shoulder When you *shoulder* something, you bring it to your shoulder.

shrill A *shrill* sound is one that is high and sharp.

shrug When you *shrug,* you lift your shoulders.

sibling Your sister or your brother is your *sibling*.

silk *Silk* is a fine material that is used to make fancy shirts and dresses.

singed Something that is *singed* is slightly burned.

sketchbook A *sketchbook* is a notebook that artists use for drawing and sketching.

slate A little chalkboard is called a *slate*.

slightest *Slightest* is another word for *smallest*.

sneer When you *sneer,* you speak with a mocking tone.

snug Something that is *snug* fits tightly.

sob *Sob* is another word for *cry*.

sober *Sober* is another word for *serious*.

social interactions *Social interactions* are the ways each member of a group responds to other members of a group.

sorceress *Sorceress* is another word for *witch*.

sorrow *Sorrow* is another word for *sadness*.

spear An old-fashioned weapon with a long shaft and a pointed tip is called a *spear*.

spectacles The glasses that people wear are sometimes called *spectacles*.

spectator *Spectators* are people who watch an event, such as a horse race.

spicy Foods that are *spicy* contain spices, such as pepper or cloves.

splendid *Splendid* is another word for *marvelous*.

spoil *Spoil* is another word for *ruin*.

sprinkled *Sprinkled* is another word for *dotted*.

stall Small rooms for horses and other animals inside a barn are called *stalls*.

startled When you are *startled*, you are frightened or surprised.

stoop A porch with stairs in front of a house is called a *stoop*.

strain When you make your body work as hard as it can, you *strain* your body.

strides *Strides* are long steps.

studded *Studded* is another word for *decorated*.

stunned When you are knocked out, you are *stunned*.

suede *Suede* is leather with a soft surface.

sunburnt *Sunburnt* is another word for *sunburned*.

supplies When you go camping, the food and other items you take with you are called your *supplies*.

suspected *Suspected* is another word for *thought*.

suspend When you hold something in the air, you *suspend* it.

tempt When you *tempt* people, you try to get them to do things by offering them something they really want.

tenderly When you act *tenderly*, you act gently and lovingly.

terror *Terror* is another way of saying *great fear*.

therefore *Therefore* is another word for *so*.

Thoroughbred A *Thoroughbred* is a special breed of horse that is used for racing.

throne A *throne* is a fancy chair for a queen, a king, or a very important person.

timid When you are *timid*, you lack courage or confidence.

tint A *tint* is a very slight color.

tremendous *Tremendous* is another way of saying *very great*.

trot *Trot* is another way of saying *run slowly*.

tug When you *tug* at something, you pull very hard.

turf Grass and the soil underneath the grass is called *turf*.

unbearable When something is *unbearable*, you can't stand it.

untilled *Untilled* is another word for *unplowed*.

usual *Usual* is another word for *common* or *ordinary*.

utter *Utter* is another word for *say*.

vacation A *vacation* is time away from school or work.

vanish *Vanish* is another word for *disappear*.

velvet *Velvet* is a soft material that is used to make fancy coats and hats.

ventriloquist *Ventriloquists* are people who can talk without moving their lips.

weep *Weep* is another word for *cry*.

whisk When something moves quickly and suddenly, it *whisks*.

willingly When you do something *willingly*, you do it of your own free will.

Fact Game Answer Keys

Lesson 19

2. a. east
    b. south
    c. west
    d. north
    e. south

3. a. United States
    b. Kansas

4. a. Gillikins
    b. Quadlings
    c. Winkies
    d. Munchkins

5. a. Kansas
    b. Land of Oz
    c. Land of Oz
    d. Kansas

6. a. desert; the Great Desert
    b. Emerald City

7. a. cyclone
    b. eye

8. a. Land of the North
    b. Land of the West
    c. Land of the East
    d. Land of the South

9. a. yellow
    b. gray
    c. blue
    d. white

10. a. Scarecrow
    b. (Cowardly) Lion
    c. Dorothy
    d. Tin Woodman

11. a. Kalidah
    b. Oz; Wizard of Oz
    c. Toto

12. a. east
    b. north
    c. west
    d. east

Lesson 29

2. a. south
    b. west
    c. west
    d. south
    e. east

3. a. cyclone
    b. eye

4. a. Land of the North
    b. Land of the South
    c. Land of the West
    d. Land of the East

5. a. blue
    b. green
    c. gray
    d. yellow

6. a. Dorothy
    b. Scarecrow
    c. Tin Woodman
    d. (Cowardly) Lion

7. a. Kansas
    b. Indiana
    c. Maine

8. a. east
    b. west
    c. east
    d. south

9. a. (The) Emerald City
    b. Oz; Wizard of Oz
    c. desert; the Great Desert

10. a. Winkies
    b. field mice
    c. Kalidahs

11. a. third
    b. second
    c. first

12. a. Land of the West
    b. Land of the East
    c. Land of the North